IMAGES
of America

MIDLAND
THE WAY WE WERE

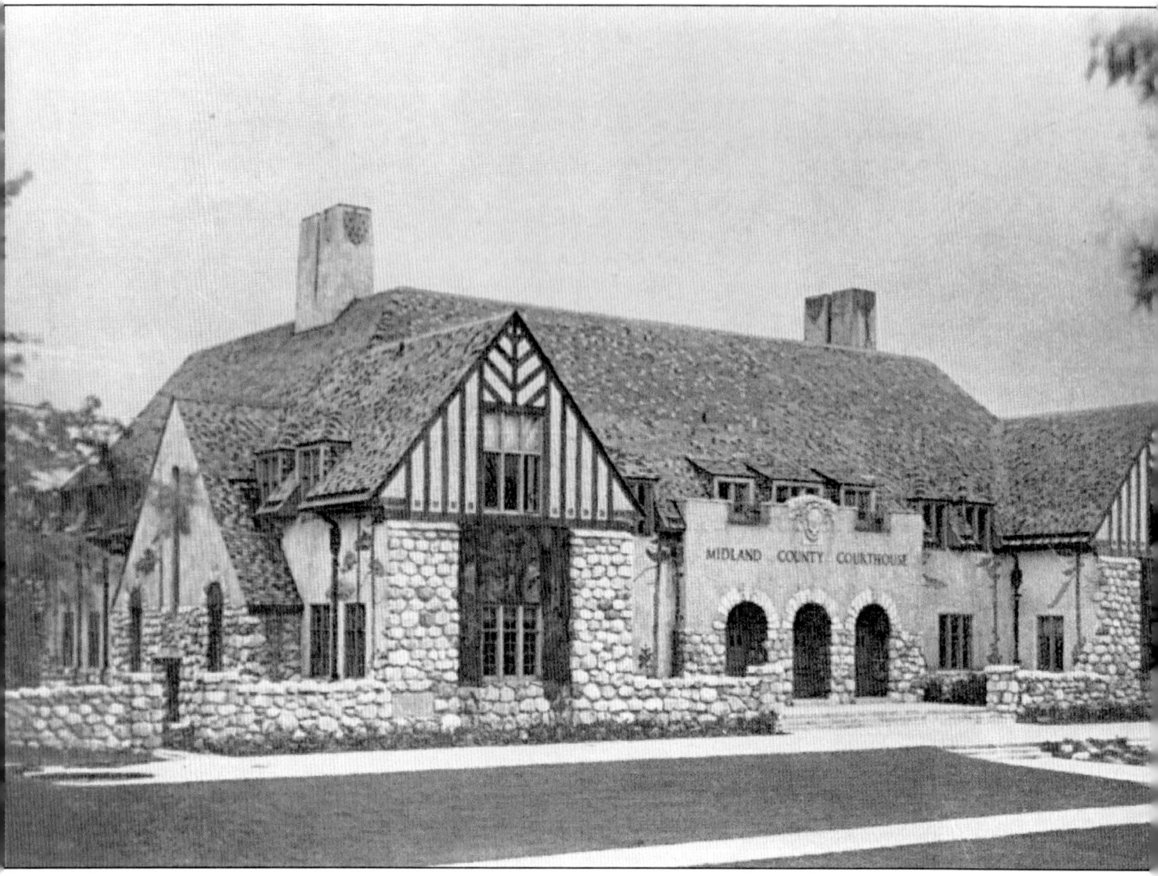
MIDLAND COUNTY COURTHOUSE

IMAGES
of America

MIDLAND
THE WAY WE WERE

Virginia Florey
Edited by Leona Seamster

ARCADIA
PUBLISHING

ISBN 978-0-7385-1886-2

Published by Arcadia Publishing
Charleston, South Carolina

Printed in the United States of America

Library of Congress Catalog Card Number: 2001091937

For all general information contact Arcadia Publishing at:
Telephone 843-853-2070
Fax 843-853-0044
E-mail sales@arcadiapublishing.com
For customer service and orders:
Toll-Free 1-888-313-2665

Visit us on the Internet at www.arcadiapublishing.com

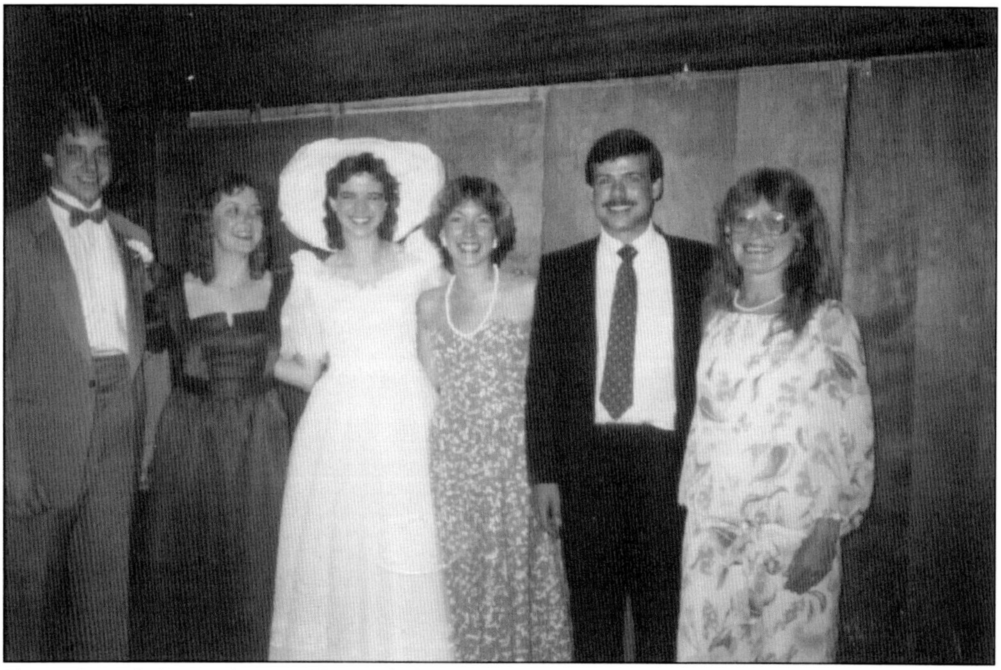

Shown here, left to right, are: Kenneth Groves, Tamara Groves Muir, Robbyn Groves Durance, Pamela Merritt Innocent, Greg Merritt and Kerry Moore Cebluski. These are children of my sisters Delores Groves and Jean Moore and my brother Dean Merritt. They are descendants of Henry White, who came to Midland in 1869 and married Catherine Coty, a young immigrant from Canada in 1871. They, too, are a part of Midland's history.

Contents

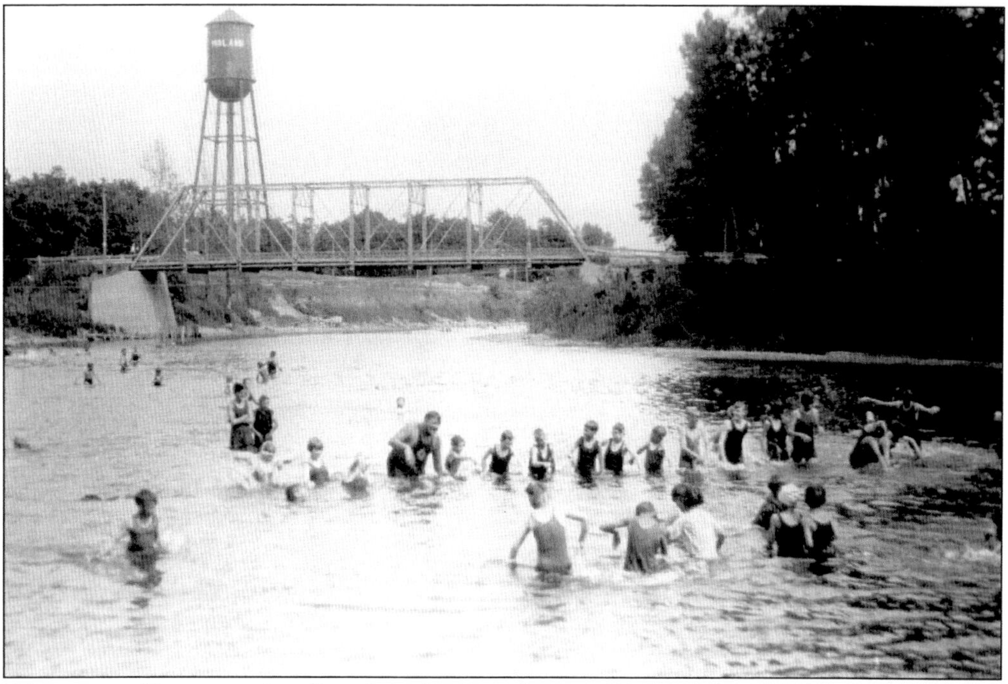

Happiness is like manna. It will not keep. It cannot be accumulated. It has rained down from heaven at our very door.

—Tryon Edwards

ACKNOWLEDGMENTS

This book could not have been created without generous support from many people. I especially want to thank all those who went through their family pictures and so generously loaned them for this book. Special thanks go to Kathy Thomas and Ned Brandt of the Post Street Archives who were so generous in letting me go through the hundreds of photos of the Dow family. Thank you to Craig McDonald and Daria Potts of the Alden Dow Archives for giving me access to their files and photos. Thank you to Jack Telfer, editor of the *Midland Daily News*, who said, yes, I could borrow some pictures, and then thank you to Doug Winger, who patiently dug through old files to find those pictures for me. Thank you to Gary Skory of the Midland Historical Society who generously looked for, and loaned me, pictures that I couldn't locate elsewhere. A special thank you to Susan Weisenberger of the Dow Corning Photo Department for the early photo of Dow Corning and some of the men so important in the early history of Dow Corning. A thank you to my sister Delores Groves who helped with the initial organization and to Amy Lindesmith who scanned all the photos for this book. A big thank you to Pastor John Seifert who always knew what was wrong when the computer wasn't cooperating. And last of all, special thanks to Leona Seamster who edited the book you are reading.

INTRODUCTION

My love affair with the small town that I was born in began at a very early age and has continued unabatedly to the present time. My great-grandfather Henry White came to the Village of Midland City in 1869. He, his wife Elmira, and their two sons followed his daughter Emma, who had just married George Covert, to Midland. George Covert scaled timber for a living in the thriving lumber camps that were flourishing in the area at the time.

Shortly after their move to the Village of Midland City, Elmira died at what today would be a relatively young age—43. Henry White then met a young woman named Catherine Coty and they were married in 1871 with their only child—my grandmother—born on June 26, 1872. Henry White's descendants continue living in Midland today, 132 years after he first came to a small village sprawling along the banks of the Tittabawassee River.

Listening to the stories of people who were my ancestors began my love of history, of wanting to know about people and why they came to the little town of Midland, of a fascination with the stories that marked the history of the town where I was born. From my grandmother I heard about the fire at the Findlater Hotel that burned 52 houses and buildings in Midland in 1876 when she was just four years old. The fire that devastated Midland began when a young girl threw out the old straw from the bed ticks into the pigpen behind the hotel. A passing train blew cinders out that ignited the straw and 52 businesses and residences were burned to the ground. Alex Findlater, who owned the hotel, was my grandmother's uncle. And so the history of the town became entwined with my family's history. As I grew up listening to these stories of Midland, it gave me a sense of both time and eternity.

When people first drifted to the Midland area it was known as The Forks because it's where two rivers come together, the Tittabawassee and the Chippewa. James Eastman established a trading post on the banks of the Tittabawassee. Later the cement abutments to support what was called the Lower Bridge (or the Benson Street Bridge as most of us called it) rested on the site of that original trading post.

While the first families who came here farmed, the men usually worked in the lumbering business in one way or another. They were lumberjacks or they worked in the camps cooking, scaling timber, or blacksmithing for the horses necessary to haul the timber.

For a short time, the small village was famous for its mineral springs. Lewis Eastman, J.S. Eastman, Alex Findlater, William Harris, Roderick Russell, Benjamin Dean and a Mr. Baker formed a joint stock company and built the Mineral Well in 1867. A large bathhouse was built. Mrs. Maggie Cunningham was in charge of the ladies' part of the new bathhouse. A little later the property was transferred to William Stearns who built a boarding house and the bathhouse was operated in the summertime for the most part.

In 1877 John Larkin and William Patrick formed a partnership to build the Larkin and Patrick saw mill, where they turned out lumber and shingles. They also sank the first salt well in the village.

By the end of the century lumbering was giving out as timber barons looked for more lucrative fields of white pine to cut but by this time a young man named Herbert Henry Dow had come to Midland. In 1890 the Midland Chemical Company was formed and on August 14, 1890, Dow came to Midland to begin his experiment at the Evens Flour Mill. On January 2, 1891, he proved that bromine could be extracted from brine with his new process. In 1895 the Dow Process Company was formed. In 1897 The Dow Chemical Company was formed, and in 1900 Dow Chemical absorbed the Midland Chemical Company.

At the turn of the century there were other manufacturing plants in the small town of Midland but The Dow Chemical Company was to surpass them all. Dove and Stanton had a butter and tub works. The Tittabawassee Mills, owned and operated by Eesley and Sons, manufactured flour. Al Dickey had a small salt and bromine plant. There was the Patrick and Larkin saw mill and salt works. The Star Mills made flour. Still later there was a chicory plant built and operated on Bay City Road, opposite The Dow Chemical Company.

As the Dow plant continued to prosper so did the town of Midland. Even the years of the Great Depression in the Thirties barely touched our town. Men worked steadily and weekly paychecks were the norm. Foundations established by Midland philanthropists gave Midland the advantages of a large city with the ambiance of a small town. And because The Dow Chemical Company was located here, it seemed that the brightest and the best young men and women came to Midland to make their home here. We who have our roots here know that we live in a unique town. Regardless of how big Midland grows in the future, to us it will always be the small town where we grew up with our family histories woven together.

In the following pages you will see pictures of people who helped create this unique city during its first 100 years from 1850 to 1950. You will see pictures of some of the things that made headlines and you will see pictures of the families who settled here, raised their families here and in their own way and their own time, added to the rich fabric of historical Midland.

This is Midland—the way we were.

One

MAIN STREET

It is to live twice when we can enjoy the recollection of our former life.

—*Martial*

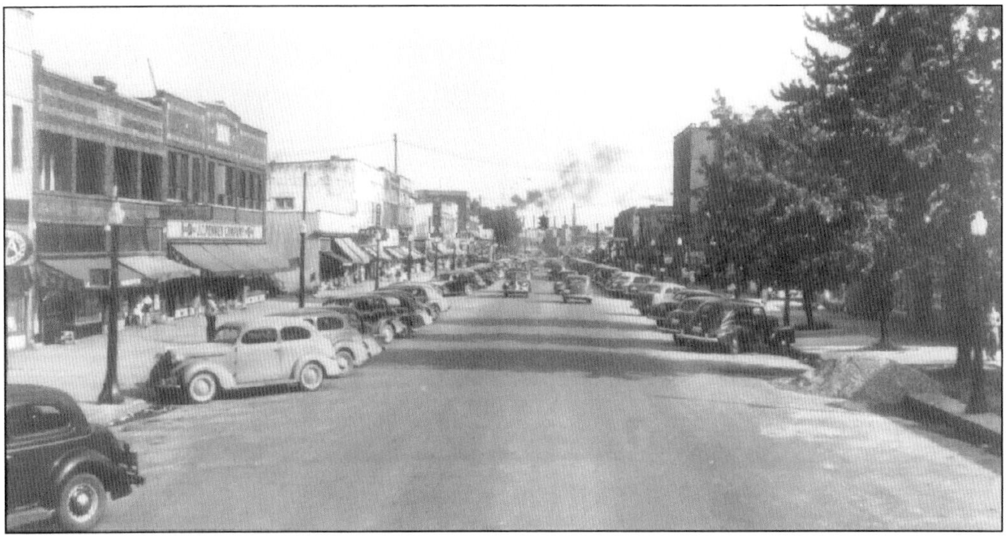

Main Street in Midland, Michigan, hugged the curves of the Tittabawassee River and for a hundred years everything of importance took place on Main Street. There were two theatres, a post office, Consumers Power, the Bell Telephone Company (when operators asked you what number you wanted and connected you to that person), doctors, lawyers and dentists, insurance companies and furniture stores, grocery stores and super markets, drug stores and candy stores, barber and beauty shops, music stores and appliance stores, car sales and gasoline stations. Everything you needed was right there on one street.

When we were growing up Main Street had just two directions: up and down. Up Main Street was the Frolic Theatre, the First Methodist Church, the Frolic Sweet Shop, Rod's Hamburgers, the Courtesy Meat Market, Consumers Power Company, the Midland Post Office, the J.C. Penney store and a residential section consisting of old Victorian-style homes. Down Main Street was the Mecca Theatre, Knepps, Beckwith & Reardon, the Chemical Savings Bank, Levine's Mattress and Furniture Company, The Dow Chemical Company, and a den of iniquity simply called Shorty's Pool Hall.

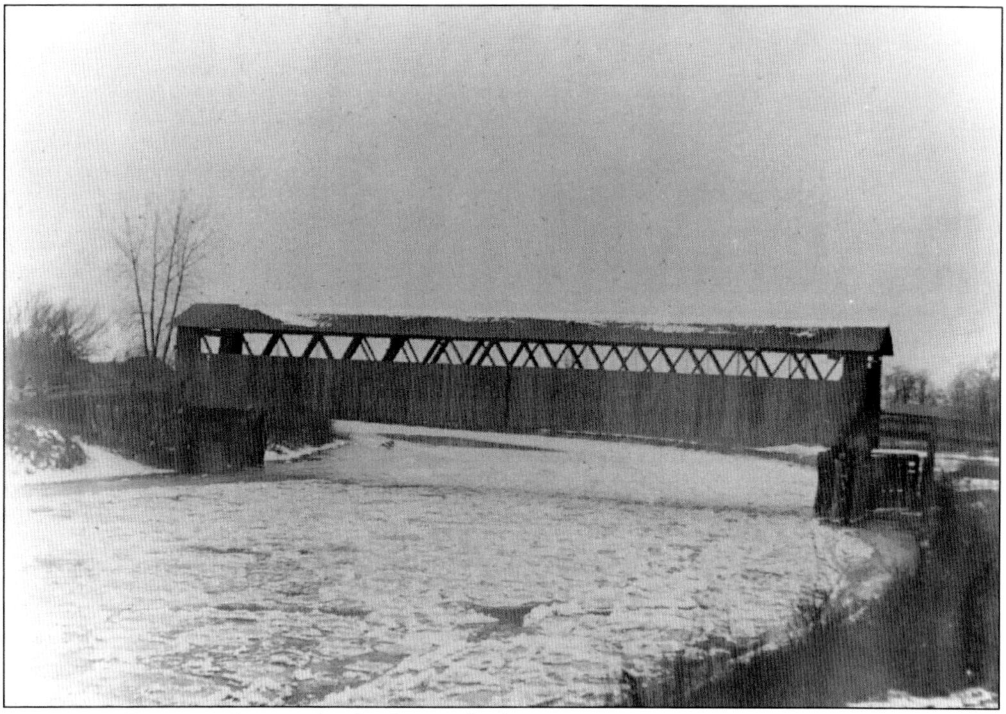

The Upper Bridge. This wooden bridge was built in 1871 to span the Tittabawassee connecting Main Street and Isabella Road. A similar wooden bridge spanned the Tittabawassee at the other end of Main Street and was called the Lower Bridge. Both bridges were carried away in the flood of 1907 in spite of gallant efforts by the village men and boys to hold them in place with ropes.

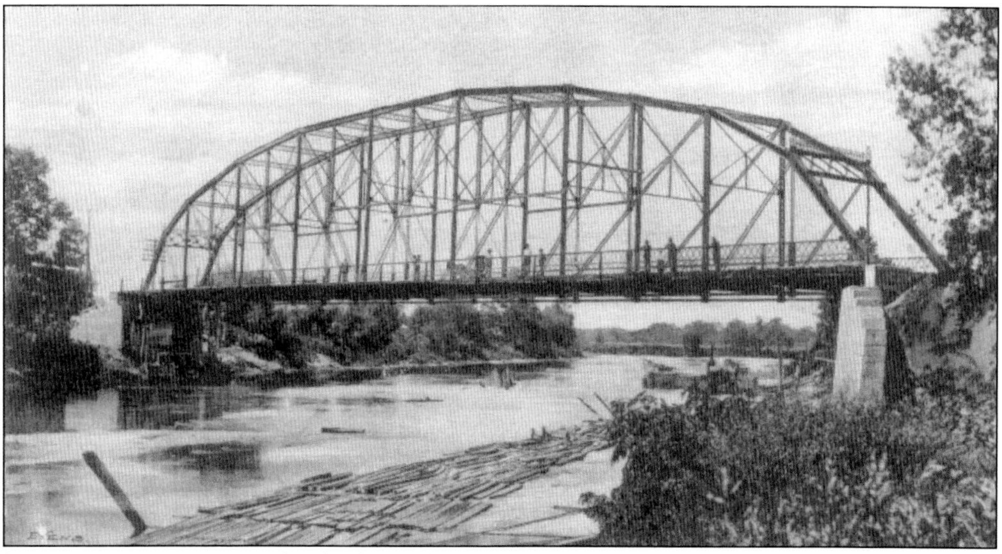

Benson Street Bridge. This bridge replaced the covered wooden bridge that was washed out in the flood of 1907. Built in 1908, it connected Main Street with Benson Street and was called the Lower Bridge. A similar metal bridge was built at the other end of Main Street once again connecting Main Street and Isabella Road.

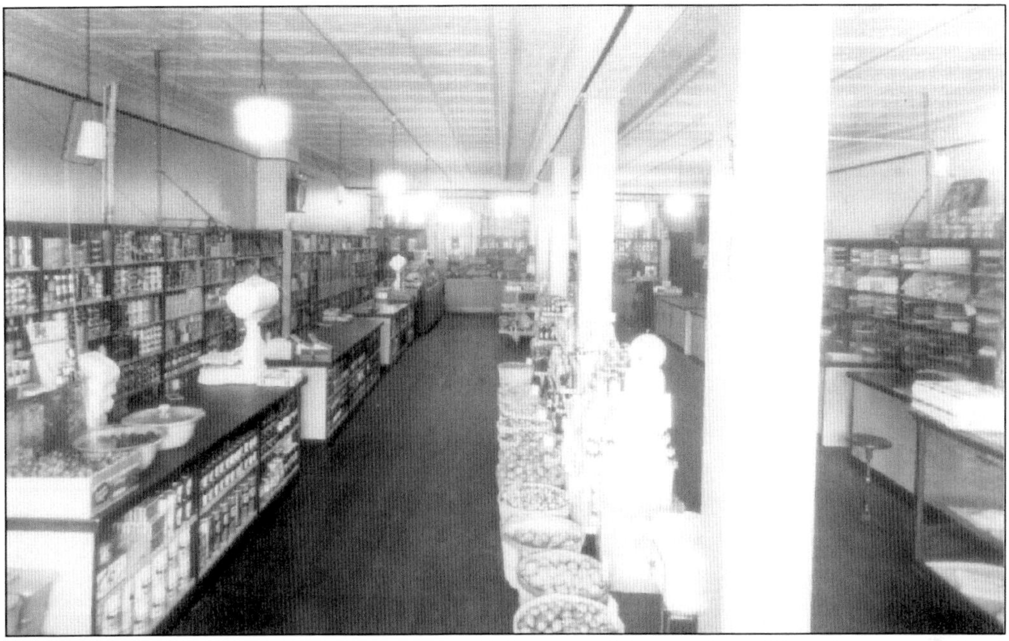

THOMPSON MERCANTILE. This is the interior of Thompson Mercantile on Main Street in Midland in 1939. The small town of Midland, Michigan managed to support seven grocery stores and two super markets—all on Main Street—which certainly made it easy for the housewife. It was the last store to carry both groceries and dry goods and it always smelled like oranges when you walked in the door.

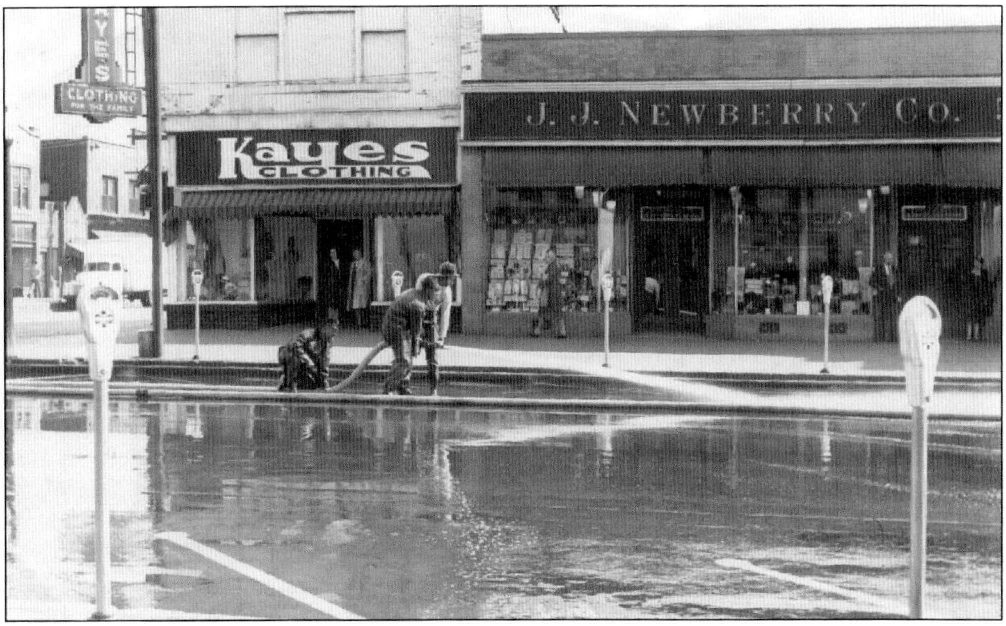

KAYE'S AND NEWBERRY'S. Kaye's Clothing Store and the J.J. Newberry Five & Dime were next to each other on Main Street. At Kaye's you could lay clothing away for as little as 50¢ a week and pay something on it every week. Their slogan was "It's Okay to Owe Kaye's." Newberry's really had things for a nickel and a dime.

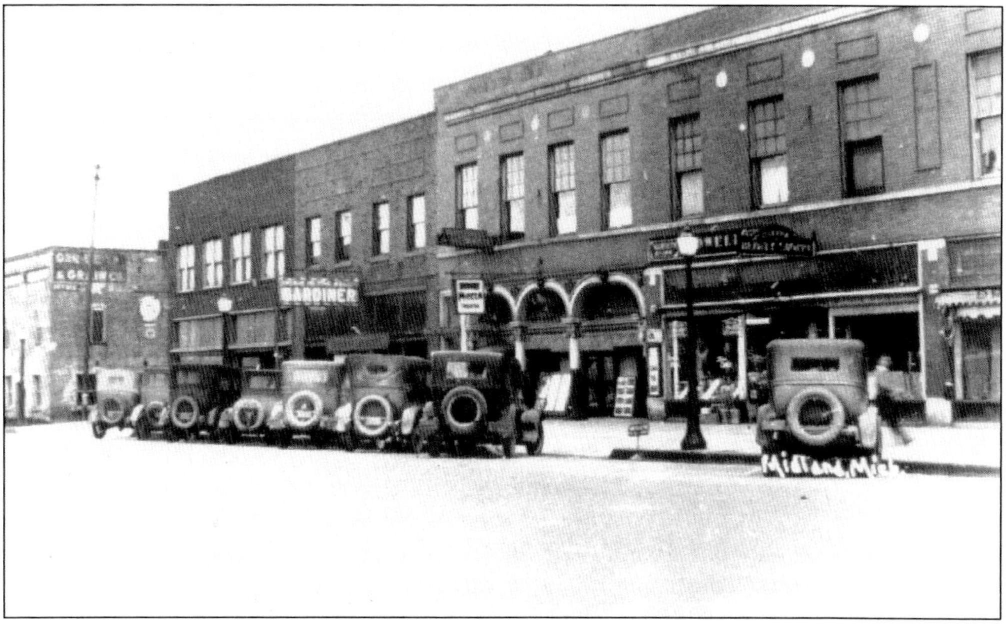

The Mecca Theatre. The Mecca Theatre was considered Down Main Street. Tickets were 10¢ and 25¢. And you saw Lash LaRue, Hopalong Cassiday, Gene Autry and Roy Rogers in feature films. The Lone Ranger and Tonto were in never-ending serials. We thought the *William Tell Overture* had been written just for them.

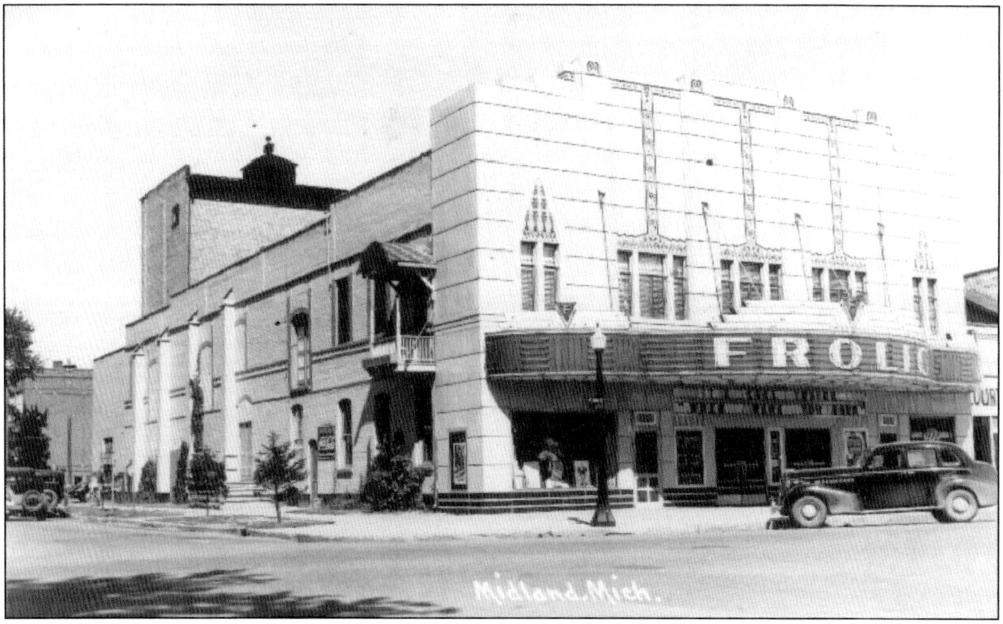

The Frolic Theatre. The Frolic Theatre was considered Up Main Street. Tickets were 10¢ and 25¢ here too, but you got to see Clark Gable, Vivien Leigh, Robert Taylor, and Tyrone Power. We usually went to the Frolic because Mom couldn't see paying 25¢ to see Gene Autry riding a horse when for the same 25¢ she could see Clark Gable or Robert Taylor.

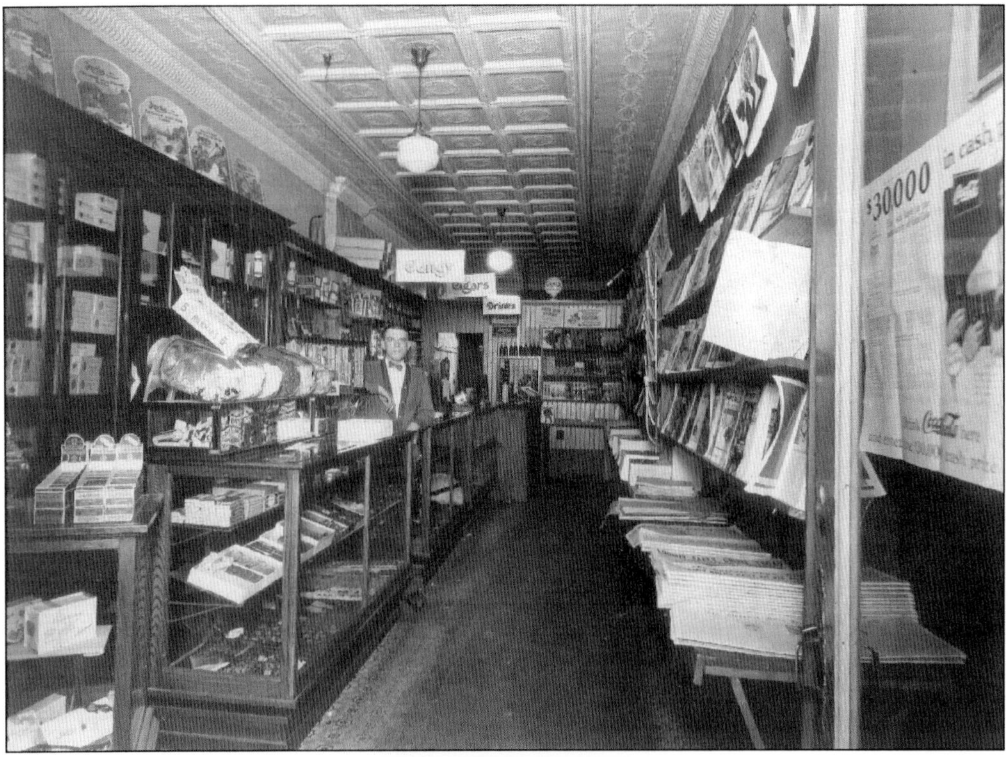

McCandless News Agency. Wayne McCandless came to Midland in 1926 to run a news agency that had been run by a Mr. Anderson. Through the years the business changed direction keeping up with the times. Today the business is known as McCandless Hallmark, and Wayne's son Jack still runs the family business. Gertrude McCandless took the business over after Wayne's death until Jack was home from the service.

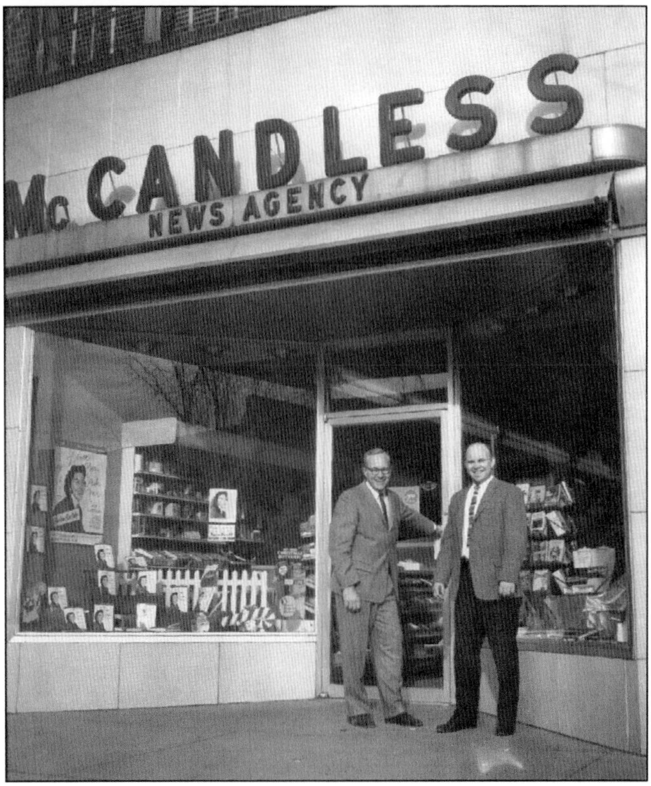

McCandless News Agency. Bob Brines and Jack McCandless stand at the door of the McCandless News Agency after a remodeling project had been completed. Still located on Main Street in Midland, it is the oldest family-operated business on Main Street.

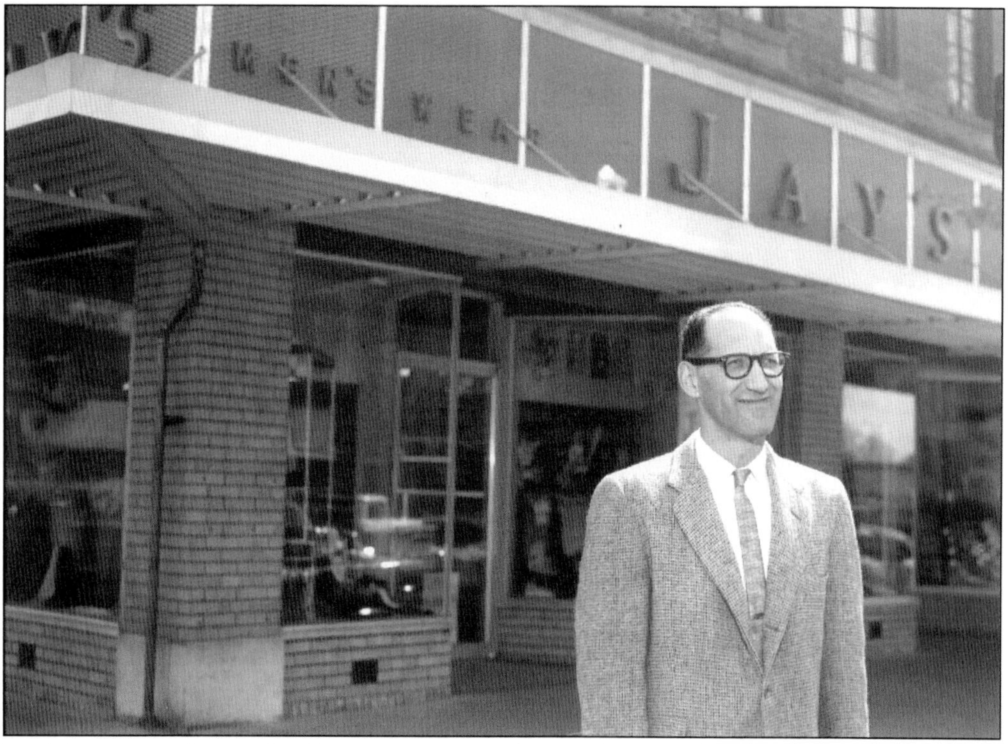

JAY'S CLOTHING STORE. Jay Grosberg came to the small town of Midland in March of 1941 and opened Jay's Men's and Boys' Wear. He made the grand sum of $5.45 the first day. Known for his civic accomplishments as well as a great clothing store, he was given the nickname "Mr. Main Street."

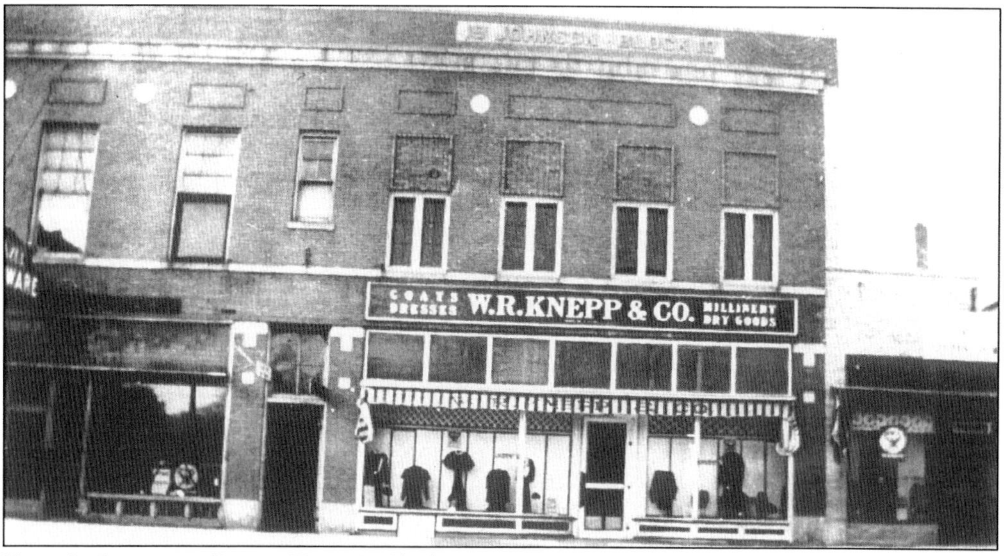

KNEPP'S CLOTHING STORE. Knepp's Clothing Store on Main Street was considered one of the nicest clothing stores in town. Generous with their merchandise, you could take home an outfit or two, try them on and if you weren't satisfied, and return the merchandise the next day. No money exchanged.

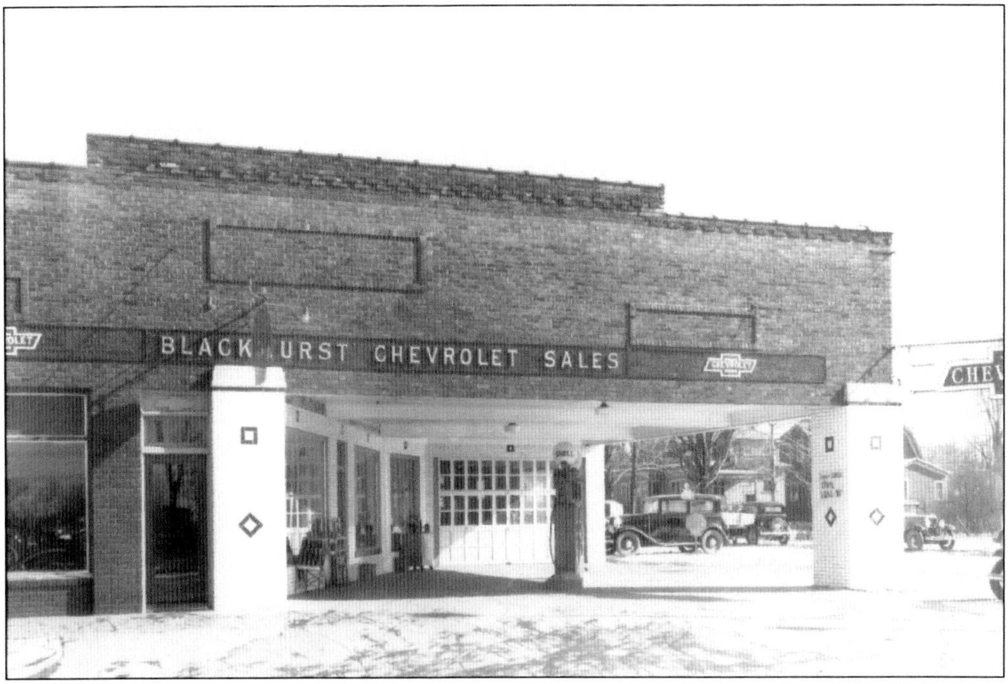

Blackhurst Chevrolet Sales. Morley Blackhurst sold Chevrolets at 433 E. Main Street in Midland. Otto Weineke sold Fords on the corner of E. Main and Benson streets. The J.W. Hackett Motor Sales at 448 E. Main Street sold Buicks. Oscar and Sheldon Hepinstall sold the old Graham car and McCarl Motor Sales sold Terraplanes. John Millar sold Dodges and Plymouths. Lloyd Mahar sold Oldsmobiles, DeSotos and Plymouths.

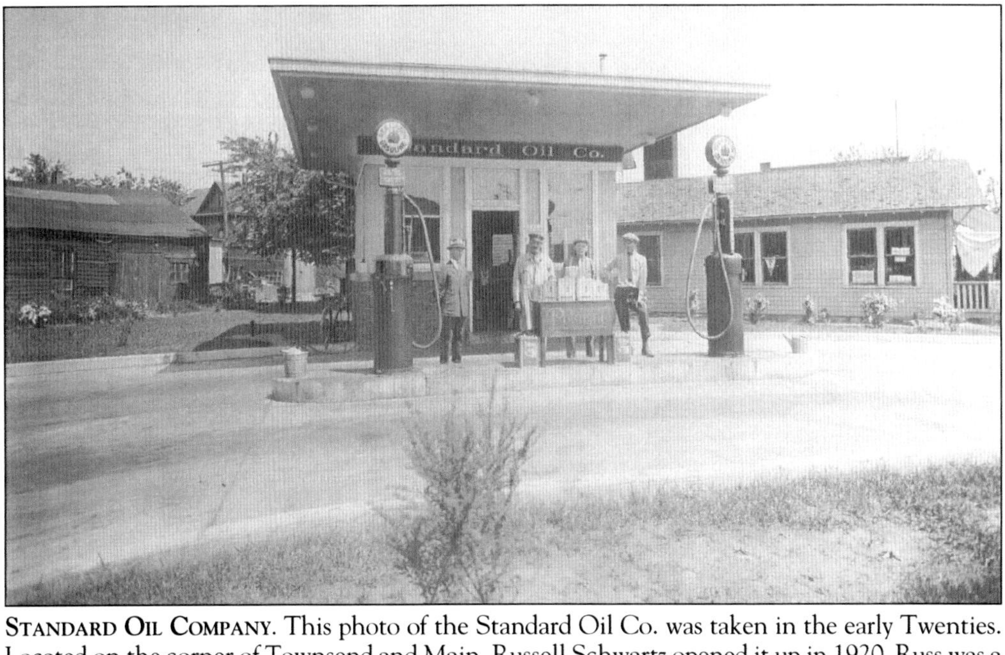

Standard Oil Company. This photo of the Standard Oil Co. was taken in the early Twenties. Located on the corner of Townsend and Main, Russell Schwartz opened it up in 1920. Russ was a son of Charles and Clara Duffett Schwartz, early settlers in the Gray-Ashby roads area.

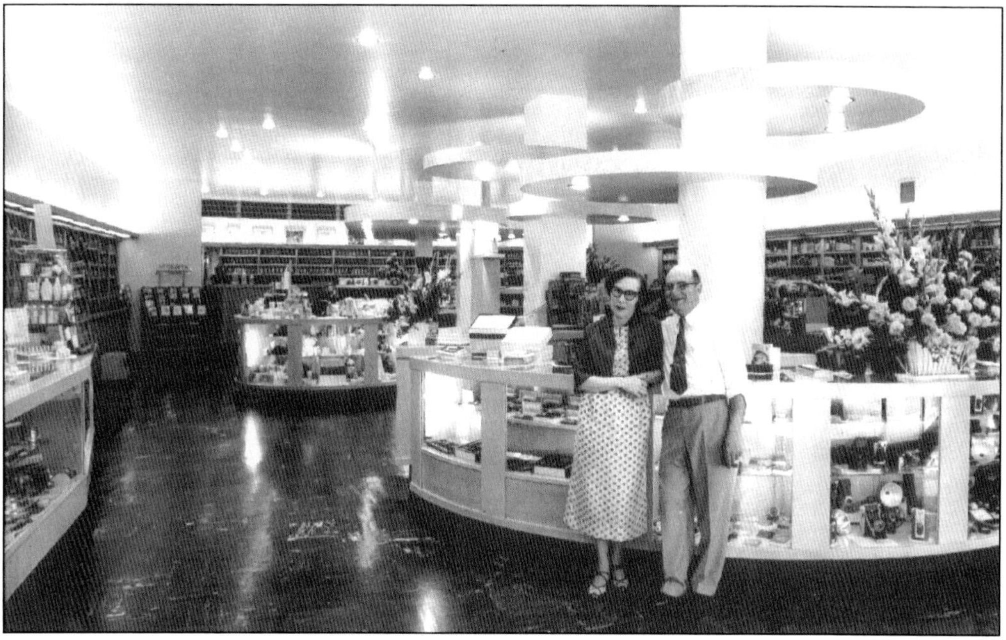

Community Drugs. Leonard Bergstein came to Midland in 1930 opening his first drug store at 311 East Main Street. Always ready to improve service to his customers, in 1938 he decided to take out the soda fountain and put in cosmetics. His wife Esther couldn't sleep for three weeks. She said, "Whoever heard of a drug store without a soda fountain?"

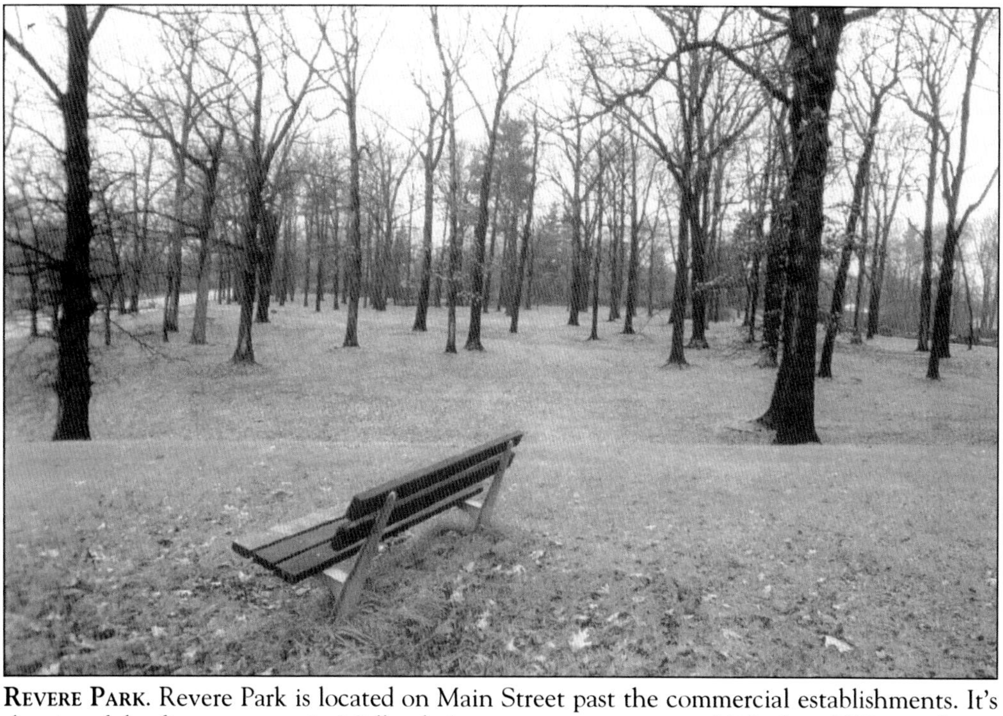

Revere Park. Revere Park is located on Main Street past the commercial establishments. It's the site of the first cemetery in Midland. A new cemetery was established in 1873 on what is today Orchard Drive.

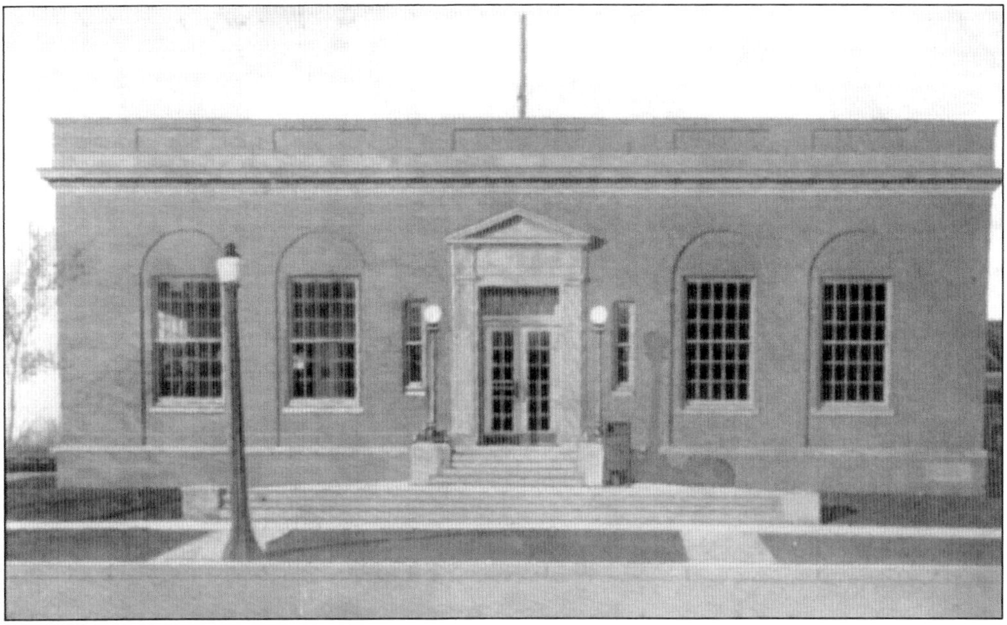

The Midland Post Office. The first post office in Midland was in John Larkin's hotel in 1856. The next 62 years saw the post office occupying various locations. This is the new post office c. 1918. It was razed to make room for a new post office in 1940. Today the main post office is located near the Circle, not on Main Street.

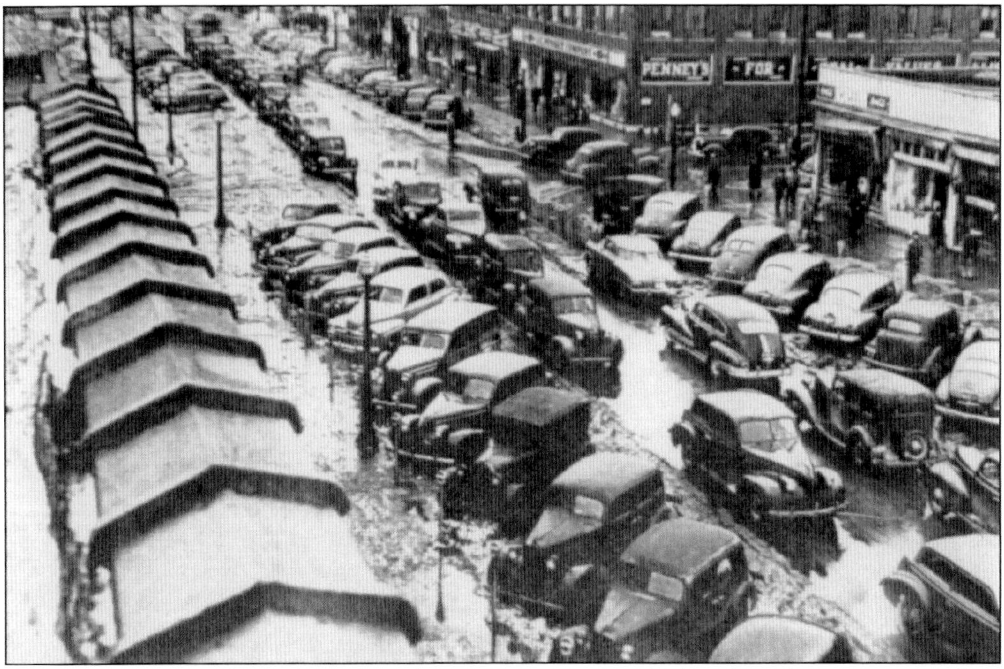

Traffic Jam. This photo shows how busy Main Street could be when the men got paid on Thursday night at The Dow Chemical Company and on Saturdays when shopping was a "must" for families in Midland. Statistics show that in 1927, Midland County's population was 27,188 people and there were 4,650 cars licensed.

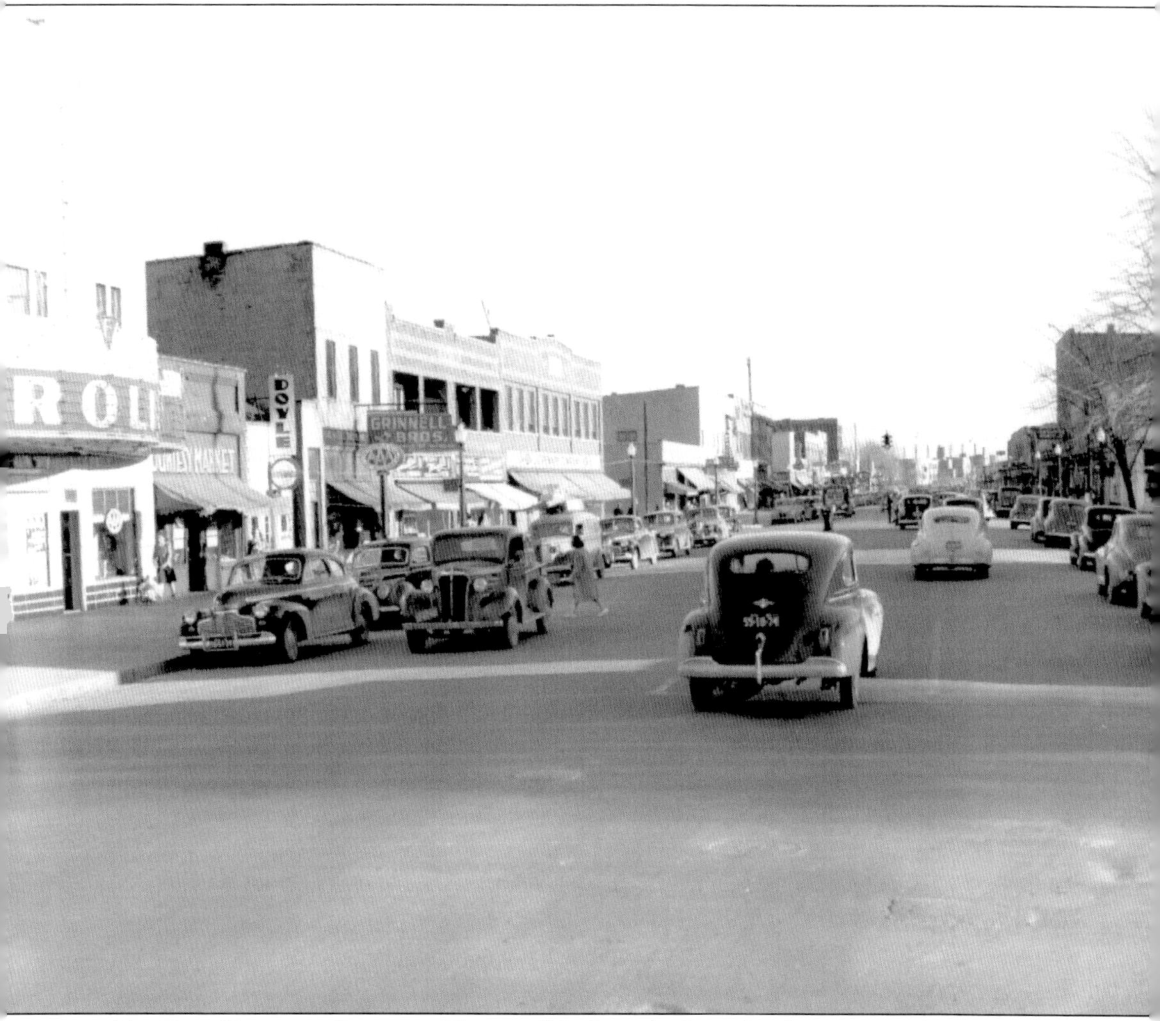

The Dow Chemical Company. Plumes of black smoke from the chimneys at The Dow Chemical Company at the end of Main Street were a familiar sight to us growing up in Midland. While the rest of the country suffered through the Great Depression, Midland had steady employment thanks to Herbert Dow. (Photo courtesy of Post Street Archives)

Two

MIDLAND LANDMARKS

Progress is the activity of today and the assurance of tomorrow.

—Emerson

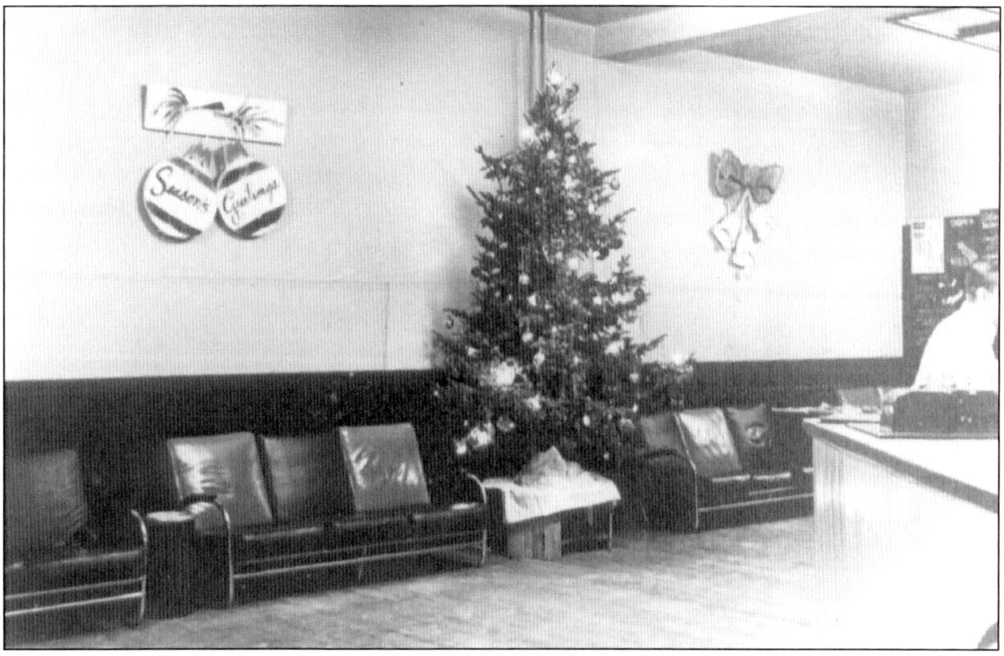

Nothing quite evokes the Thirties and how Christmas used to be as this photo of the main lobby at the old Community Center on Townsend Street in Midland. Pasteboard cutouts are on the wall. It's a real Christmas tree and the bulbs were so big you could burn your hand on them.

To those of us growing up in Midland, certain buildings became landmarks that can never be replaced. Many have been torn down to make way for progress: The Frolic Theatre, the Mecca Theatre, the first airport, the Midland Theatre on the Circle, Del's Drive-Inn on the Circle, the old Carnegie Library on Townsend and next door to it the Community Center, the first radio station in Midland—WMDN, the City Hall on Ashman Street, the old Junior High and Senior High on Grove Street. Photographs are all that remain of that part of our lives lived in the last century.

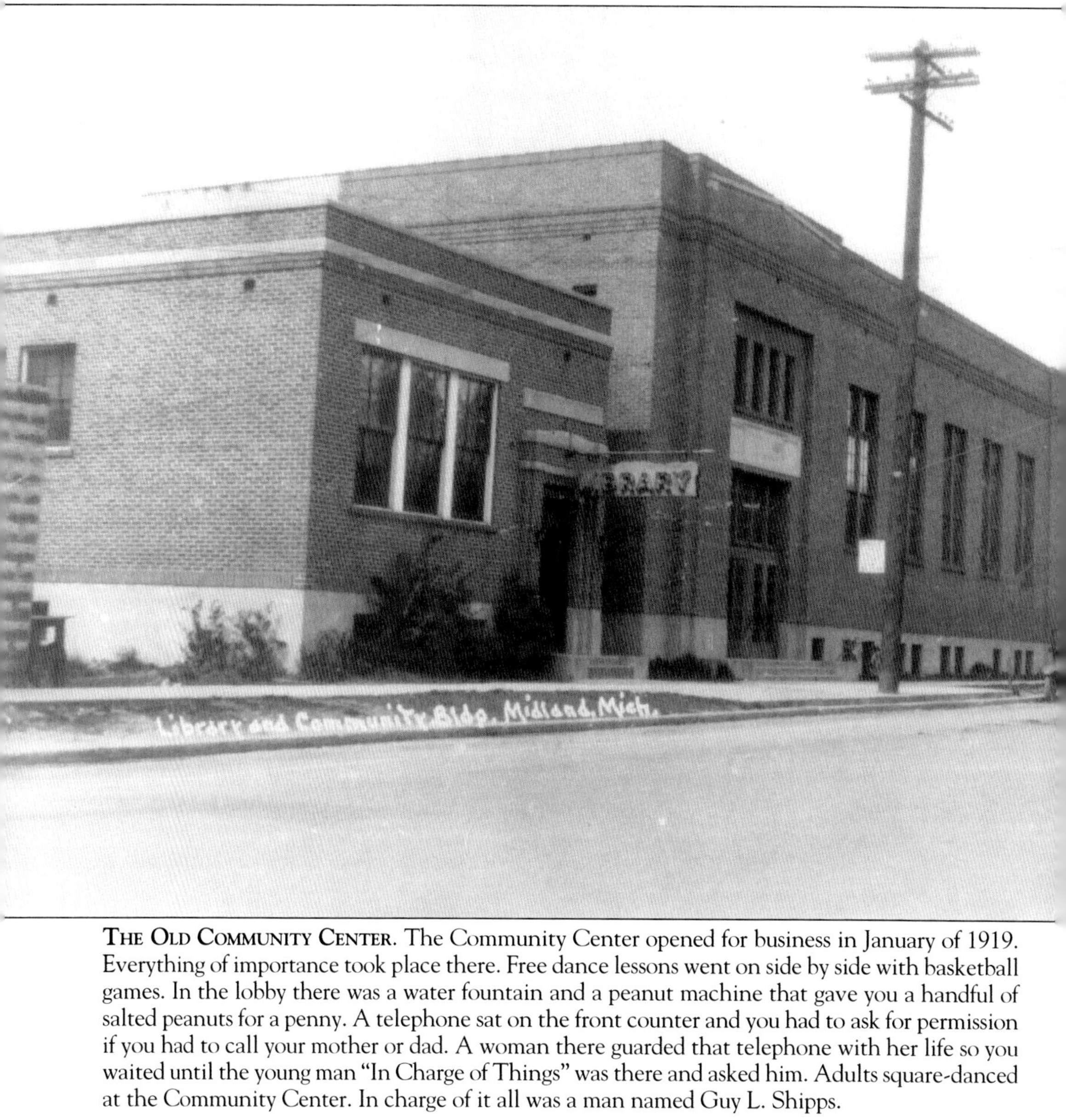

The Old Community Center. The Community Center opened for business in January of 1919. Everything of importance took place there. Free dance lessons went on side by side with basketball games. In the lobby there was a water fountain and a peanut machine that gave you a handful of salted peanuts for a penny. A telephone sat on the front counter and you had to ask for permission if you had to call your mother or dad. A woman there guarded that telephone with her life so you waited until the young man "In Charge of Things" was there and asked him. Adults square-danced at the Community Center. In charge of it all was a man named Guy L. Shipps.

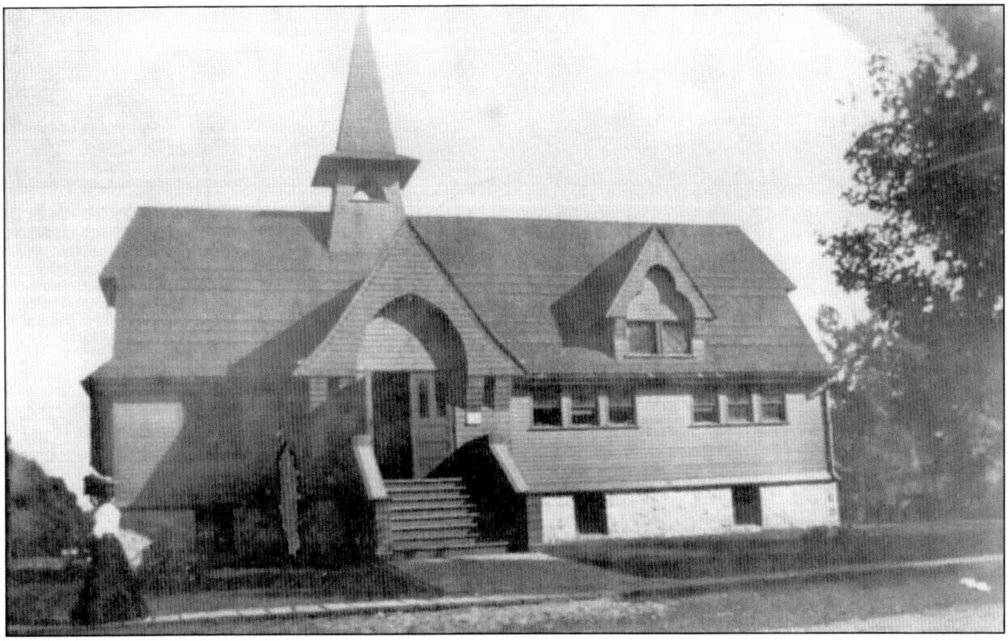

Midland's First Library. On March 10, 1900, a subscription library opened up in space rented from the Unitarian Church on the corner of Ashman and Ellsworth streets. Two hundred books made up the total inventory.

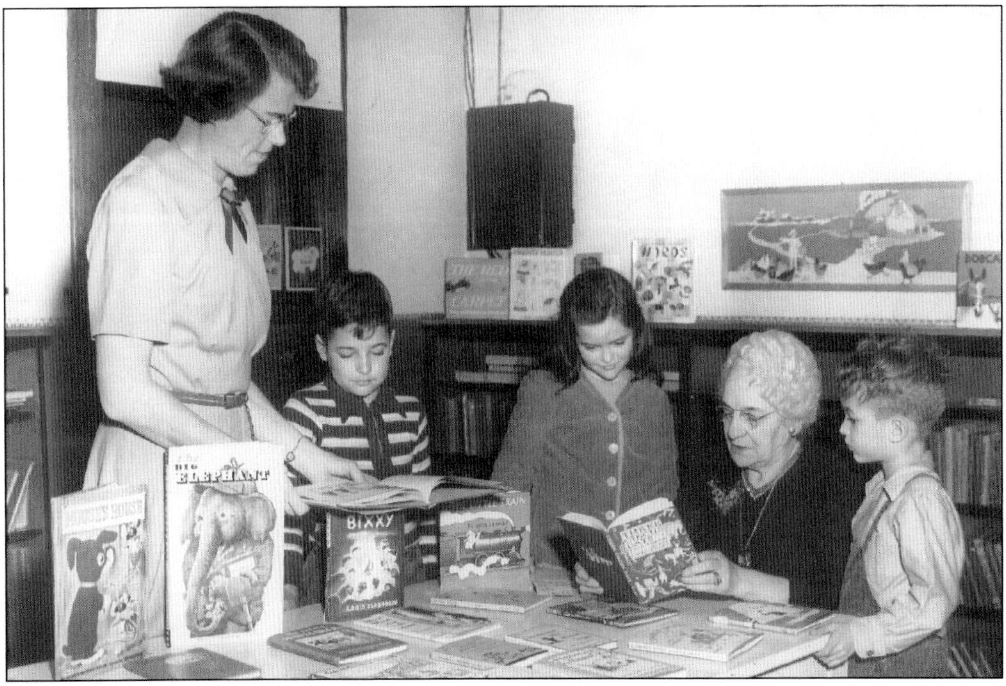

The Carnegie Library. The Andrew Carnegie Library on Townsend Street was located next to the Community Center. In this photo Mrs. Mildred Stanford is seated with Garnetta Simansky on the far left. The children, left to right, are Nelson LeRoy Smith, Denice Jones and Russell Tommy Smith. Signs reading SILENCE were on every table.

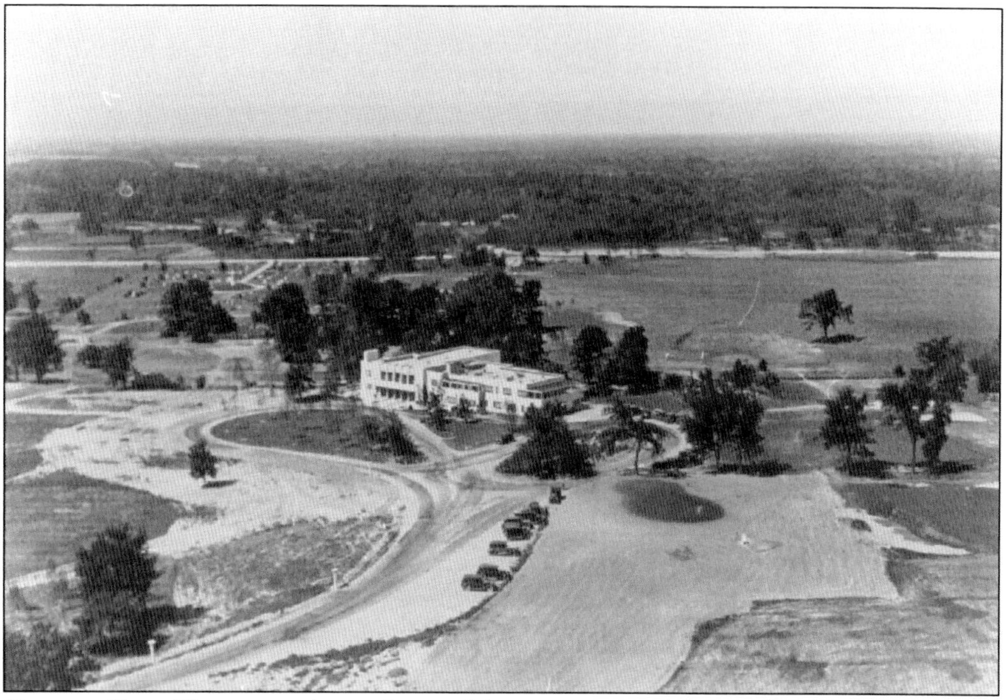

Country Club. This is an early aerial view of the new country club in Midland. Gilbert Currie, a local lawyer and philanthropist, got tired of driving to Saginaw to play golf and it wasn't long before a country club and golf course were on the drawing board. It officially opened May 1, 1931.

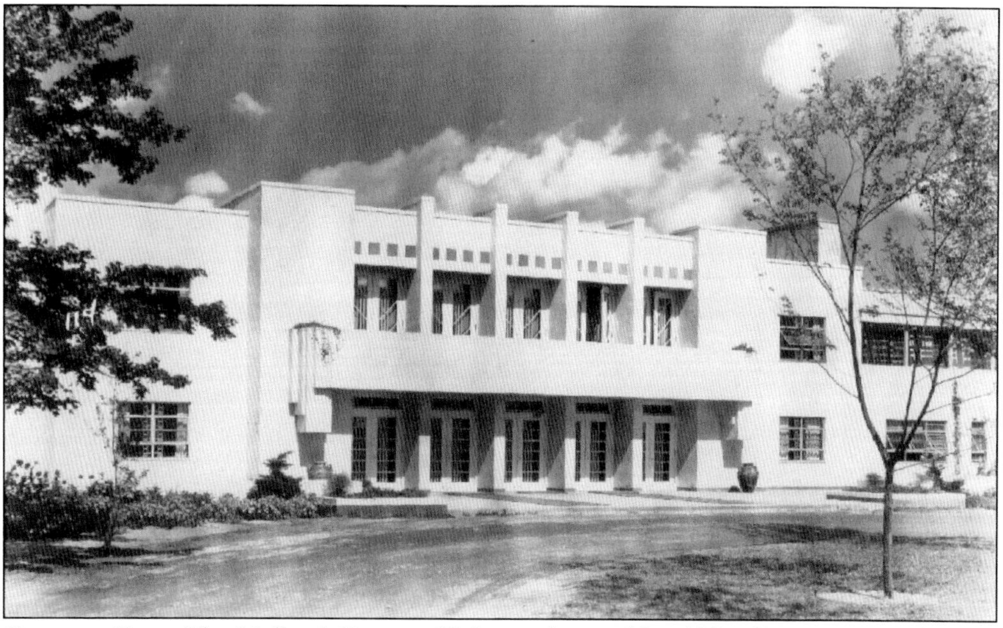

Country Club. The Midland Country Club was designed by Alden Dow in 1931 when he was attending Columbia University. The property for the country club and the surrounding golf course was purchased from the Petersen family (80 acres) and the Haley family (40 acres). Designed in the new Art Deco style, it was labeled "different" by conservative Midlanders.

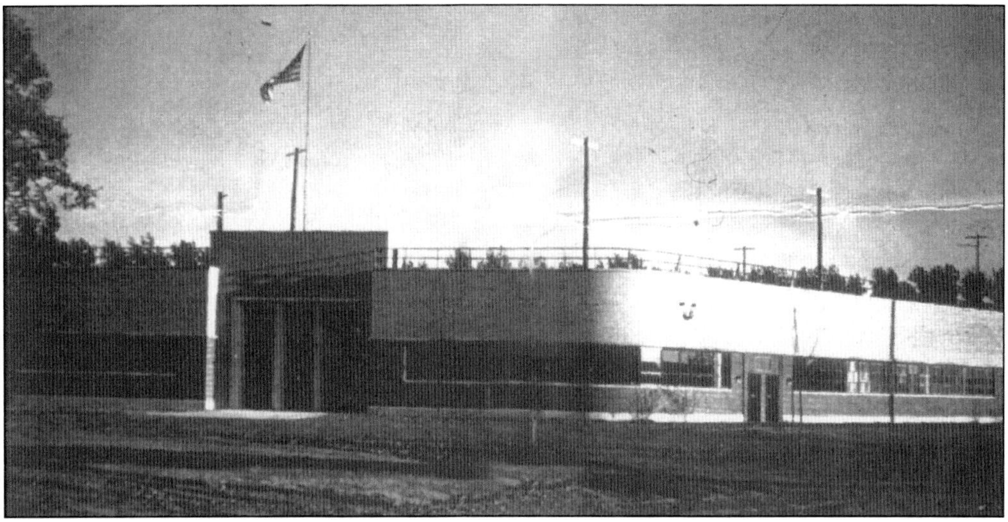

Currie Stadium. On May 23, 1942, Currie Stadium was dedicated in Emerson Park. The Dow AC's ball team played to a standing room only crowd that night. A lawyer by profession, Gilbert Currie was a leading philanthropist in Midland. After donating Currie Stadium to the city of Midland, he made the stipulation that no admission would ever be charged at the stadium and this was honored for many years.

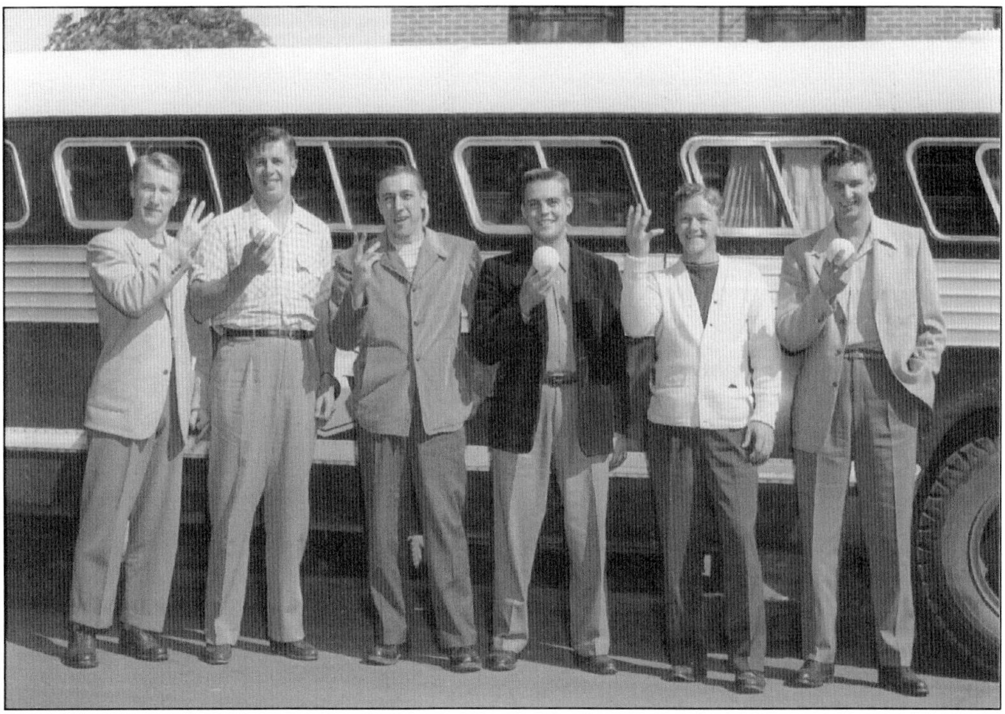

Dow ACs. The Dow Chemical Company sponsored a softball team named the Dow Athletic Club but it was shortened to Dow ACs. They quickly became celebrities in our small town and it was standing room only when they played at Currie Stadium. In 1948 they won the world softball championship. Left to right, the players shown here are: Bob Wright, Al Linde, Jim Hall, Clyde Dexter, Bill Berryman, and Don McDonald.

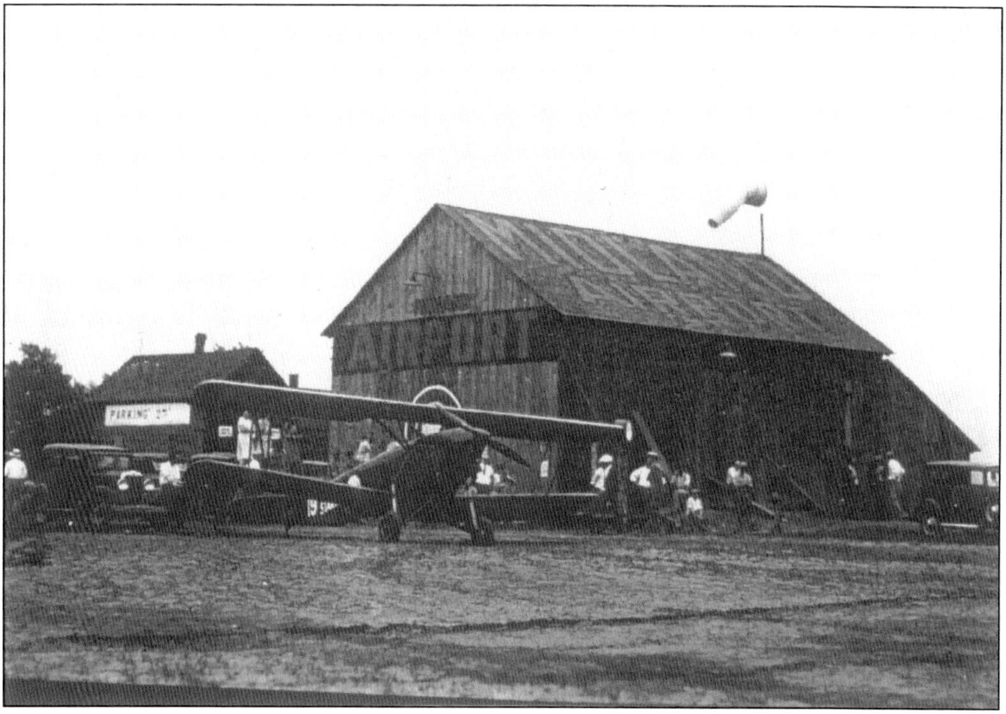

BARSTOW AIRPORT. The first airport in Midland was simply called the Midland Airport and was located in the Swede and Eastlawn area. It was renamed Barstow Airport in honor of Jack Barstow, a young Midland man who died in a plane crash during a homecoming celebration in Corpus Christi, Texas.

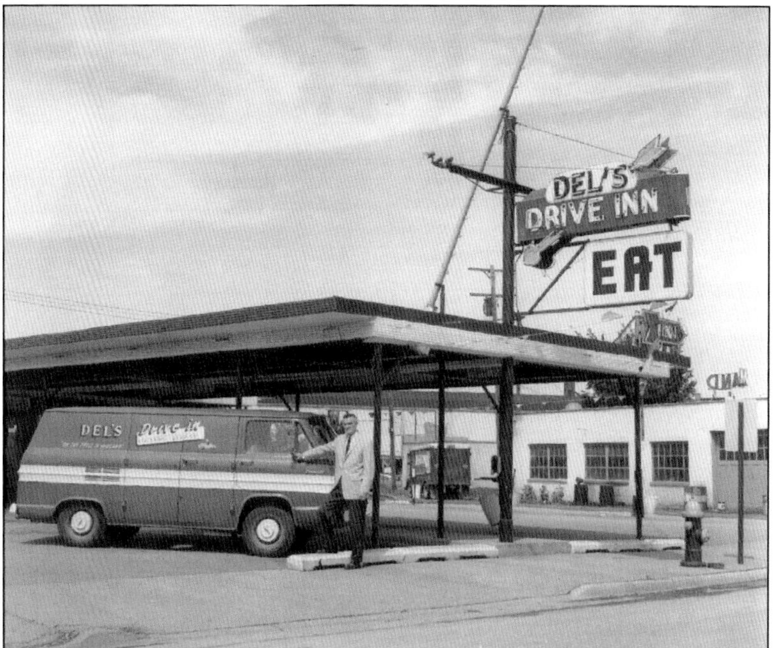

DEL'S DRIVE-INN ON THE CIRCLE. It was the first drive-in to conquer the small town of Midland, Michigan. Such a novelty. You ordered by speaking into a box. A tray was hooked on the car door with your order on it. You didn't have to get out of your car. How easy could life get?

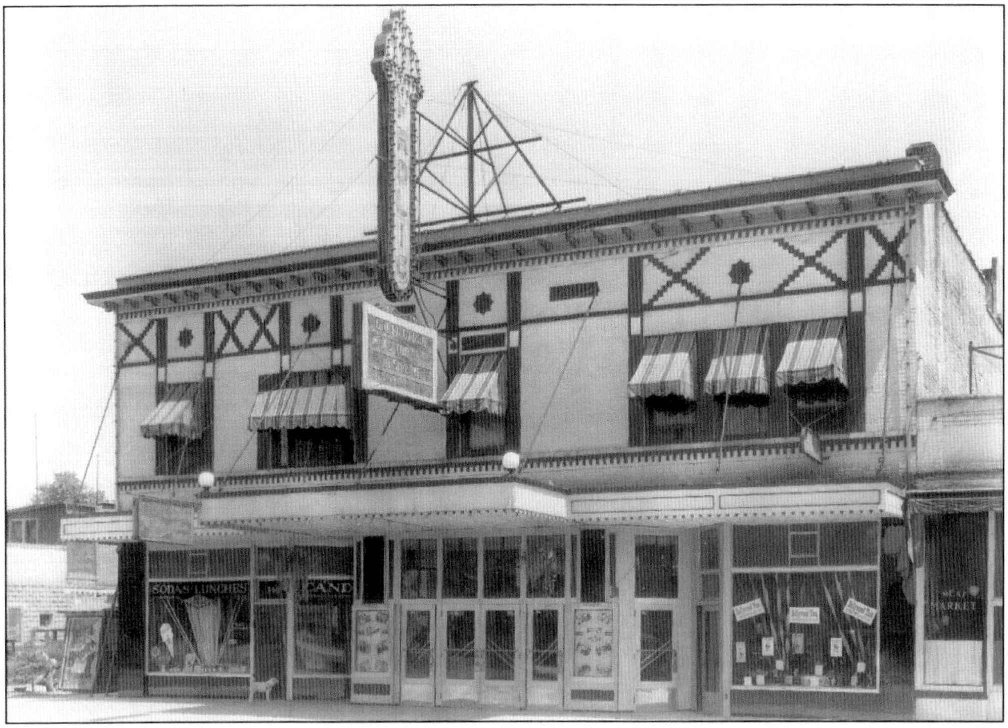

THE FIRST FROLIC THEATRE. This is the Frolic Theatre built by Bill Cassidy on Main Street in 1924. An organist named Mr. Bath played music to accompany the "Silent" movies that were being shown. In 1929 the first "Talkie" came out and always eager to be up to date, Bill Cassidy remodeled this theatre into one that would carry sound.

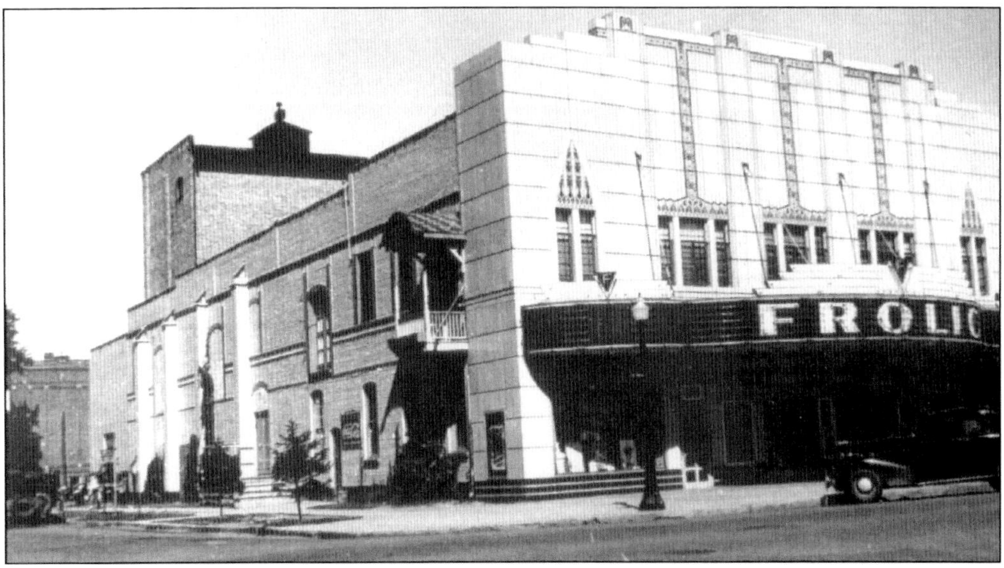

THE REMODELED FROLIC THEATRE. The Frolic Theatre on Main Street was remodeled to provide the new "Talkies" to the movie-going public. No expense was spared to make the renovated movie house elegant. Tickets were a dime for children and a quarter for adults. And next door was the Frolic Sweet Shop.

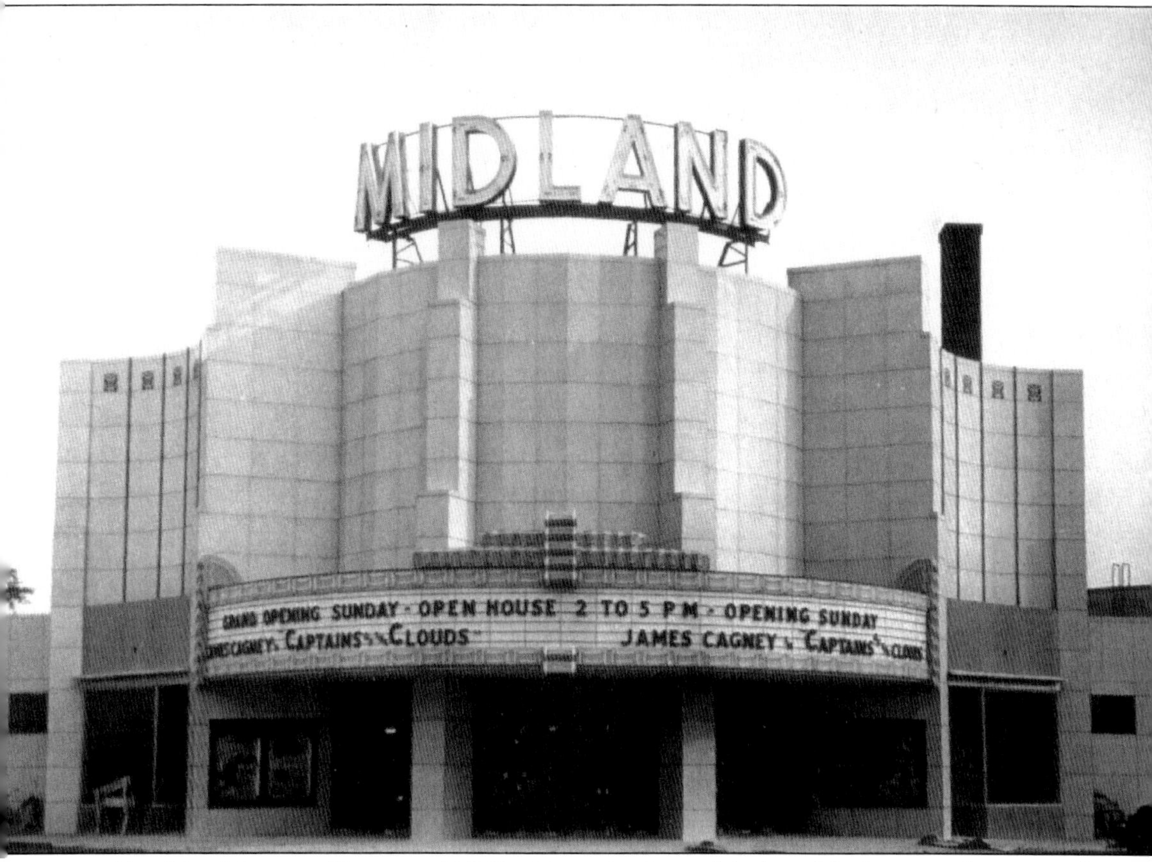

THE NEW MIDLAND THEATRE. Bill Cassidy took a leap of faith and built a new theatre on the Circle when the Circle was still in its infancy. It opened in May of 1942 with James Cagney in *Captain of the Clouds*. Spacious and elegant with red plush seats, imitation Grecian urns, and lighted mirrors—all designed to make a special world for a couple of hours for the price of a movie ticket. Everyone agreed it was a beautiful theatre but a lot of people said, "Who's going to drive all the way out there just to see a movie?"

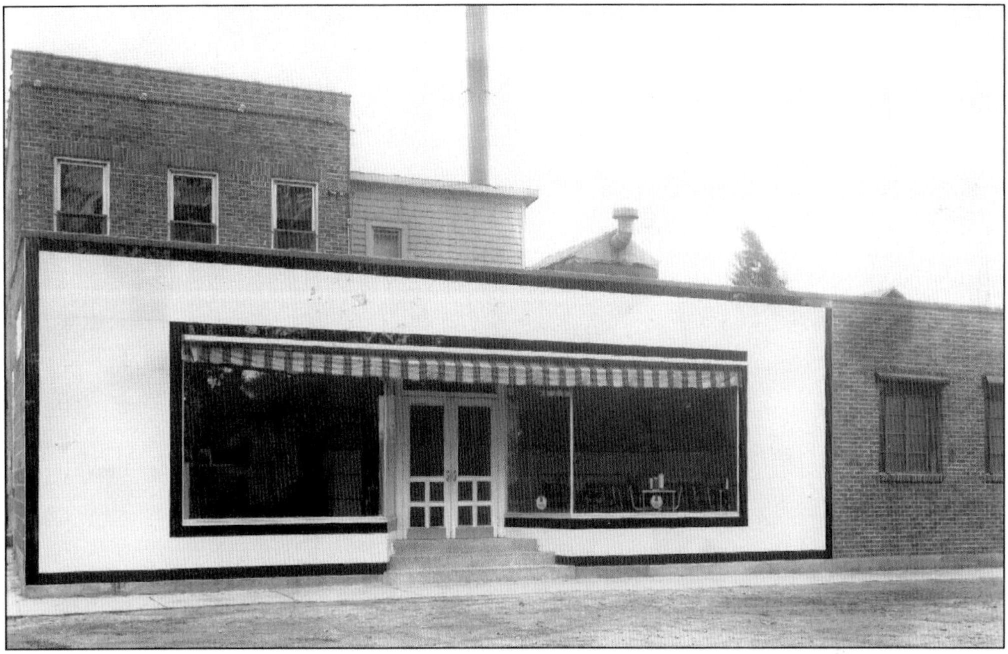

Smith Dairy Exterior. Smith Dairy was located on George Street making it close to elementary schools, the Junior High and the Senior High. There may have been other places that sold ice cream but everyone agreed that Smith Dairy was the best. Summer nights found the sidewalks lined with people waiting to get inside for an ice cream cone. Business was brisk!

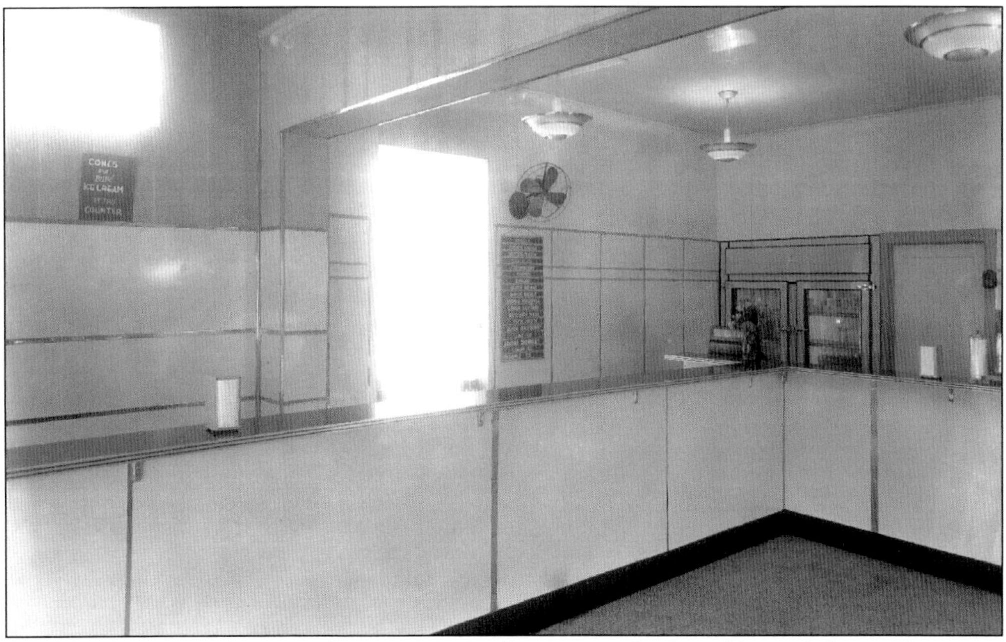

Smith Dairy Interior. Everything was stark white except for the tables and chairs. The young women who dished out the ice cream wore white uniforms and little hats that they pinned in their hair with bobby pins. Cones were 5¢. Sodas and sundaes 10 ¢. Banana splits cost a whopping 15¢!

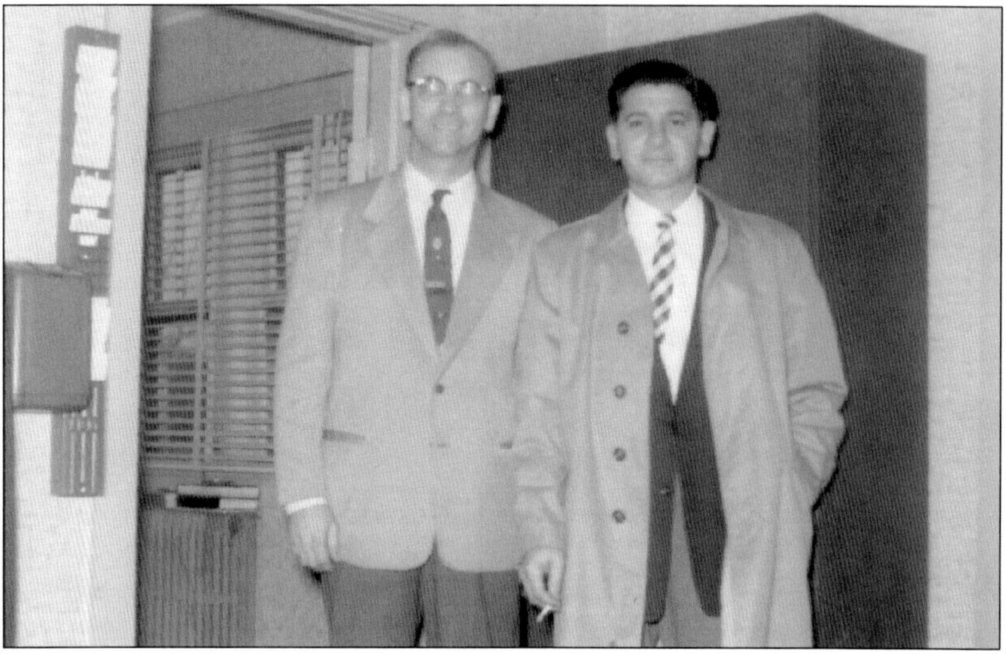

WMDN, THE FIRST RADIO STATION. It was on Swede Road in an old farm house. It went on the air in 1948 with a young man from North Dakota, Pete Wolf, its first engineer. He soon became the station manager. Here Pete, as station manager, poses with his one full-time salesman, Pete Buffa.

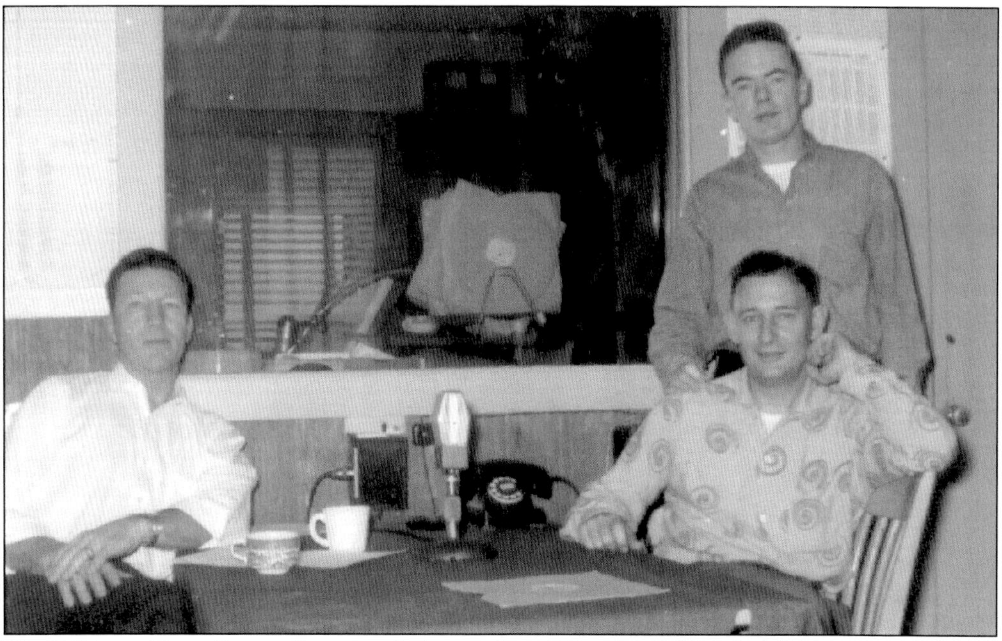

WMDN, THE FIRST RADIO STATION. Left to right are Ernie Strickland and Art Sauve with Bob Morgan standing in back of Art in the room where interviews took place and live musicians performed (free of charge). Space was so crowded that new records were put in the bathtub until there was time to file them in the record room.

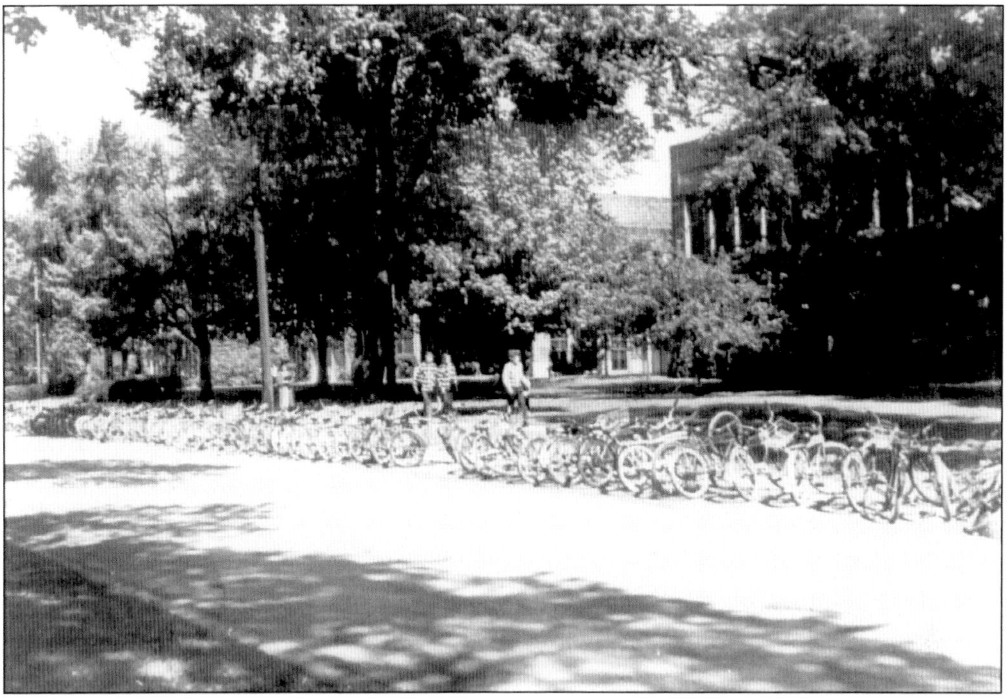

Junior High. After the Union School burned down in 1908, a new senior high school was built on Grove Street by 1909. Before long an elementary school known as Second Ward and a Junior High were added. In 1937 a new Senior High was built on Rodd Street and just the elementary and junior high schools remained on Grove.

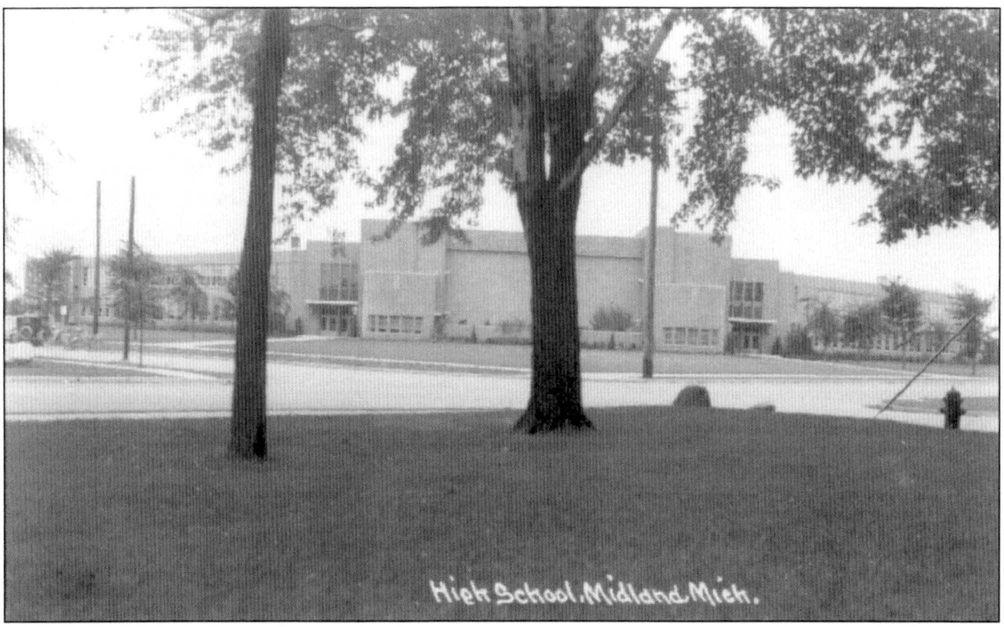

The New Senior High School on Rodd. As the school population continued to grow, a new Senior High School was built on Rodd Street and occupied in 1937 with the class of 1938 being the first graduating class.

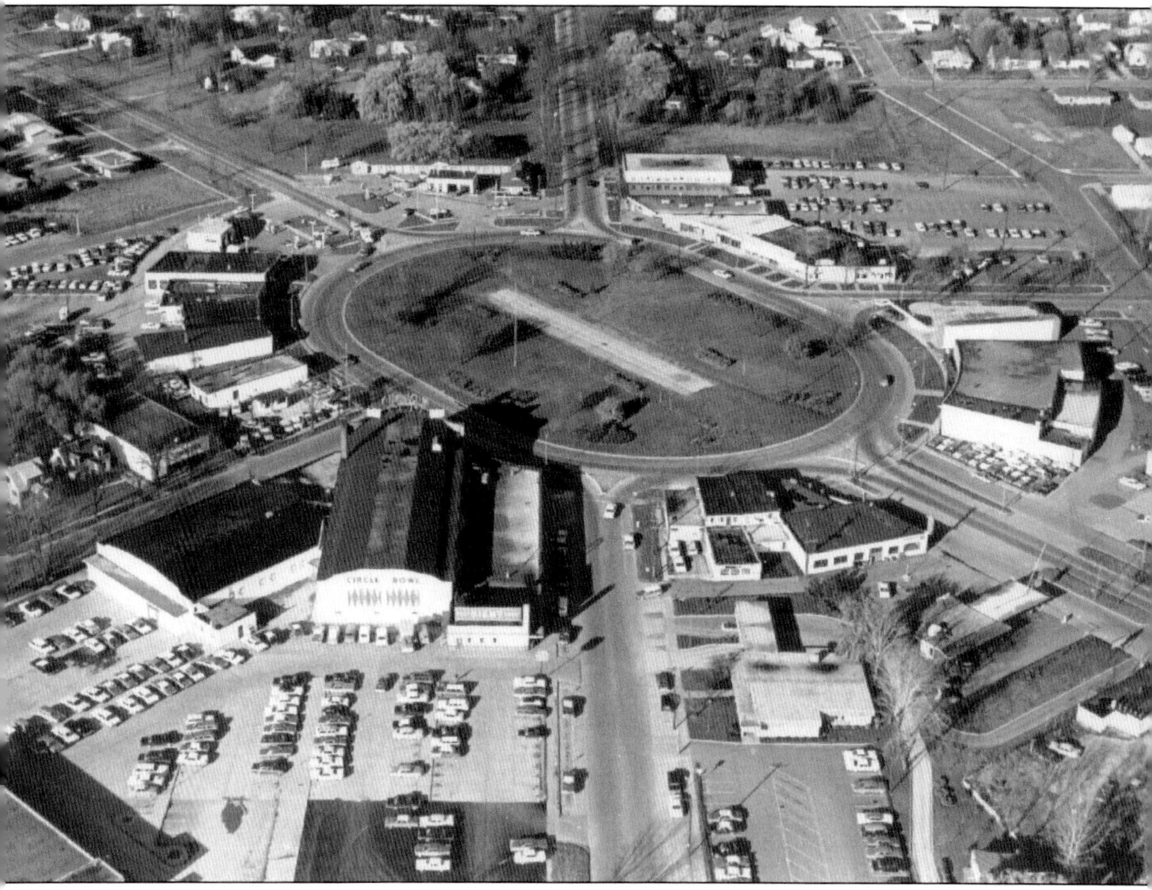

The Circle, Gateway to the North. A man by the name of Anthony Dagle first platted the Circle area in the town's infancy. Eventually, businesses began stretching out there since there was no more room on Main Street for new businesses. Designed to improve the flow of traffic, it proved to be a bottleneck and eventually the park was taken out and Saginaw Road went straight through. If you're an old-time Midlander you should be able to pick out the Midland Theatre, the Chemical Bank, Jess Mudd's gas station and overnight cabins, Miller's Furniture Store, the Community Drug Store, Otway Autos, Knopics' Hardware and Smith's Flowers and Gifts.

Three

Dow Legacy

The greatest truths are the simplest and so are the greatest men.

—Hare

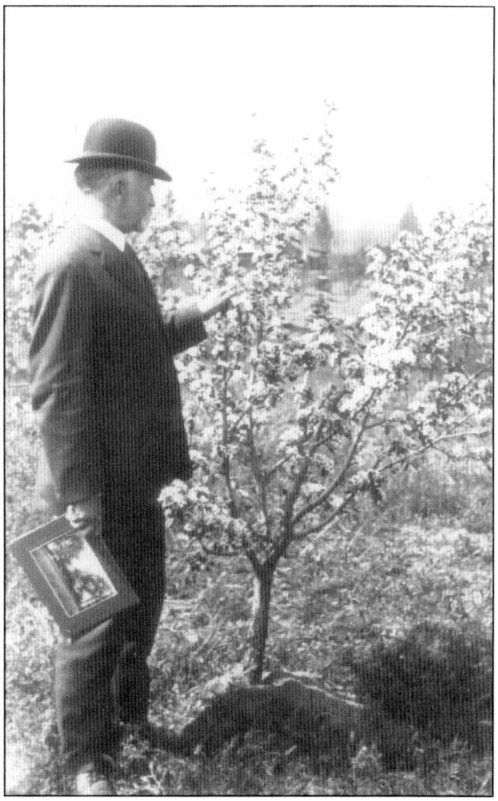

Herbert Henry Dow was born on February 26, 1866, to Joseph and Sarah Dow in Belleville, Ontario, Canada where his dad had been sent temporarily to work.

In 1888 he made his first trip to Midland, Michigan to take samples from the brine sea that lay beneath the flatlands of this small village on the banks of the Tittabawassee River. On January 4, 1891, he proved that bromine could be produced electrolytically and on September 29 that same year he got a patent on the process of extracting bromine from brine. By May 18, 1897, Herbert Henry Dow had persuaded 57 investors to put up the magnificent sum of $200,000 to start a new business named The Dow Chemical Company in the small town of Midland, Michigan. He was 31 years old at the time and no one expected great things from him. But his chemical company was to succeed beyond anyone's wildest expectations into a chemical conglomerate spanning the world and make the Dow name famous world-wide.

His death in 1930 at the age of 64 has not diminished the work he accomplished and Midland is all the richer because he lived here. (Photo courtesy of Post Street Archives)

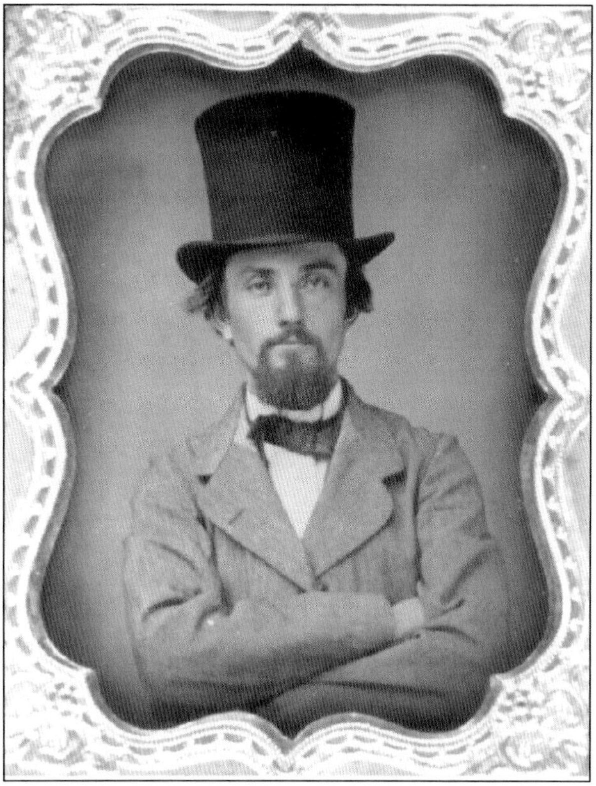

JOSEPH HENRY DOW. Dated 1860, this is Joseph Henry Dow, Herbert's father. He was born in 1836 and died in 1901. He married Sarah Bunnell on Thanksgiving Day, 1863, and that marriage produced three children: Herbert Henry, Mary, and Helen. Joseph Dow was a master mechanic and his son Herbert learned early on from his father to seek inventive solutions to problems. (Photo courtesy of Post Street Archives)

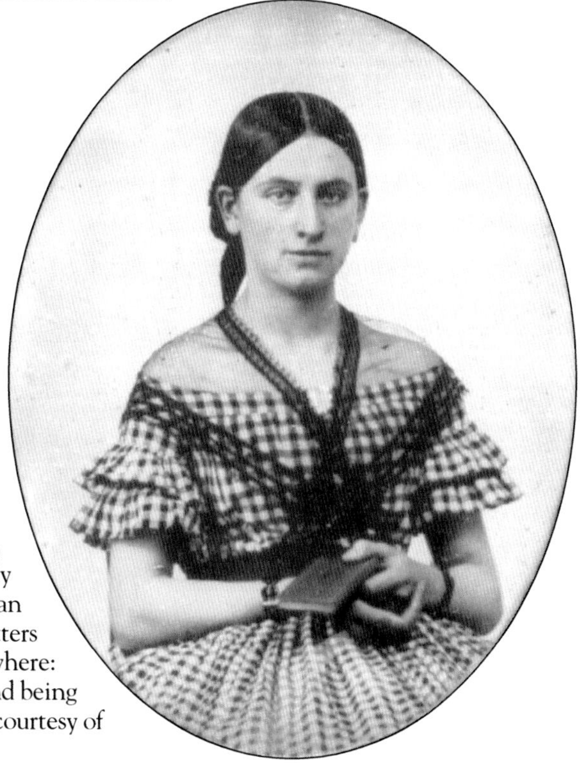

SARAH BUNNELL DOW. Sarah Bunnell Dow was born in 1838 and married Joseph Henry Dow on Thanksgiving Day, 1863. She died in 1909. When her only son, Herbert, moved to Midland, Michigan to begin a chemical business her letters reflected the worries of mothers everywhere: infrequent letters home, extravagance, and being a young bachelor in a new town. (Photo courtesy of Post Street Archives)

GRIST MILL. This is the grist mill that Herbert Henry Dow rented in 1890 to prove that bromine could be extracted from brine electrolytically. The mill was owned by Evens, Eesley and Harris. Dow began operations on a 24-hour basis with a three-man crew. William Andres was the miller, Malcolm McDonald was the cooper, and John McDonald was the salt maker. The grist mill was located on West Main Street. The grist mill is long gone and the site is now known as Hart Park.

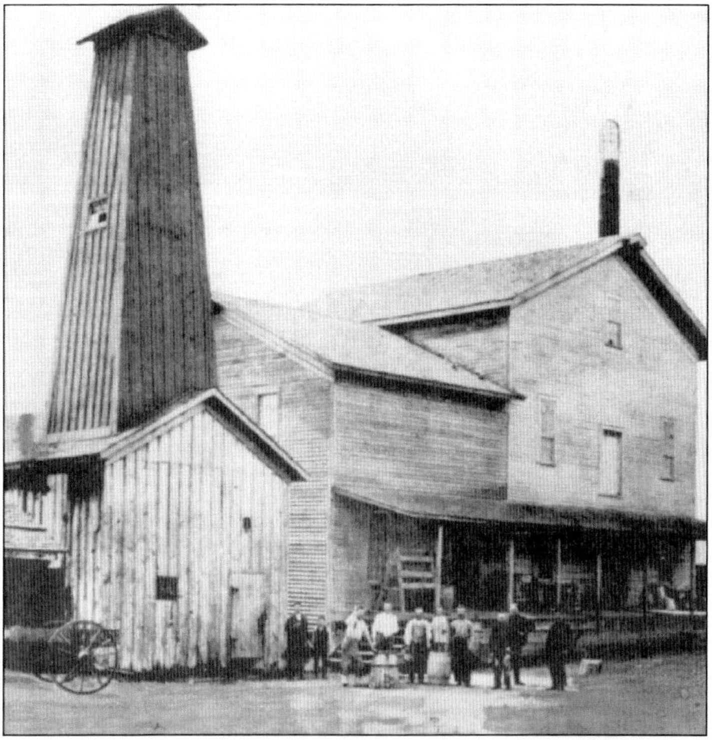

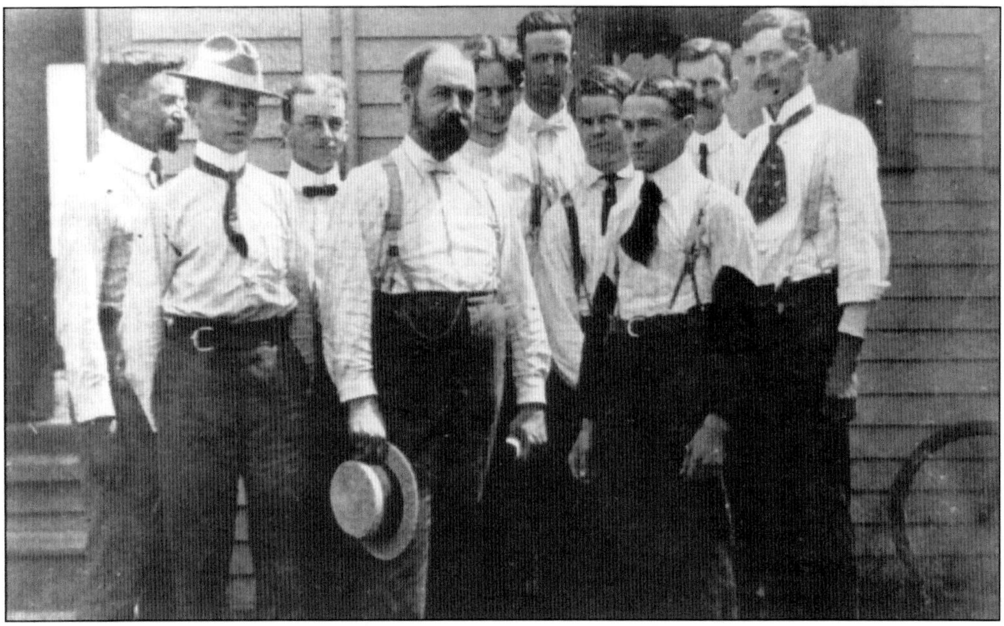

OFFICE STAFF. Dated 1901, this photo shows the men involved in the creation of the fledgling Dow Chemical Company. Left to right, the men are: Herbert Henry Dow, E.O. Cross (wearing a hat), F.N. Lowry (behind Cross), A.E. Convers (holding his hat), J.E. LeFevre, J.C. Graves (tallest man in picture), D.Richardson (in front of Graves), E.W. Bennett (in the very front of picture), T. Griswold (partially hidden by Bennett), and M.B. Johnson. (Photo courtesy of the Post Street Archives)

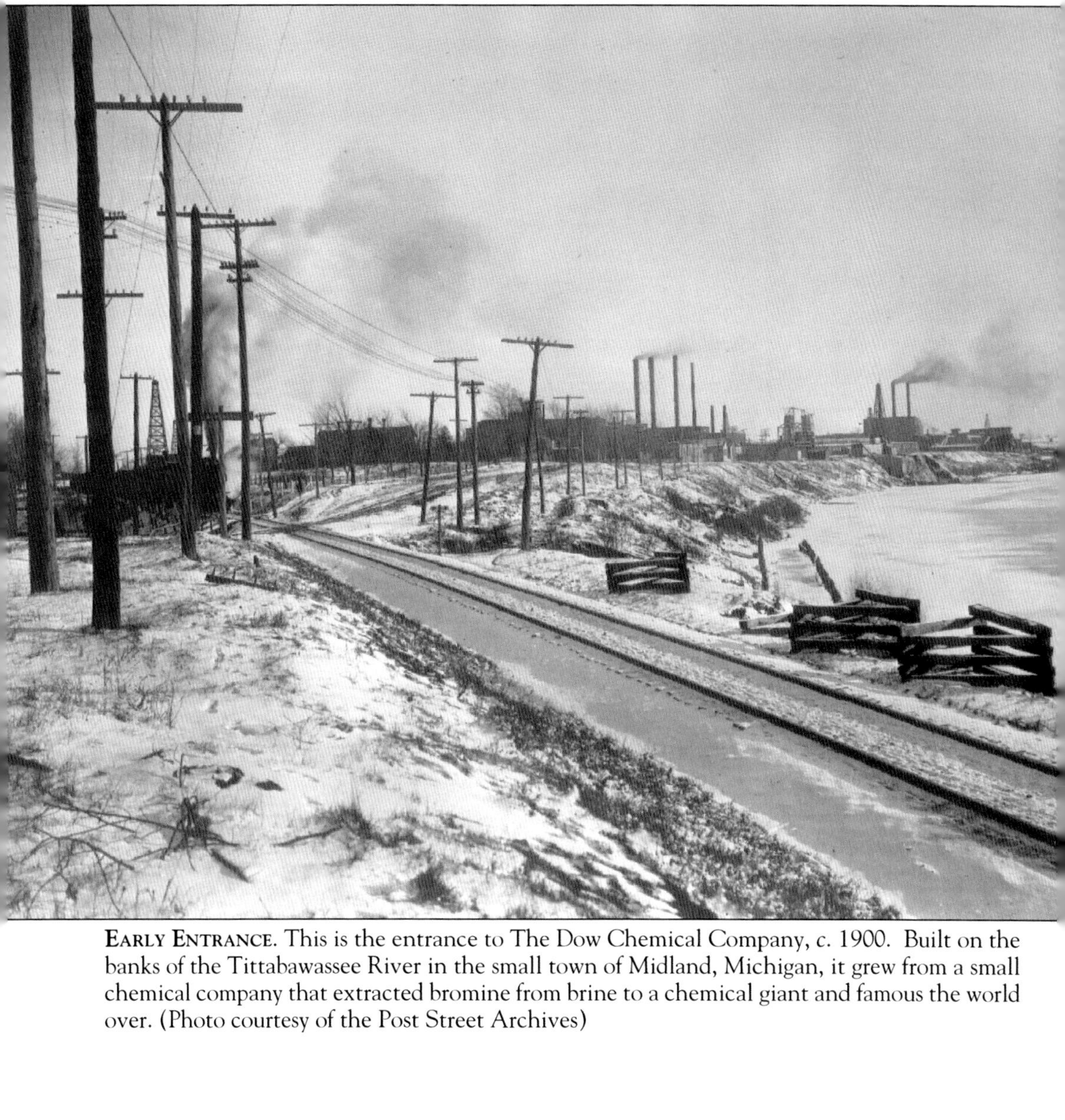

Early Entrance. This is the entrance to The Dow Chemical Company, c. 1900. Built on the banks of the Tittabawassee River in the small town of Midland, Michigan, it grew from a small chemical company that extracted bromine from brine to a chemical giant and famous the world over. (Photo courtesy of the Post Street Archives)

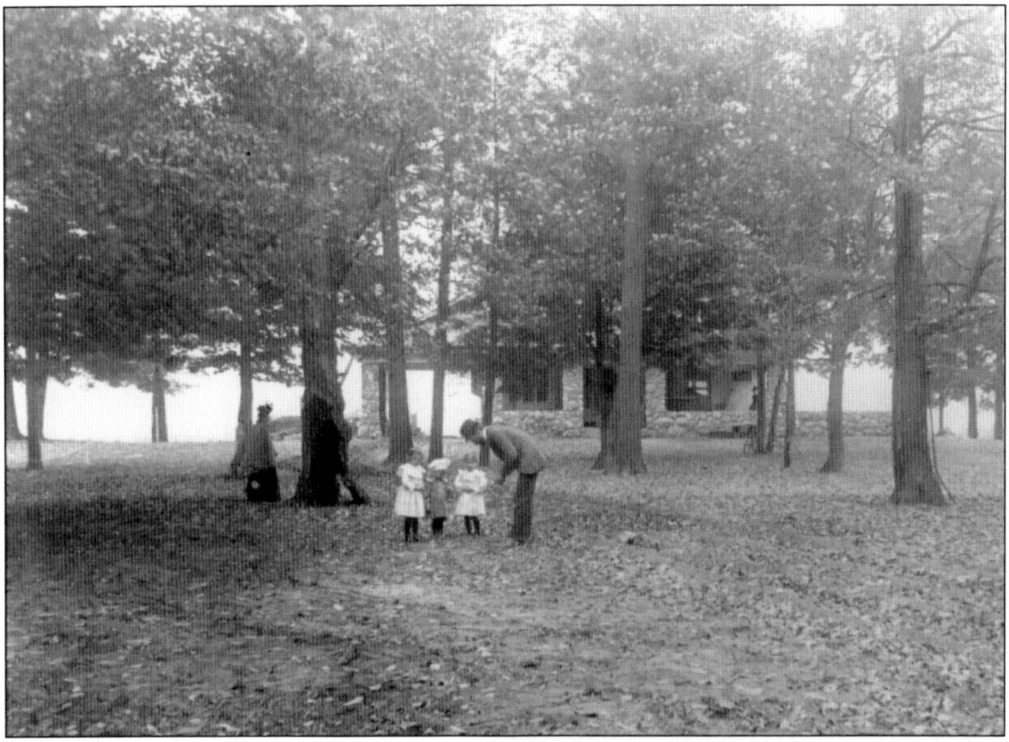

Dow Home. In 1899 Herbert Henry Dow began the building of the only home he would ever own. It was located on West Main Street. The soil was sandy and barren, but in 1900 Dow hired Elzie Cote as a full-time gardener for what became known as "The Pines." Elzie Cote was the Dow gardener for the rest of his life. (Photo courtesy of Post Street Archives)

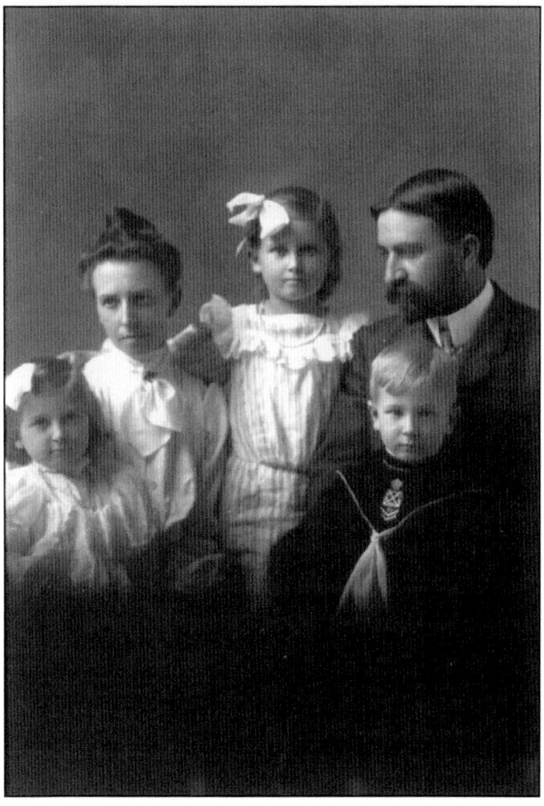

Dow and Family. Herbert Henry Dow was a doting father and the archives teem with family photos. This photo is c. 1902 and from left to right are Ruth, Grace, Helen, Herbert, and son Willard. (Photo courtesy of Post Street Archives)

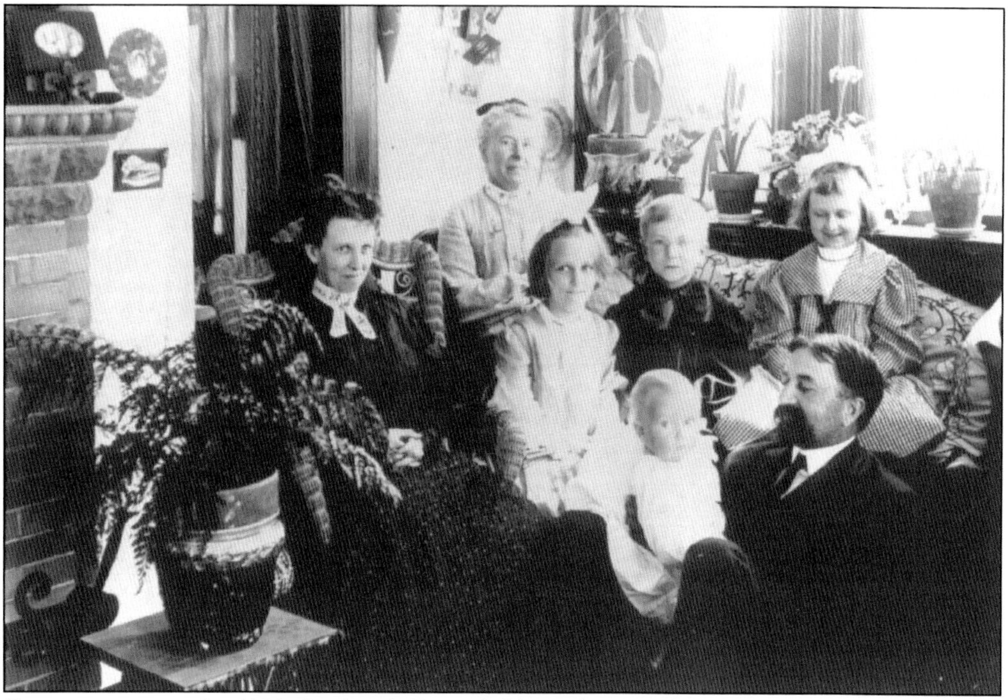

California visit. In 1899 the fourth Dow child was born and named Osborne Curtiss. This family picture shows Dow with his wife and four children when they visited J.H. Osborn and his wife in California, a long-time family friend. Left to right are Grace Dow, Ruth, Willard, Helen, and Herbert (holding Osborne). Mrs Osborn sits in the rear. (Photo courtesy of Post Street Archives)

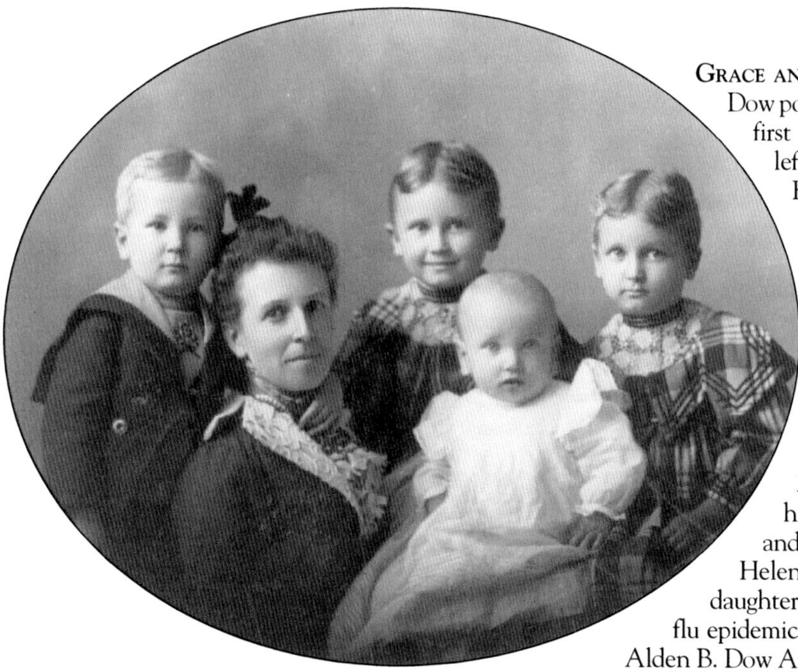

Grace and Children. Grace Dow poses proudly with her first four children. From left to right are Willard Henry, Grace (holding Osborne Curtiss), Helen and Ruth Alden. The picture dated 1902 was one of the last of the baby, Osborne, who died on October 3, 1902, devastating his parents Grace and Herbert. In 1918 Helen, the Dows' oldest daughter, died during the flu epidemic. (Photo courtesy of Alden B. Dow Archives)

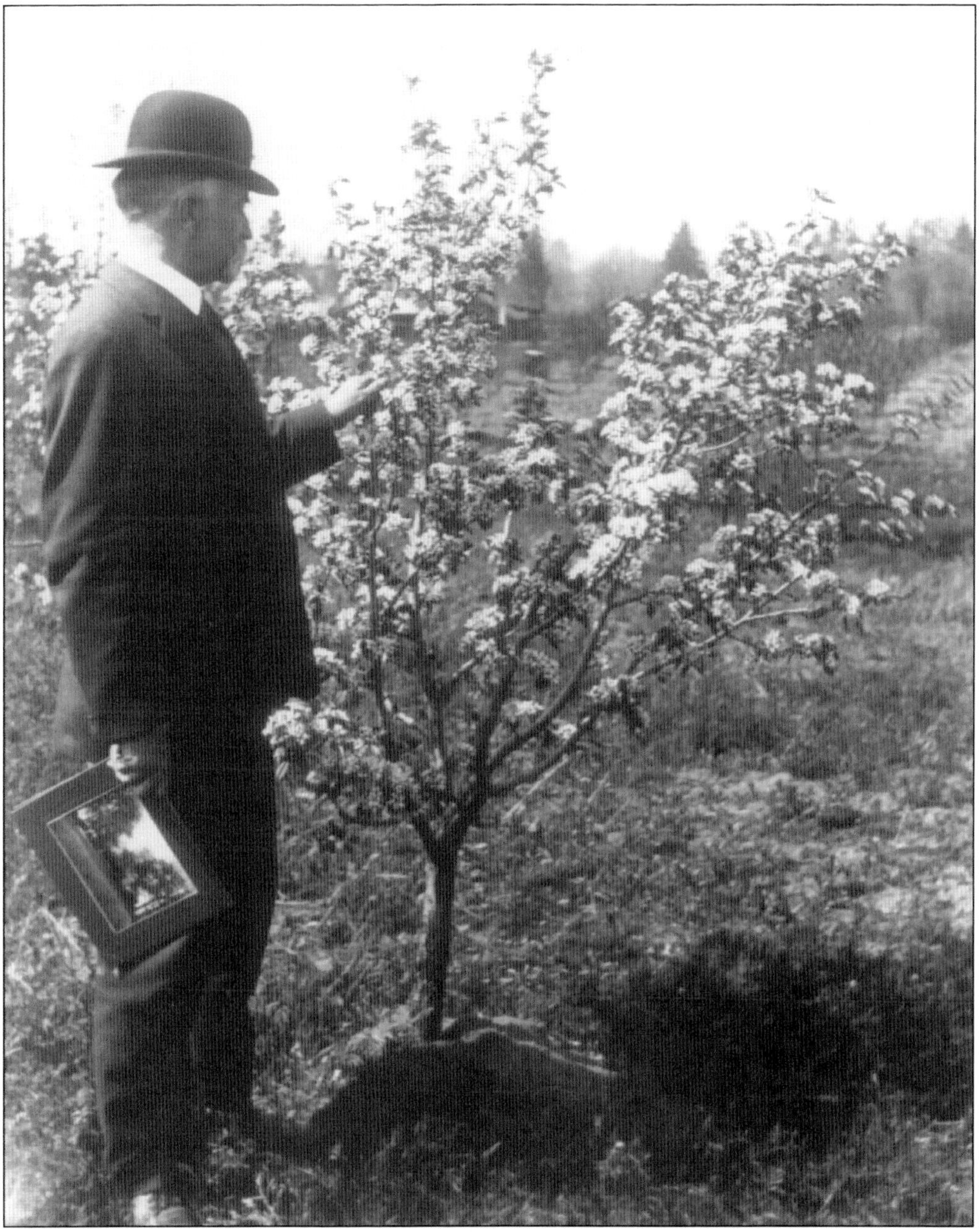

ORCHARD PICTURE. On May 3, 1899, Herbert Dow wrote his father Joseph: "I planted an orchard yesterday...92 fruit trees of 35 varieties, 1 vine of 10 varieties of grapes and 1 of 4 varieties of lilacs..." That letter typifies the way that Herbert Henry Dow thought. Another man might have written, "I planted some trees yesterday." But Herbert Henry Dow planted "an orchard." This photo shows Herbert Dow in 1913 inspecting part of his orchard. (Photo courtesy of Post Street Archives)

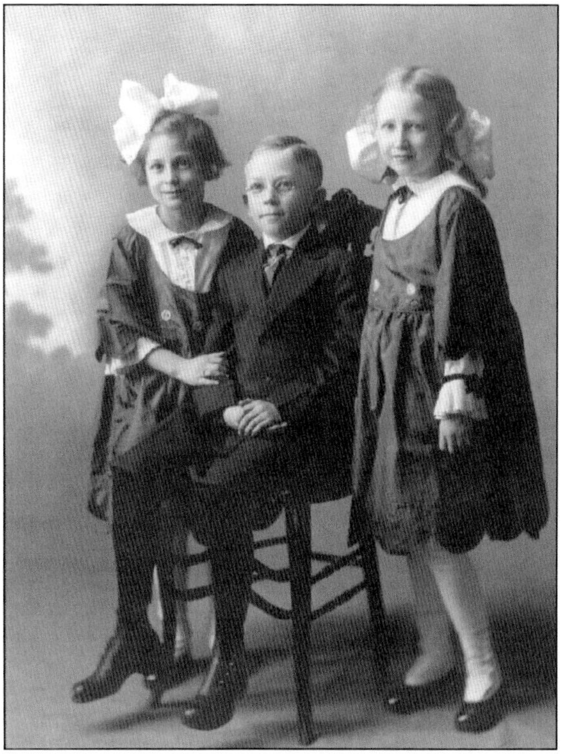

DOW CHILDREN. This family portrait shows the three youngest Dow children. From left to right are Dorothy, Alden, and Margaret. Dorothy would grow up and marry Dr. Anderson Arbury. Margaret would marry Dr. Harry Towsley and Alden would become a world famous architect. (Photo courtesy of Alden B. Dow Archives)

DOW AND SONS. Herbert Henry Dow poses with his two sons, Willard Henry on the left and Alden Ball on the right. Both sons continued their father's illustrious legacy. Willard became president of The Dow Chemical Company upon the death of his father in 1930, guiding it through the Depression and World War II and Alden became world-famous in the field of architecture. (Photo courtesy of Post Street Archives)

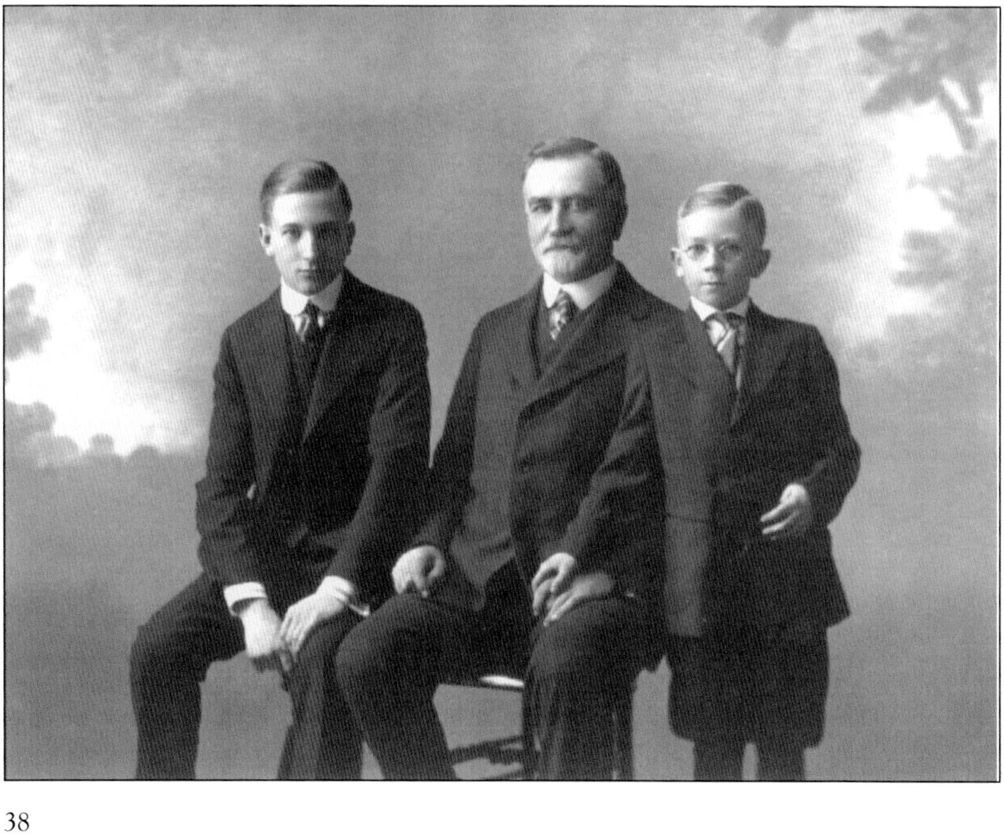

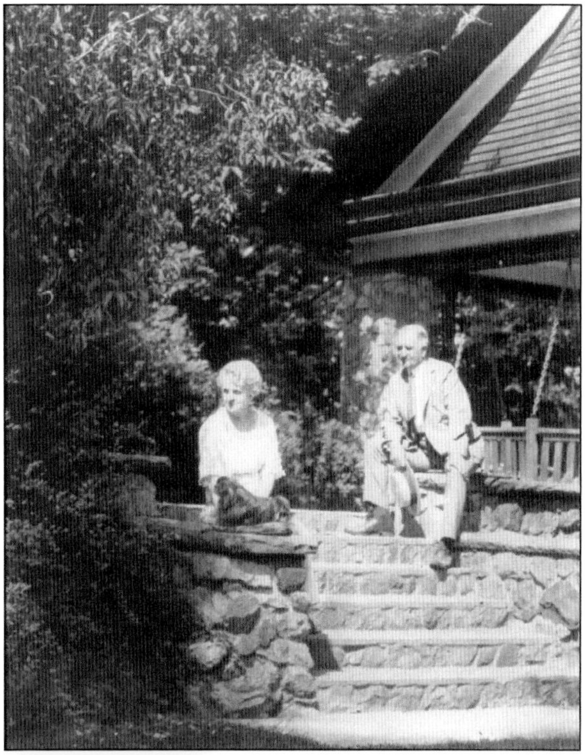

AT HOME. Herbert and Grace Dow take a moment to relax in the sunshine with their little dog at their home on West Main Street. Through the years Dow working with his gardener Elzie Cote created the Dow Gardens that eventually surrounded that home, a small Eden set in the little town of Midland, Michigan. (Photo courtesy of Post Street Archives)

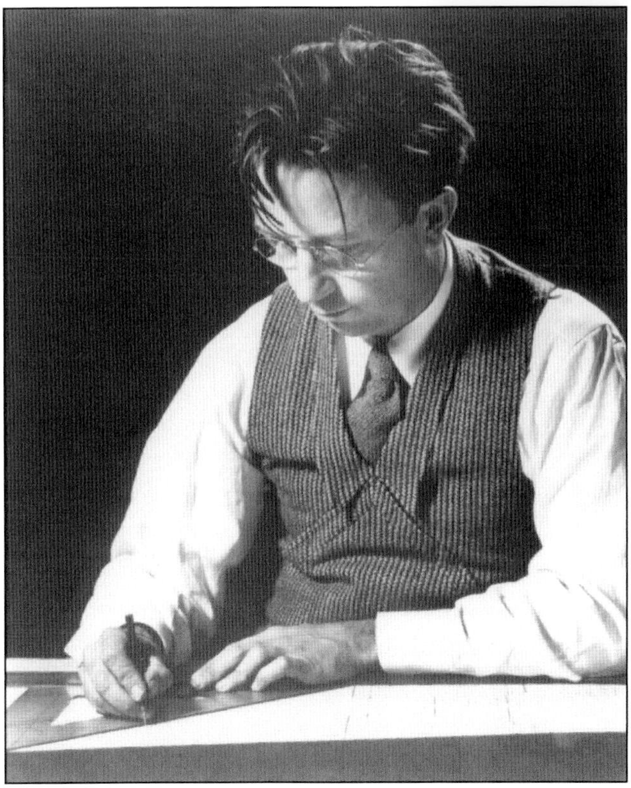

ALDEN DOW. This is Alden Dow bent over his drawing board, intent on the job in front of him. After spending three years in college on an engineering curriculum he told his father that he wanted to be an architect. In 1931 he graduated from Columbia University with a degree in architecture. (Photo courtesy of Alden B. Dow Archives)

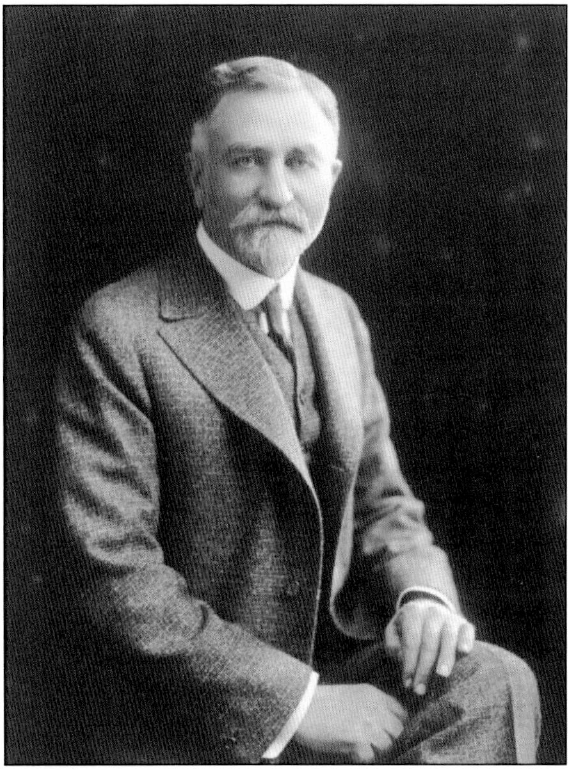

1930 Photo. This is Herbert Henry Dow shortly before his unexpected death in 1930 at the Mayo Clinic in Rochester, Minnesota. His life was summed up in a letter that he received from the Reverend John Naramore on December 16, 1927, praising him for what he had accomplished and ending with, "You remembered your ideals." (Photo courtesy of Post Street Archives)

Alden Dow Studios. This is a photo taken in the Forties of the famous Alden B. Dow Studios located in Midland, Michigan. Greatly influenced by his 1933 visit to Frank Lloyd Wright at Taliesin in Spring Green, Wisconsin, Alden Dow was awarded the first Frank Lloyd Wright Creativity Award in 1982. Mrs. Wright called Alden, "my late husband's spiritual son." (Photo by Bill Hedrich, Hedrich-Blessing, courtesy of Alden B. Dow Archives)

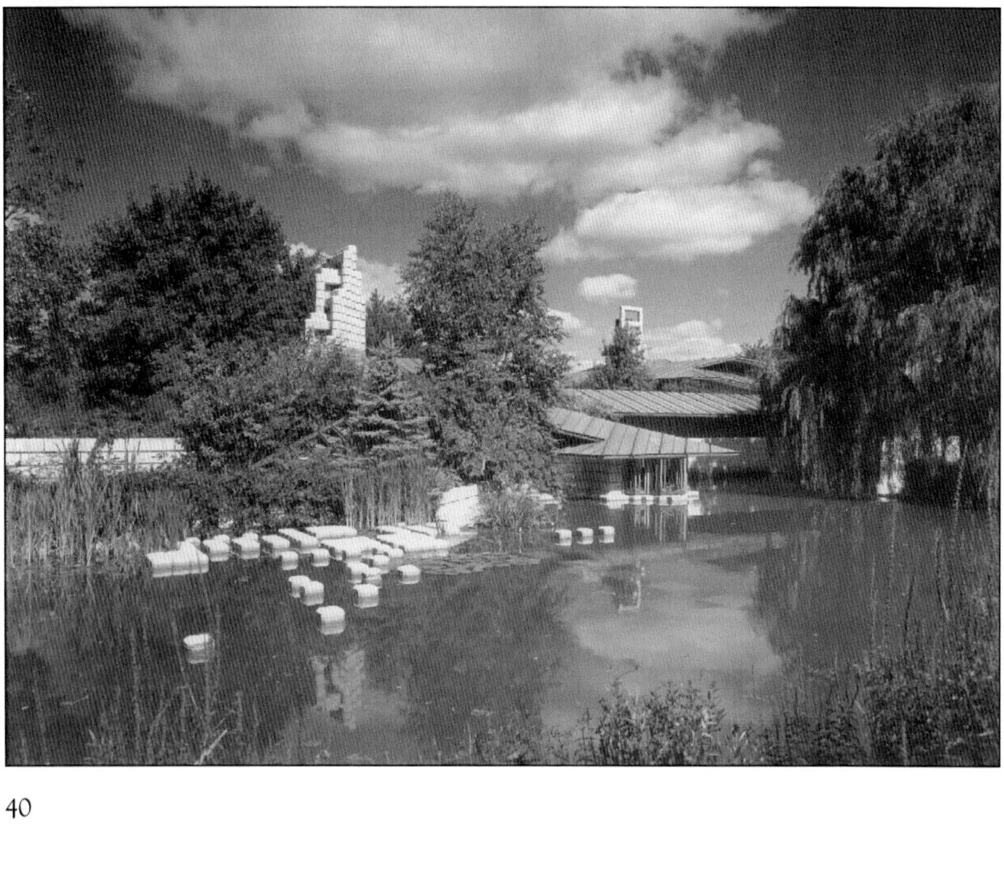

Four

HEADLINES

History is never history when we are living through it.

—*Anonymous*

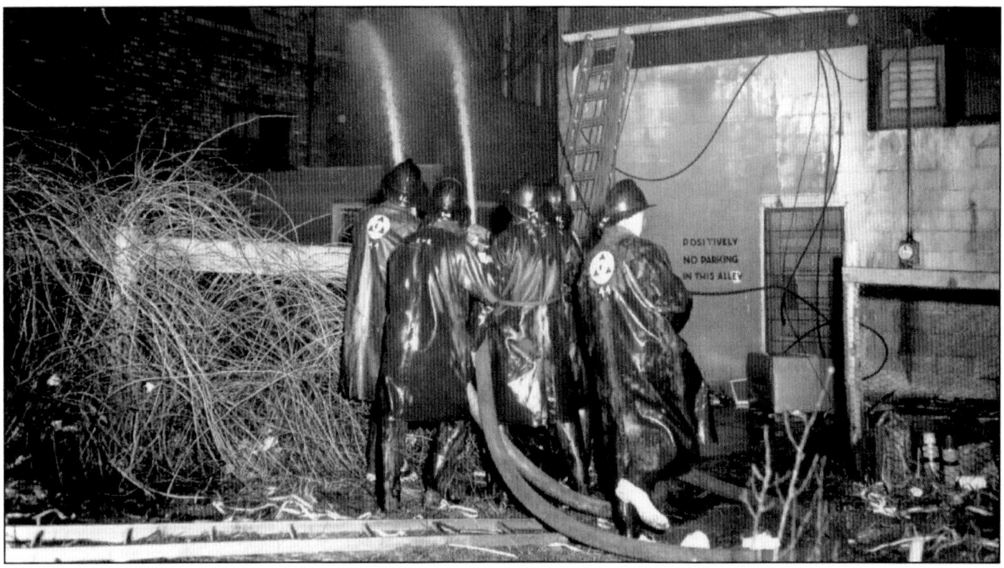

There are headlines that tell us what is happening around the world. Headlines that tell us what is happening in the United States. And headlines that tell us what is happening in the state of Michigan where we live. But it is the headlines in our local newspaper that record the history we live through.

Headlines have documented our lives in Midland for a hundred years. In 1876 a fire started at the Findlater Hotel on Main Street and burned 52 buildings and houses before it was under control. On February 16, 1916, Bill Baker and Della Taylor perished in a fire that also burned three business blocks. On April 19, 1943, the Frolic Theatre caught fire when a janitor decided to burn some trash on a windy afternoon. On December 15, 1958, Cohoon's Elevator burned to the ground. On April 27, 1959, Sears and the Midland Paper Company suffered a million dollar loss. And on January 19, 1967, weary firemen fought a fire in the Baker Building in six degree weather.

Following are some photos and more headlines that shaped our lives.

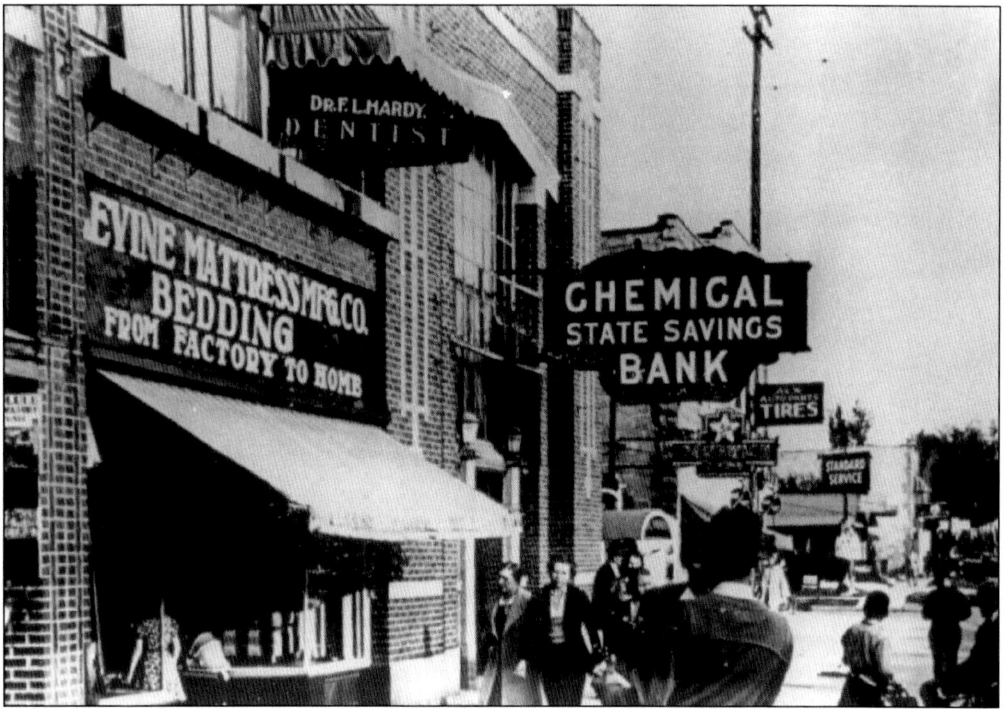

The Bank Robbery. Wednesday, September 29, 1937, was a quiet, sleepy autumn day in the small town of Midland, Michigan but it wouldn't stay that way. Jack Gracey and Tony Chebatoris drove into town that morning intending to rob The Dow Chemical Company's payroll at the Chemical Bank. (Photo courtesy of Midland Daily News)

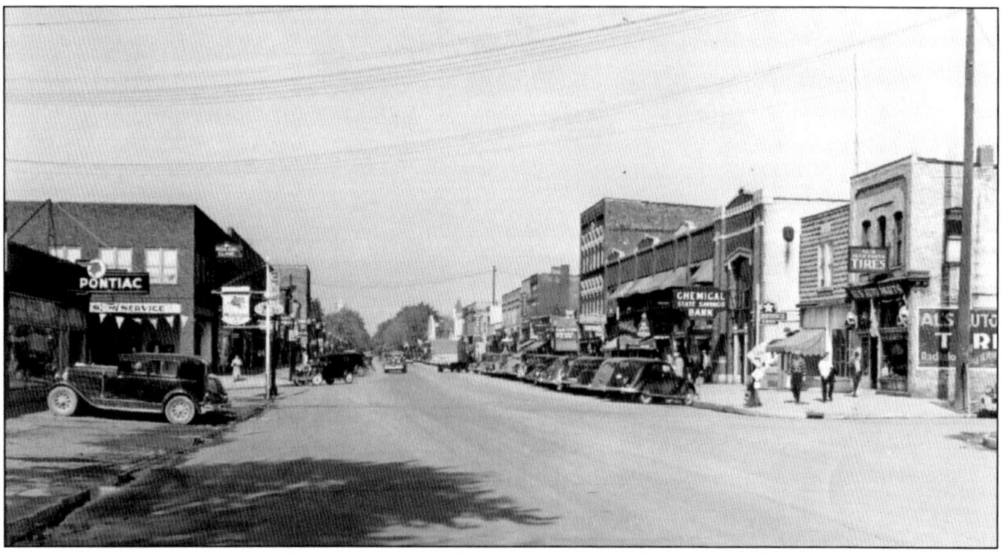

The Bank Robbery. Jack Gracey entered the bank first, pulling out a shotgun from under his overcoat. Clarence Macomber, president of the bank, grabbed the gun, forcing it downward to the floor so the customers wouldn't be hurt. Tony Chebatoris entered the bank then and seeing his partner-in-crime in trouble, opened fire hitting both Clarence Macomber and Paul Bywater. (Photo courtesy of Midland Daily News)

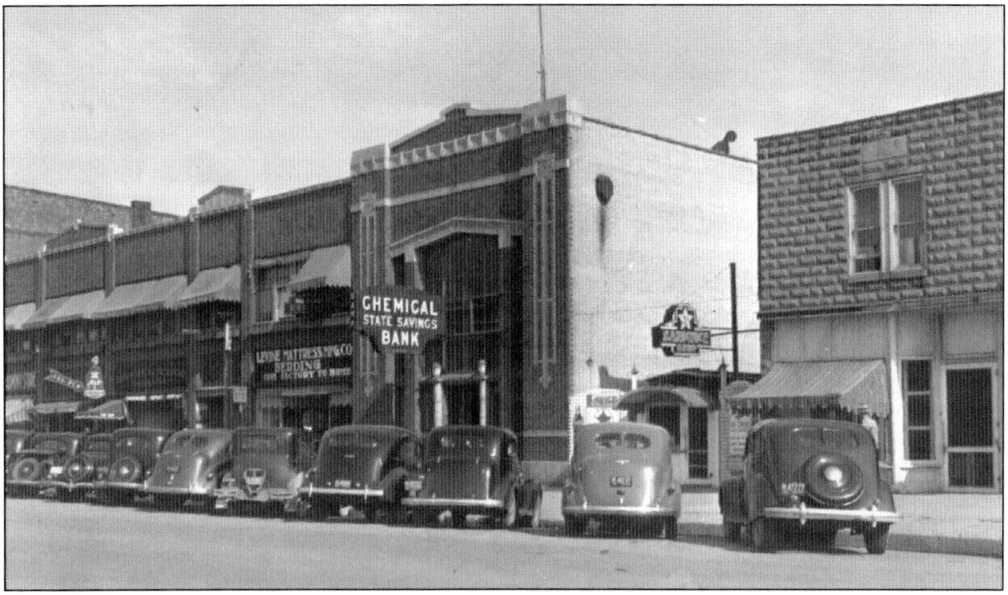

THE BANK ROBBERY. Gracey and Chebatoris fled the bank, jumped in their car and headed down Benson Street toward the bridge. Frank Hardy, a dentist above the bank and deputized by Sheriff Ira Smith, heard the shooting and grabbed the rifle in his office. Aiming out the second story window, he shot at the car, wounding Chebatoris, causing him to crash the car. (Photo courtesy of Midland Daily News)

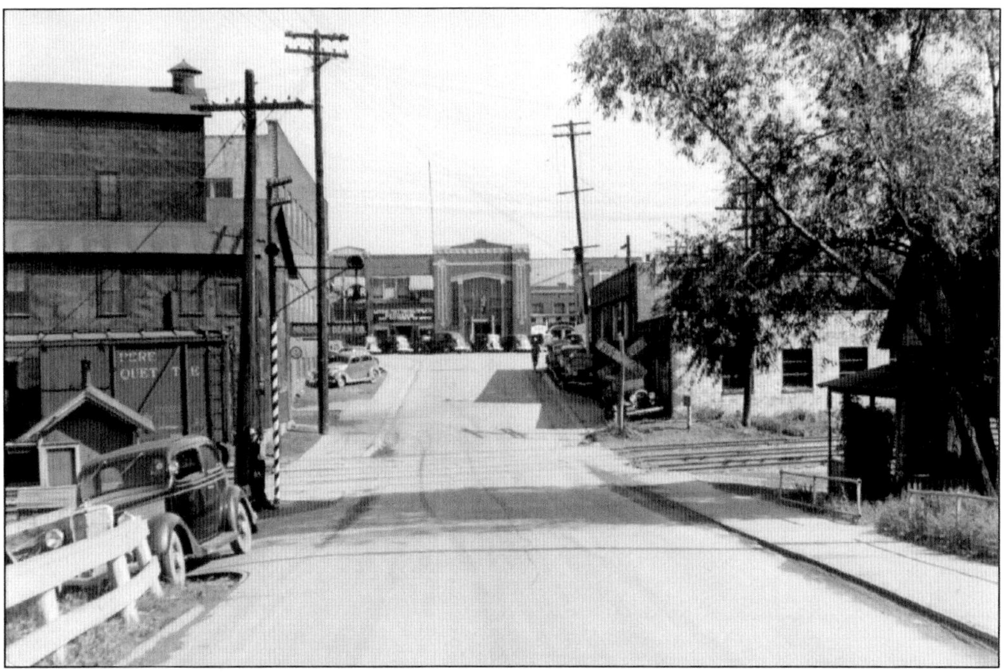

THE BANK ROBBERY. Jumping from the car, Gracey and Chebatoris began running toward the railroad tracks abandoning their car. A man in uniform was standing in the street, and thinking that he had shot at their car, Chebatoris shot him. By now Dr. Hardy had aimed again and this time hit Gracey. Gracey fell to the pavement dead. (Photo courtesy of Midland Daily News)

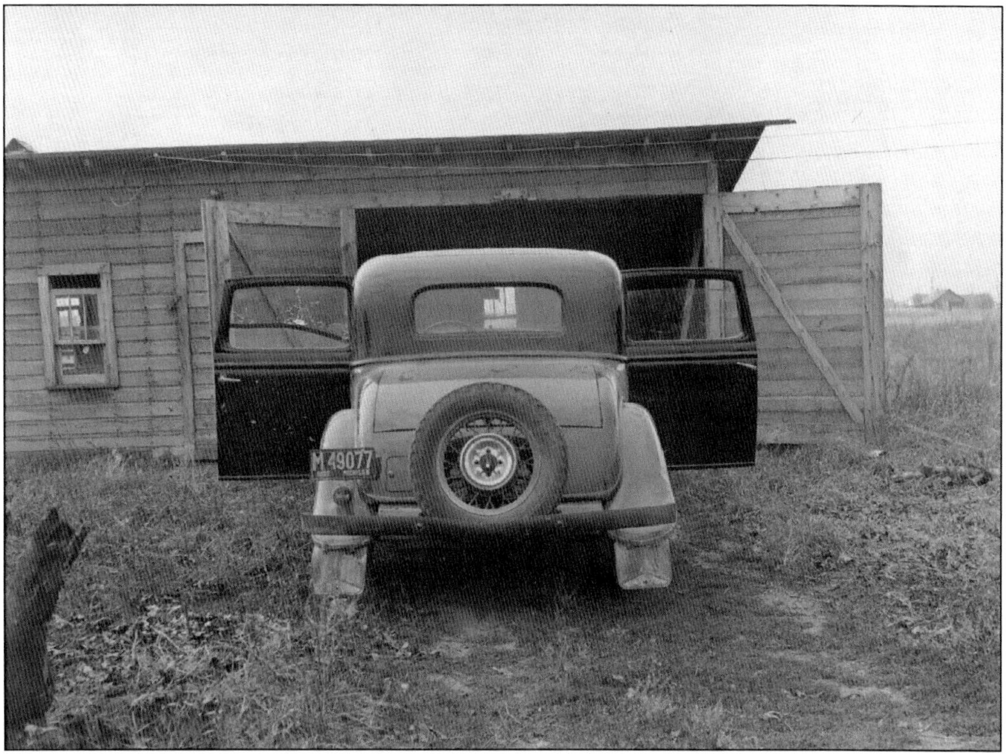

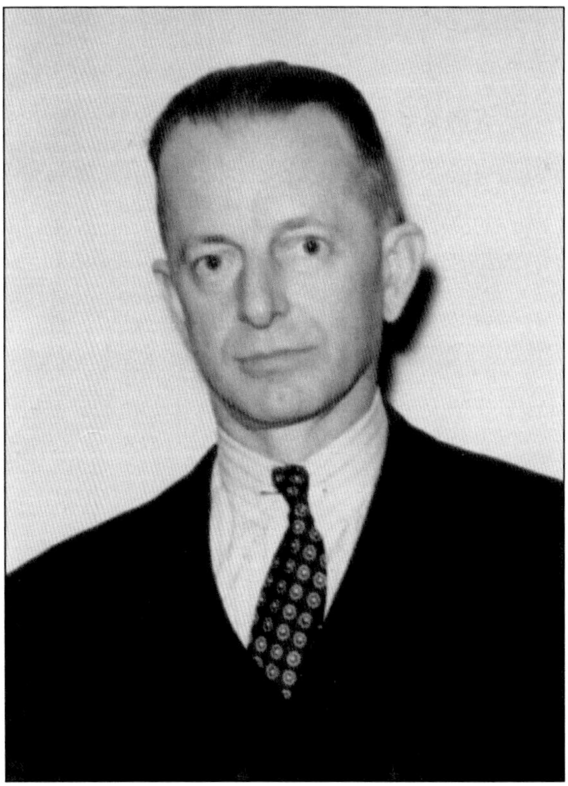

The Bank Robbery. Thoroughly rattled, Chebatoris made one mistake after another. Commandeering a car, he couldn't operate the shift. Then he jumped into another car and while backing up crashed into another car. Sheriff Ira Smith and Deputy Ben Voorhees made the arrest. Chebatoris was convicted of bank robbery and murder. He was hanged on July 8, 1938, in Milan Federal Prison. (Photo courtesy of Midland Daily News)

The Bank Robbery. This is Dr. Frank Hardy, nicknamed "the shooting dentist" after the aborted bank robbery. He received $200 from the American Surety Company and the Chemical Bank matched that amount. Hardy also received a gold medal and a personal letter from F.B.I. chief J. Edgar Hoover. (Photo courtesy of Midland Daily News)

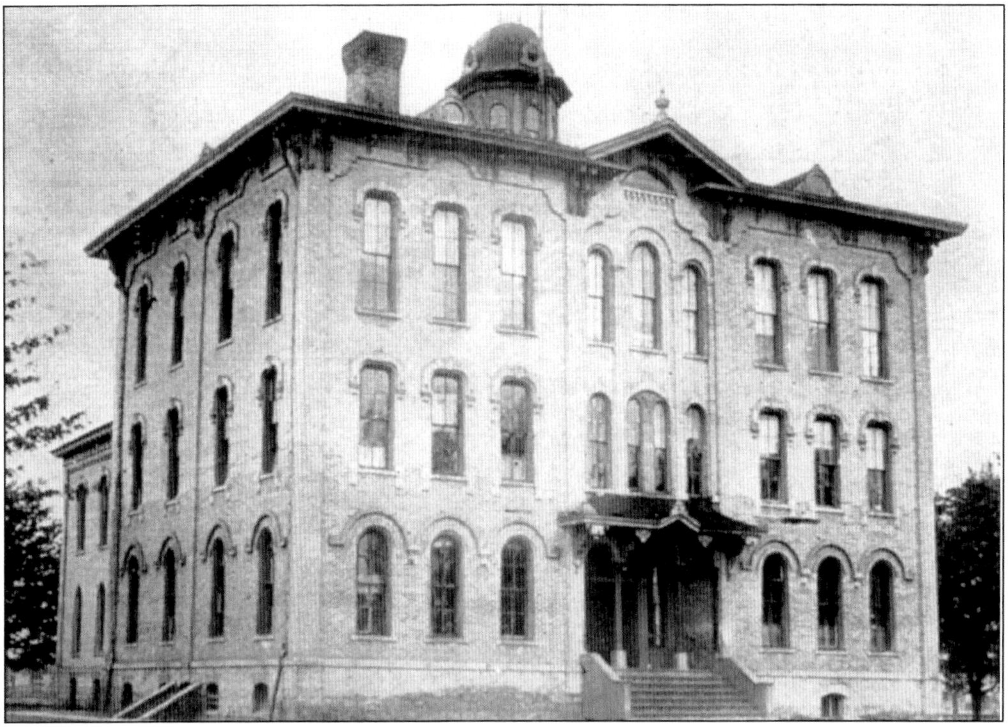

THE UNION SCHOOL. The Union School was a three-story brick building built in 1872 in the Village of Midland City. It housed grammar students, junior high students and the senior high students. In 1905 it also housed the County Normal on the third floor.

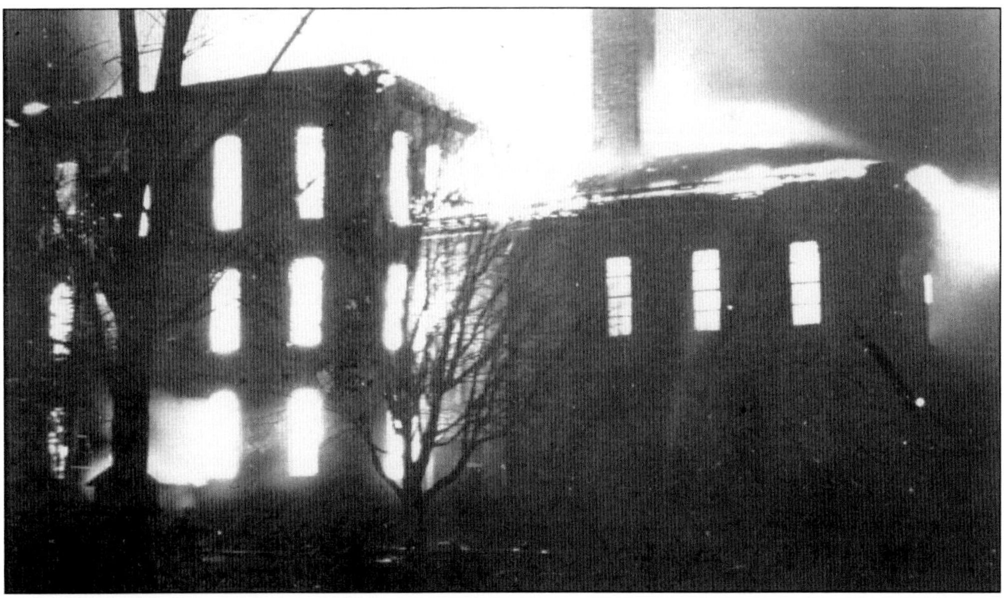

THE UNION SCHOOL. The headlines in the local newspaper on October 23, 1908 read: "The Greatest Calamity in Years in This City." Thomas E. Hinds who lived near the school saw a light in the basement, sounded an alarm and a hose cart was soon at the scene. But the fire spread to the second floor and then the third floor.

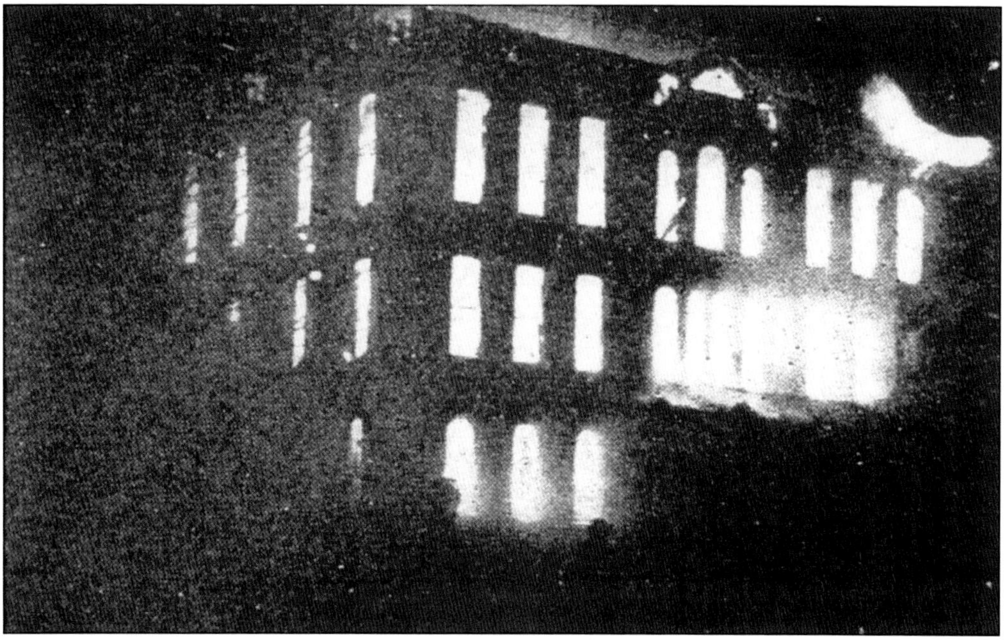

The Union School. Flames encircled the dome and then the roof fell in. Piece by piece the high walls fell inward. When the fire burned itself out, only a chimney and a few jagged pieces of wall remained standing.

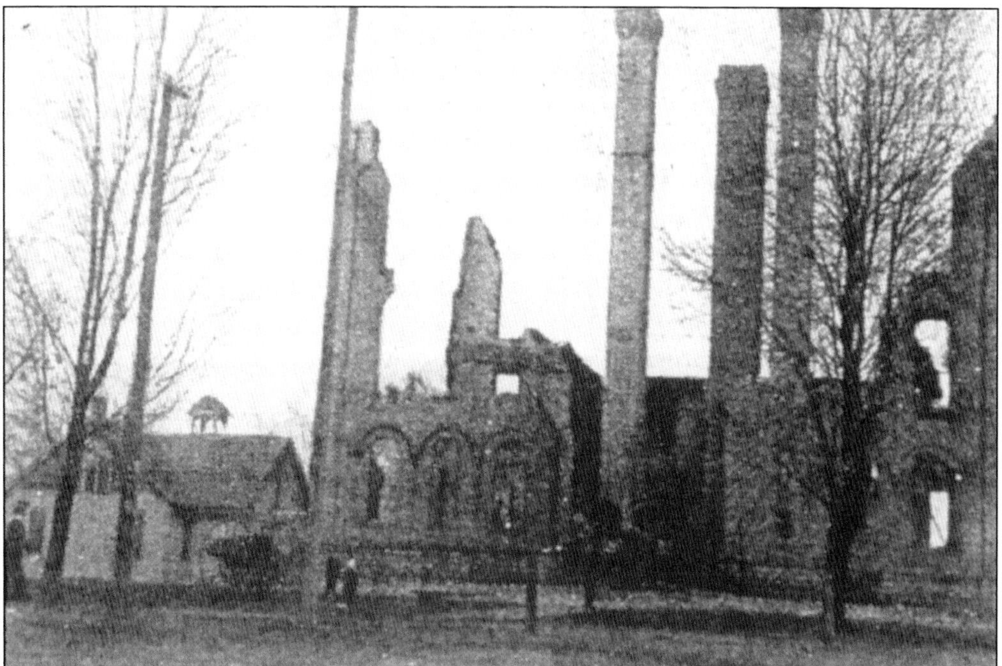

The Union School. Arson was never proven but another fire was discovered in the reading room of the Library on December 4, and shortly after that fire destroyed barns owned by Martin DeBolt and George Warner. By 1909 a new senior high school was ready for occupancy and then a junior high and an elementary school were added on each side.

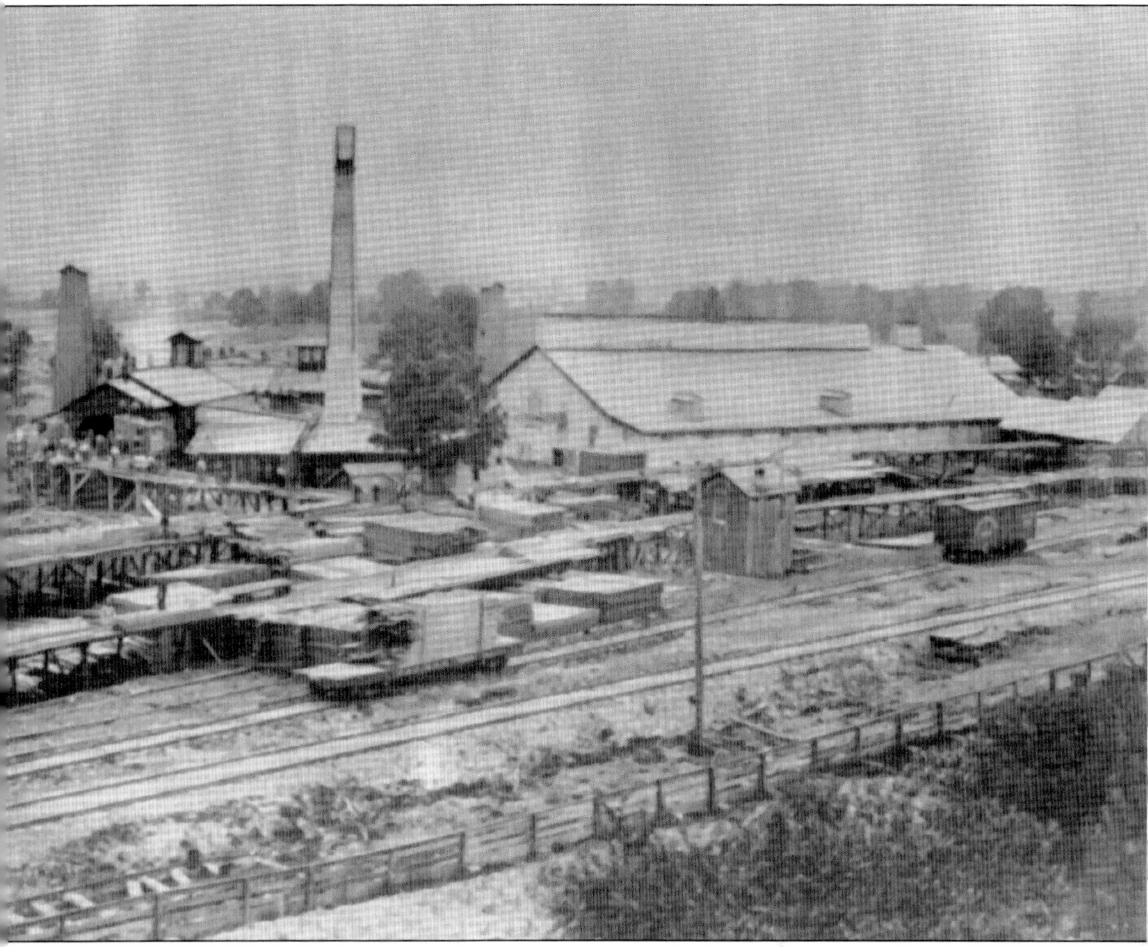

Larkin and Patrick Sawmill. This is the original Larkin and Patrick saw mill and salt block at the foot of McDonald Street. (Today it's a parking lot.) Founded by John Larkin in 1855, it was Midland's main industry in the late 1880s. In May of 1892 an explosion destroyed the mill killing Charles Allen, Richard Steers, and Eugene Van Valkenburg. Eight others were injured. The mill was rebuilt.

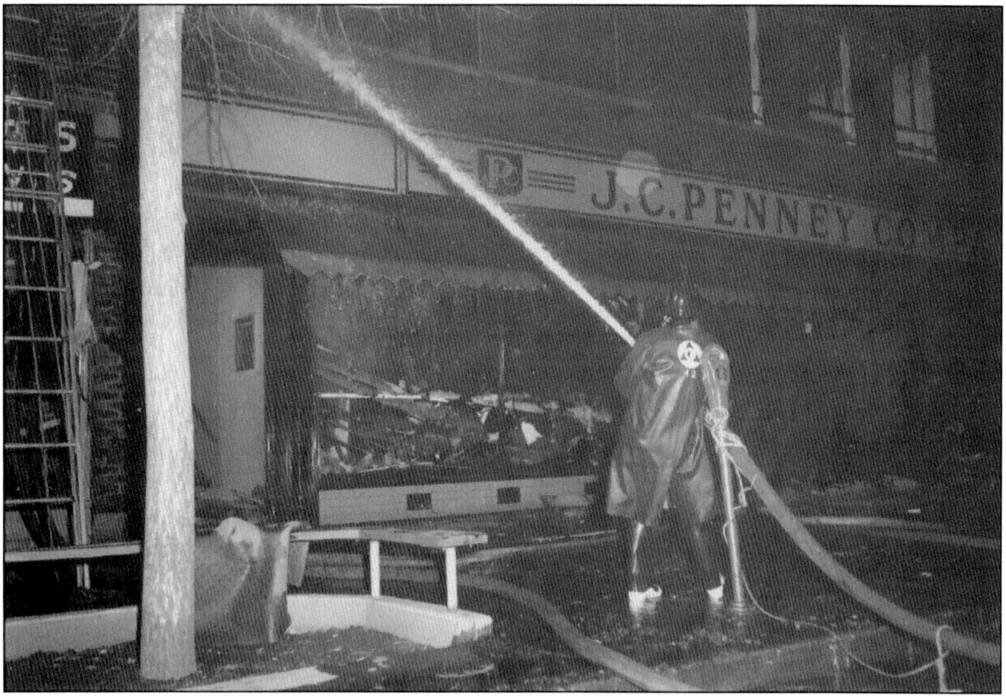

THE PENNEY FIRE. On March 26, 1954, the Reinhart Building burned but it was usually referred to as the "Penney fire" because the J.C. Penney Store was the largest tenant in the building. The Penney store was getting ready to move to a new location at the time. A total of 47 firemen fought the blaze.

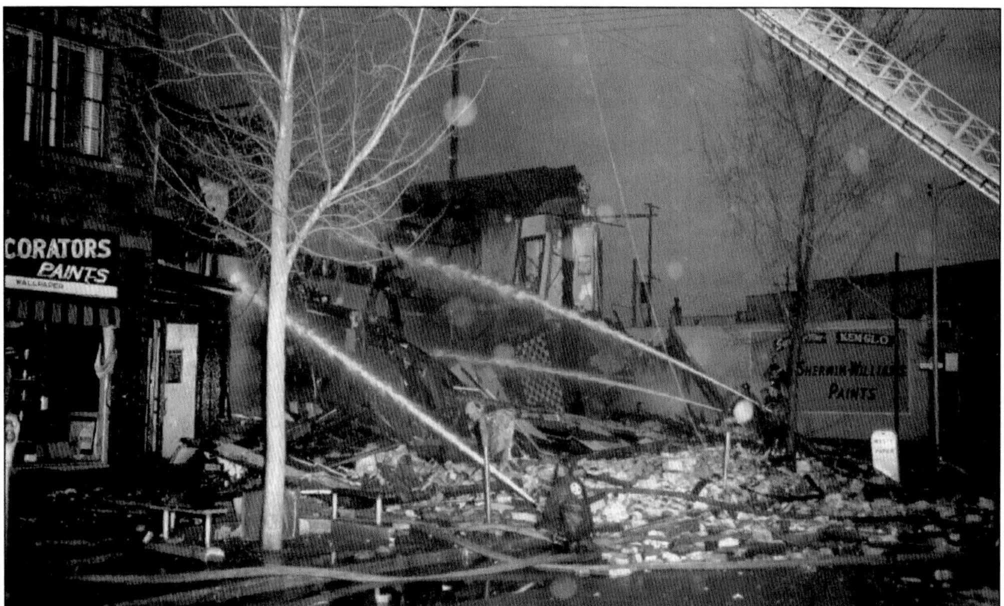

THE PENNEY FIRE. The second floor of the Reinhart building had many professional offices including those of Dr. J.W. Seeburger, Dr. L.L. Dulude, Dr. Charles Towsley, Dr. M.D. Buskirk, Dr. Irvin M. Howe, Melvin Pike, Dr. C.L. MacCullum, and Dr. E.J. Harvey.

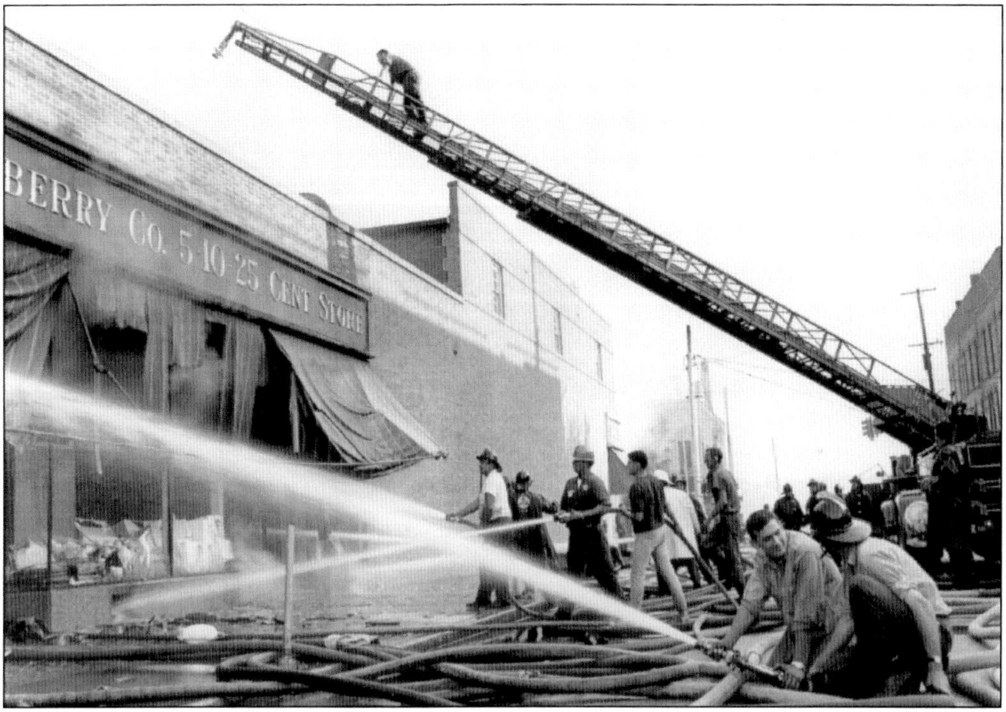

THE NEWBERRY FIRE. The fire at the J.J. Newberry store was reported at 4:52 p.m. on June 17, 1965, but the street was blockaded until 12:30 the next morning. Firefighters stayed on the scene all night to make sure that the fire didn't break out again. (Photo courtesy of Midland Daily News)

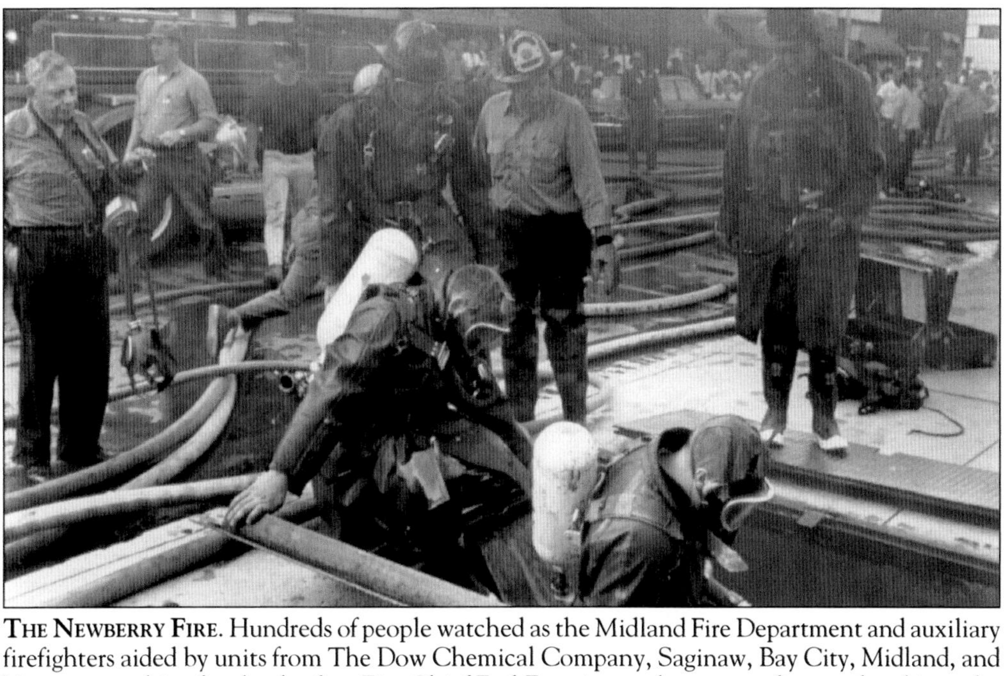

THE NEWBERRY FIRE. Hundreds of people watched as the Midland Fire Department and auxiliary firefighters aided by units from The Dow Chemical Company, Saginaw, Bay City, Midland, and Homer townships fought the fire. Fire Chief Earl Engwis watches as two firemen head into the basement of the burning building. (Photo courtesy of Midland Daily News)

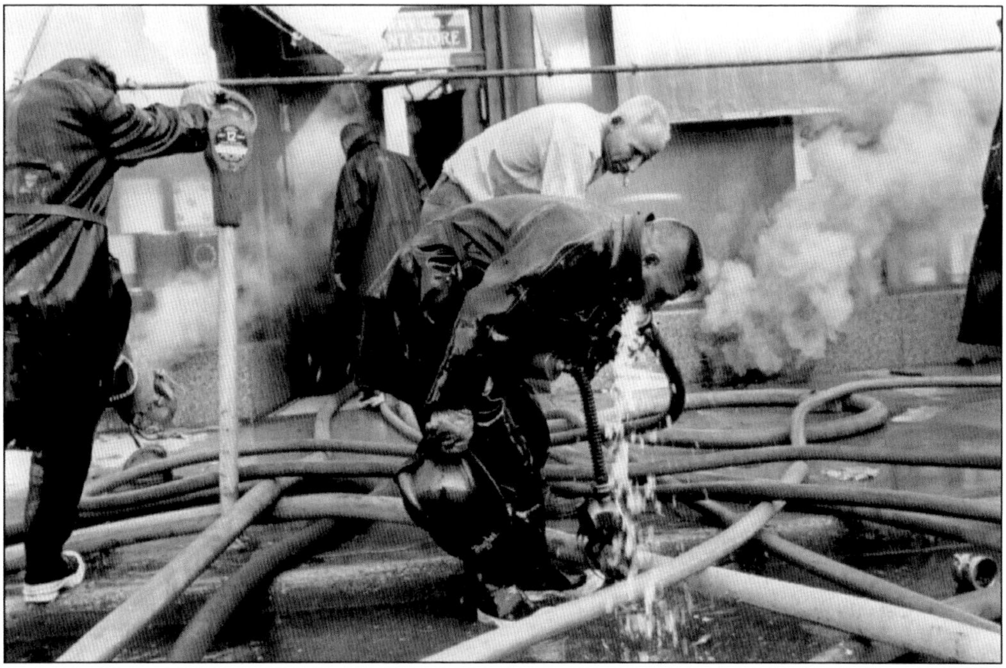

The Newberry Fire. A weary fireman leans against a parking meter getting a second breath while a second fireman takes a drink of water from a fire hose during the J.J. Newberry fire on June 17, 1965. Dense columns of smoke went skyward for hours. (Photo courtesy of Midland Daily News)

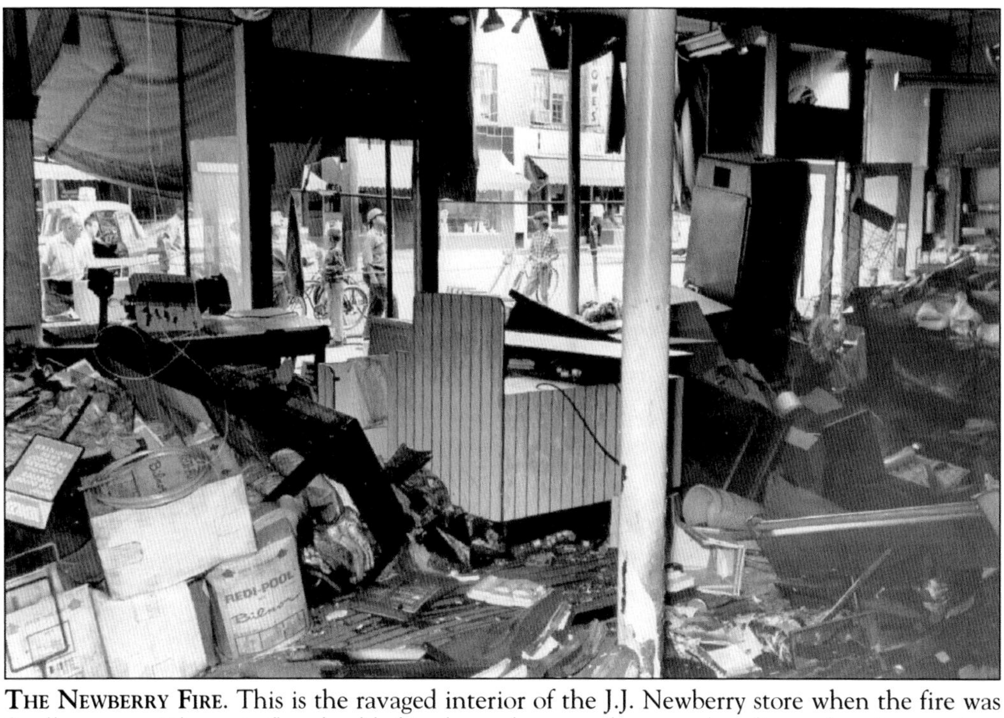

The Newberry Fire. This is the ravaged interior of the J.J. Newberry store when the fire was finally put out. The main floor buckled in three places sending merchandise and equipment into a water-filled basement (Photo courtesy of Midland Daily News)

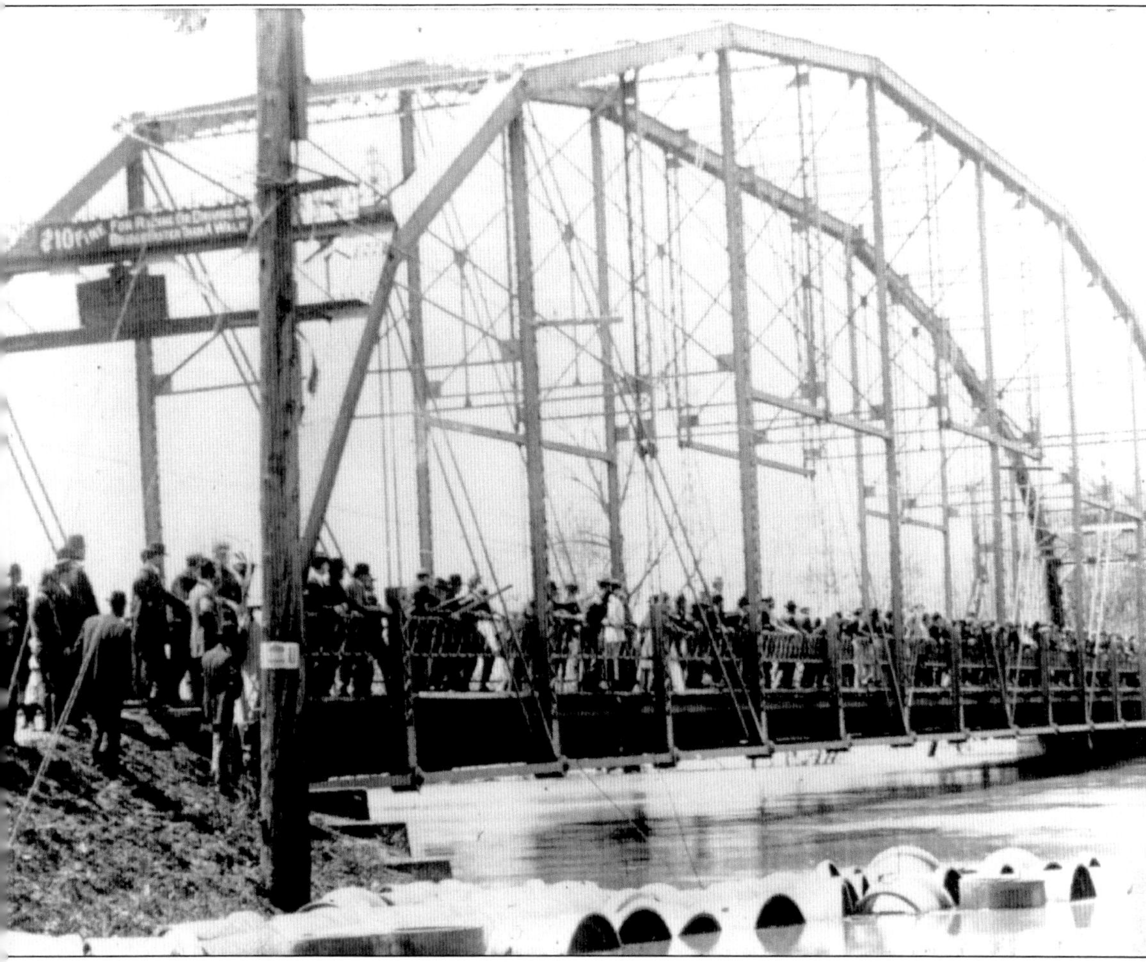

The Flood of 1912. Midland's greatest flood occurred in 1912 in May when a continuous downpour for 72 hours sent the Pine, Chippewa, and Tittabawassee rivers on a rampage. It broke the records set by the flood of April, 1876, and January of 1907. Here is a picture of the Benson Street Bridge lined with onlookers as the flood waters were finally receding. (Photo courtesy of Midland Daily News)

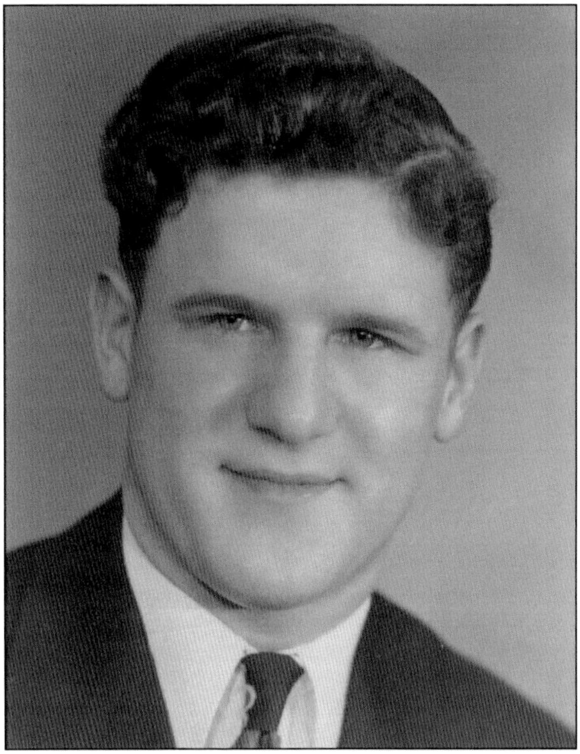

Dow Explosion, 1948. In 1948, Dale Raetz, a 19-year-old worker at The Dow Chemical Company, was killed when a blast ripped through a boiler. He was a 1948 graduate of Midland High School and was the son of Mr. and Mrs. Rudolph Raetz. In addition to his parents and his young bride, Reathel Mason, he left a twin brother, three sisters and a younger brother.

Dow Explosion, 1950. In 1950 an explosion rocked 414 Building, near the Austin clockroom. The force of the blast blew out doors and windows in buildings and nearby residences. Eight men were killed: David Brubaker, R.A. Nissila, George Riggie Jr., Floyd Schreiber, Henry Miller, H.S. Hawkins, Merle Maybee and Edward B. Clevenger. Thirteen others were injured in the blast. (Photo courtesy of Midland Daily News)

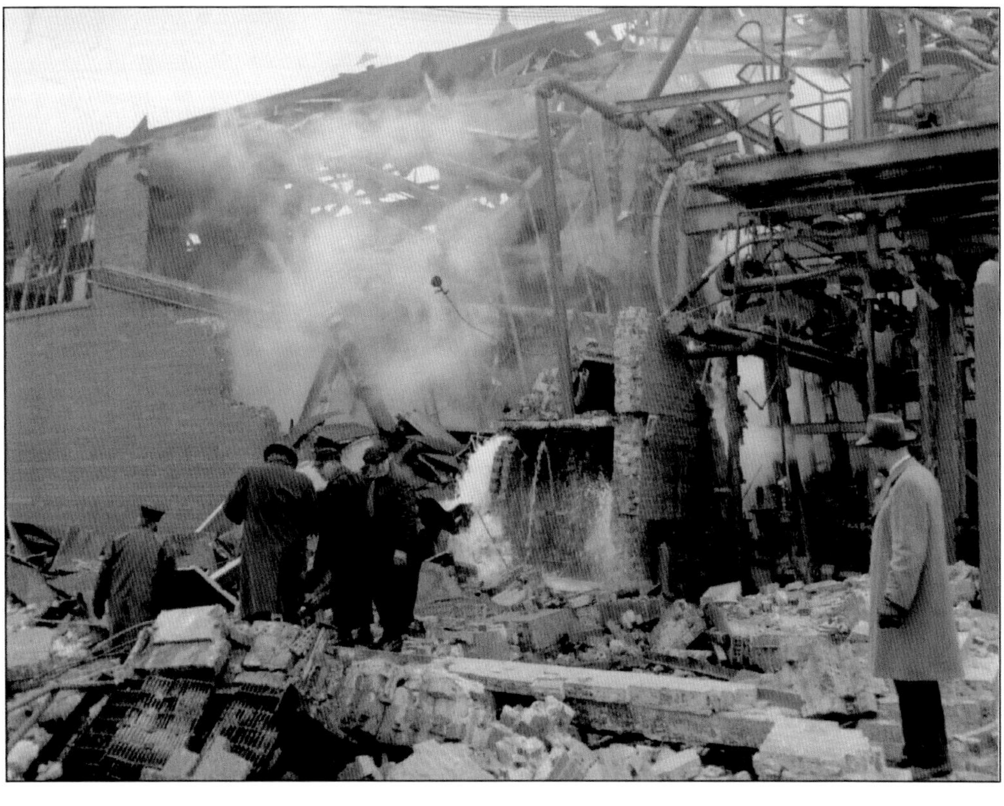

Five

Frank Wixom
He Built a Dream

One of the strongest characteristics of genius is the power of lighting its own fire.
—*John Foster*

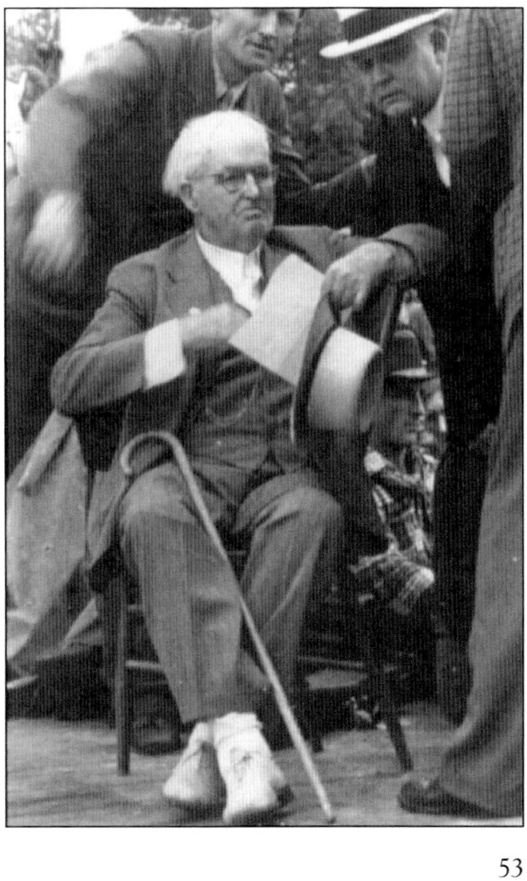

He was twenty something when he got the idea of harnessing the power of the Tittabawassee River in Midland County by building a series of dams. The dams would provide cheap electricity for industry and make the area a recreational spot. That idea was to consume most of Frank I. Wixom's life.

Born on May 31, 1863 in a log cabin in Howell township, Livingston County, Michigan he was consumed with two passions: restlessness and ambition. He started out doing magic tricks from the back of a buckboard wagon, went on to do farm work, went in the circus business, and wildcatted for oil in Canada, Illinois, and Wyoming. But on April 1, 1905, he returned to Edenville to begin a project that would take up the next 18 years of his life.

Capital and the acquisition of flowage rights from landowners along the river were formidable obstacles. Fortunately he came in contact with a family that would stick by him for four decades, lending financial as well as moral support, the Hayhurst family of Detroit, Michigan: James, Edgar, and Alice Maude.

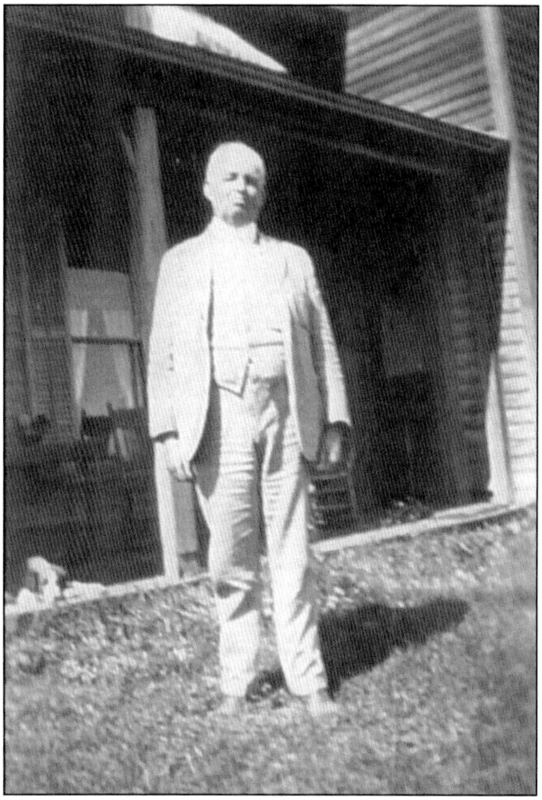

Frank Wixom. This is Frank Isaac Wixom posing in front of the home that the Hayhurst family owned in Edenville, Michigan. The Hayhurst family lent both financial support and moral support to Wixom for four decades as he worked to build his dream of putting dams on the Tittabawassee and Tobacco Rivers.

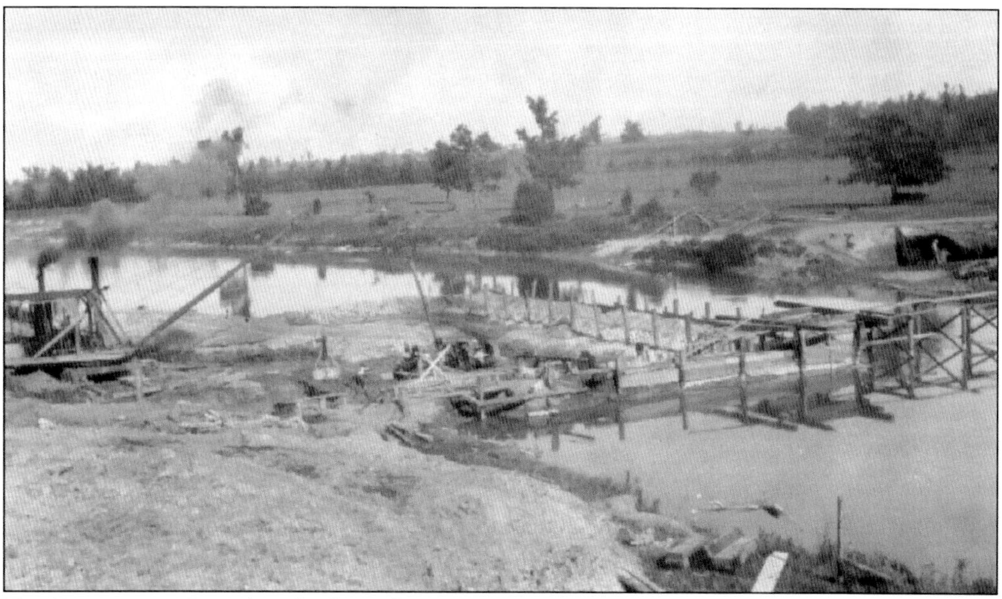

The Beginning. Traveling back roads, entertaining at lumber camps, Wixom got the idea of building dams to harness power from the Tittabawassee and Tobacco Rivers for electricity. On April 1, 1905, he moved to Edenville to begin the project that would take up the next two decades of his life. the building of five dams: Edenville (two), Sanford, Secord, and Smallwood. (Photo courtesy of Wolverine Power Company)

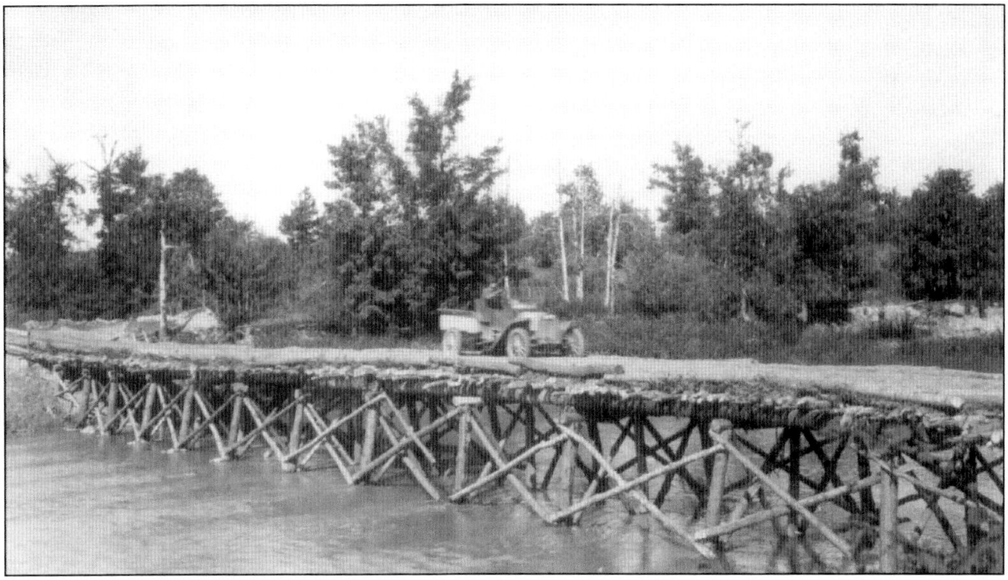

TEMPORARY BRIDGE. Bringing his dream to life meant hardships, both financial and physical for Wixom. Money was desperate. People demanded money for flowage rights along the rivers. Distraught and at the end of his rope, in a letter he wrote: "I'm not going to put up with this any longer." (Photo courtesy of Wolverine Power Company)

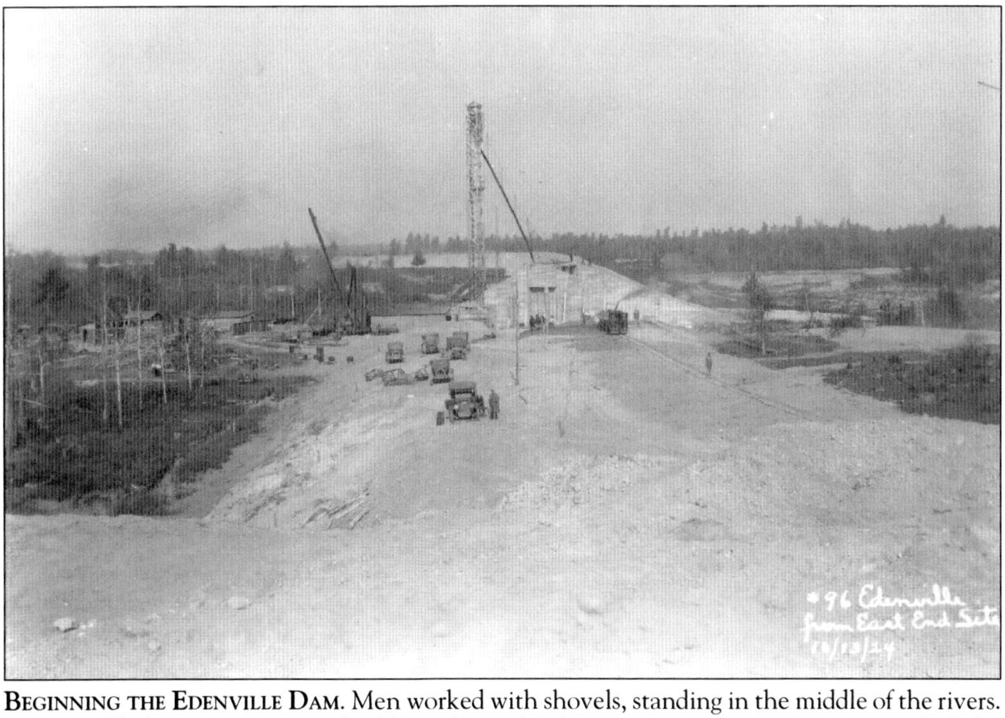

BEGINNING THE EDENVILLE DAM. Men worked with shovels, standing in the middle of the rivers. Horses pulled great scrapers to build up the embankments. Men driving tractors packed the soil down and moved the earth from place to place to make room for the enormous structures that were to house the generators to harness the power of the river water. (Photo courtesy of Wolverine Power Company)

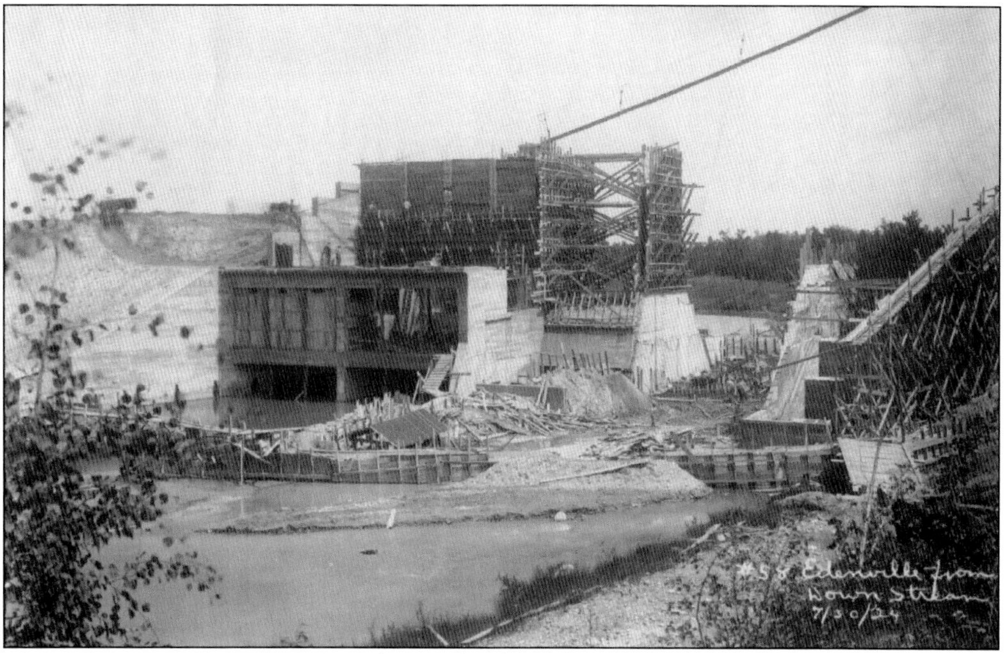

EDENVILLE DAM, JULY, 1924. Once begun, the dams were being built with crews at Sanford and Edenville. Above Edenville, two large dams were built on the Tobacco and Tittabawassee Rivers just above their confluence. This became Wixom Lake, covering 3258 acres and stretching for 10 miles on what had once been farmland. (Photo courtesy of Wolverine Power Company)

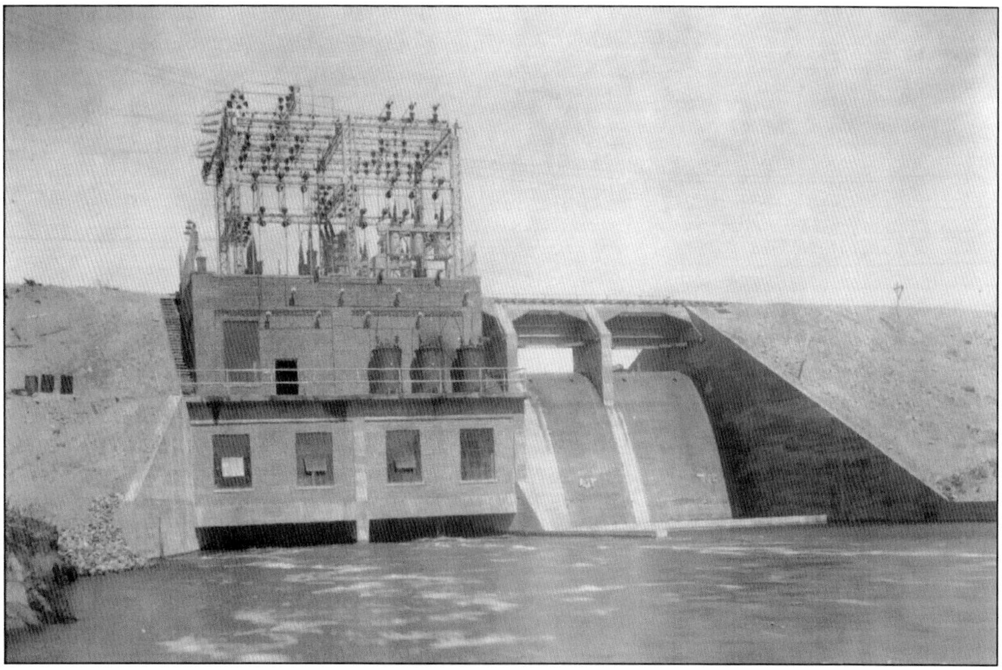

COMPLETED EDENVILLE DAM, APRIL, 1925. Wixom's dream resulted in five dams making a series of lakes almost 35 miles long and covering 9,000 acres of ground. The dams not only produced electricity but also helped with flood control. (Photo courtesy of Wolverine Power Company)

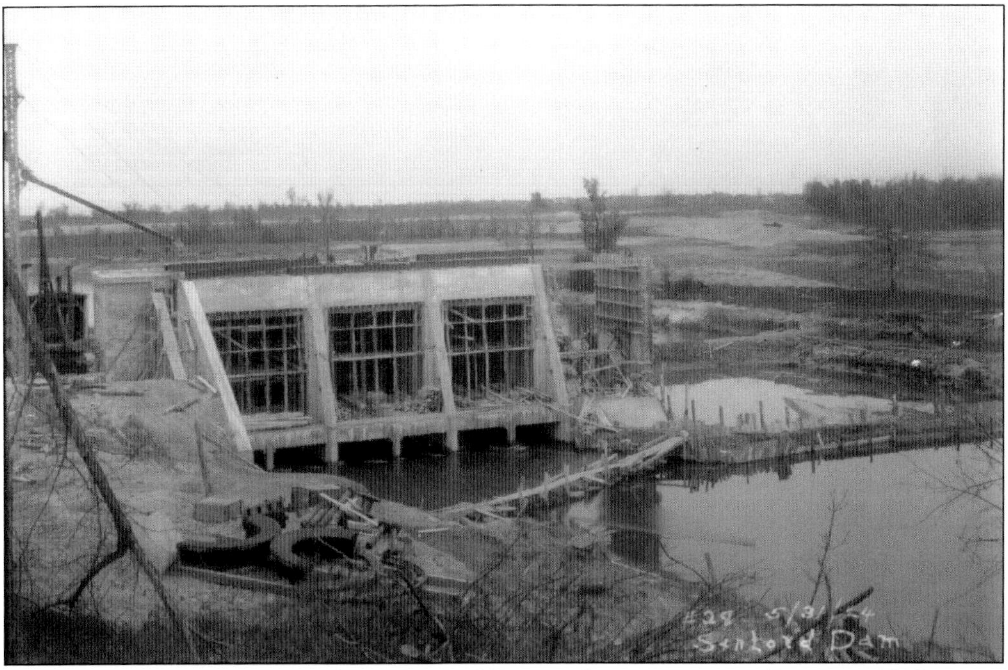

SANFORD DAM, MAY, 1924. This is Sanford Dam under construction. Begun in 1923, it was completed by 1924 and the first power was generated in October of 1925. Consumers Power signed a 99-year lease with the Wolverine Power Company to use all the power generated by the new dams. (Photo courtesy of Wolverine Power Company)

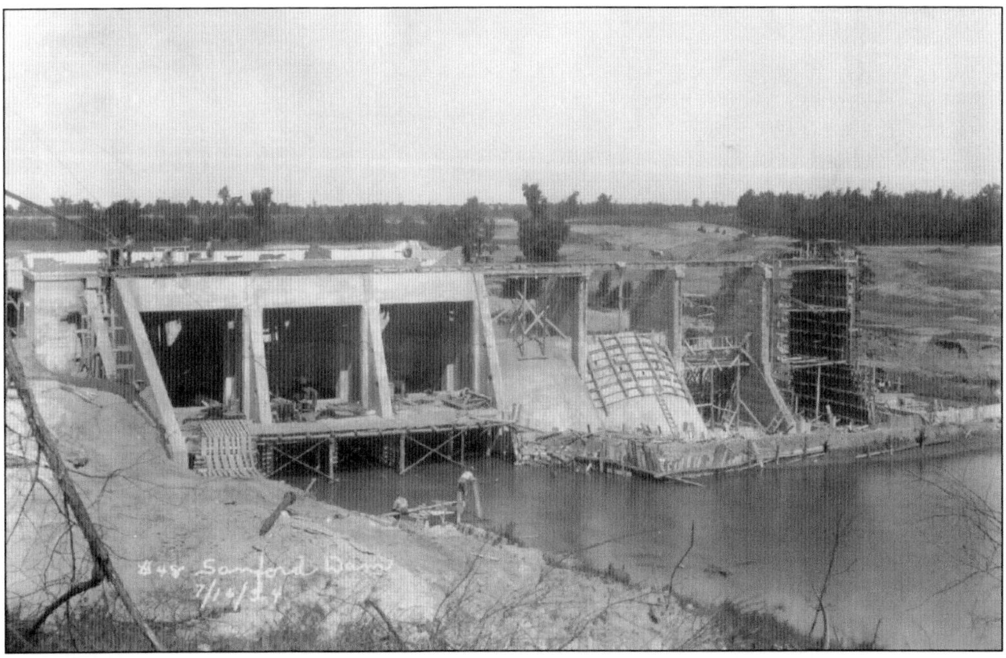

SANFORD DAM, JULY, 1924. Water was backed up from Sanford to Edenville to form Sanford Lake. Hundreds of acres of land were inundated when the dams went into operation. Farmers were paid for the flowage rights. (Photo courtesy of Wolverine Power Company)

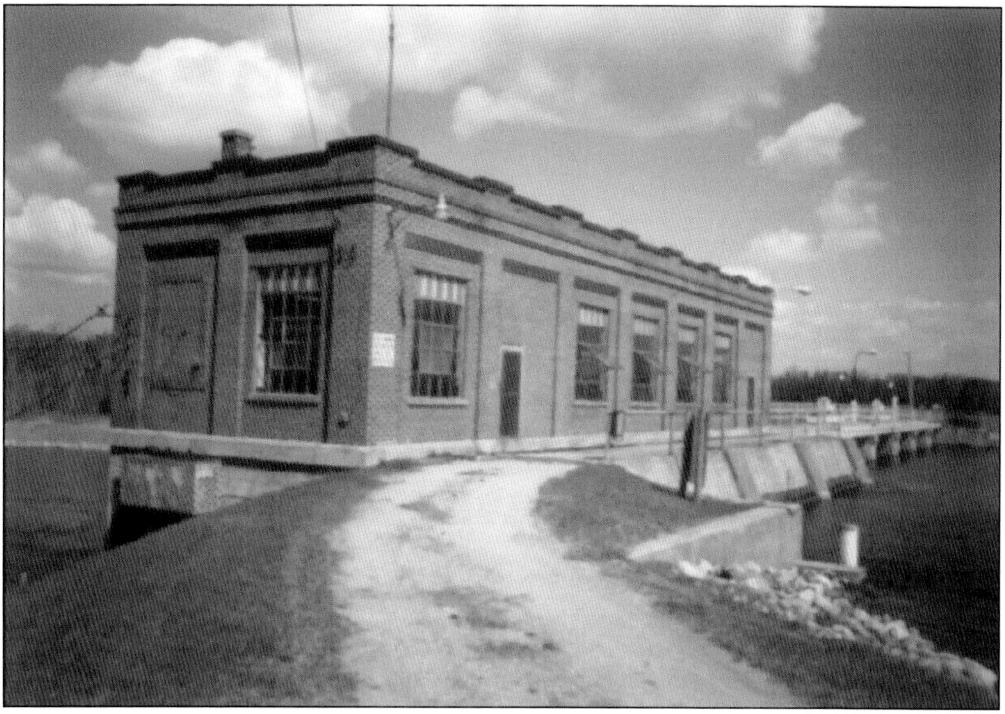

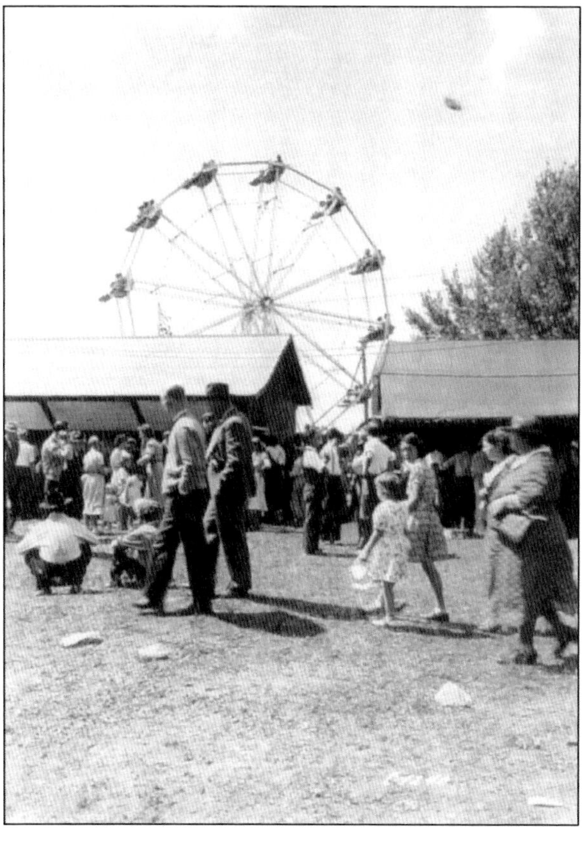

SANFORD DAM. This is the completed Sanford Dam, an enduring monument to the genius of Frank Wixom. His dream changed the topography of Midland County. (Photo courtesy of Wolverine Power Company)

FERRIS WHEEL. Once the dams were a going concern, Wixom turned to another project: the lumberjack picnics. The first one was held in 1932 and they continued until 1941. People came from all over Michigan and nearby states to enjoy the carnival, the food and the lumberjack re-enactments. One summer crowds reached 50,000 at the lumberjack picnics.

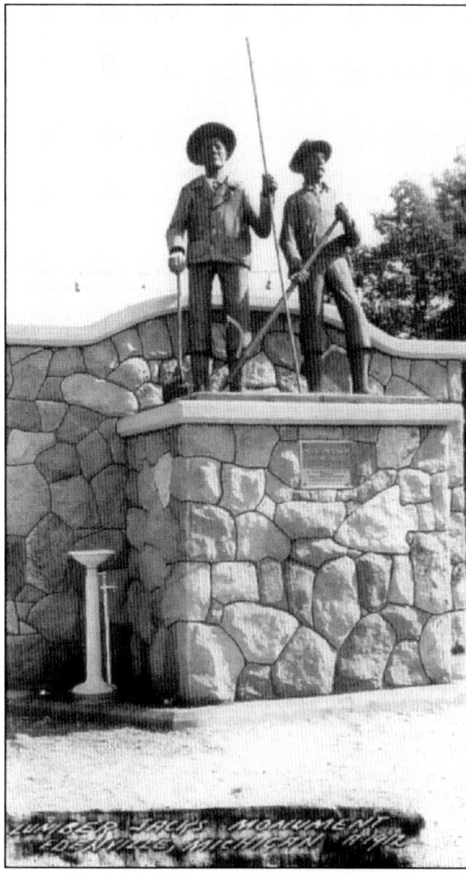

LUMBERJACK MONUMENT. This monument to the lumberjacks of Michigan was dedicated in 1937 and erected at the entrance of the lumberjack picnics held for 10 years in Edenville, Michigan. Alfred Levely carved the life-size figures of William Dundas (left) and Otis Terpenning (right). Cornelius Jackson did the stonework.

COOKING FOR THE LUMBERJACK PICNICS. Log cabins were built on the Hayhurst farmland to serve as cafeterias. Lumberjacks were hired to do the cooking and the church women from the Hope Methodist, Hope Baptist, and Edenville Methodist churches did the serving and the cleaning up. Meals were 50¢.

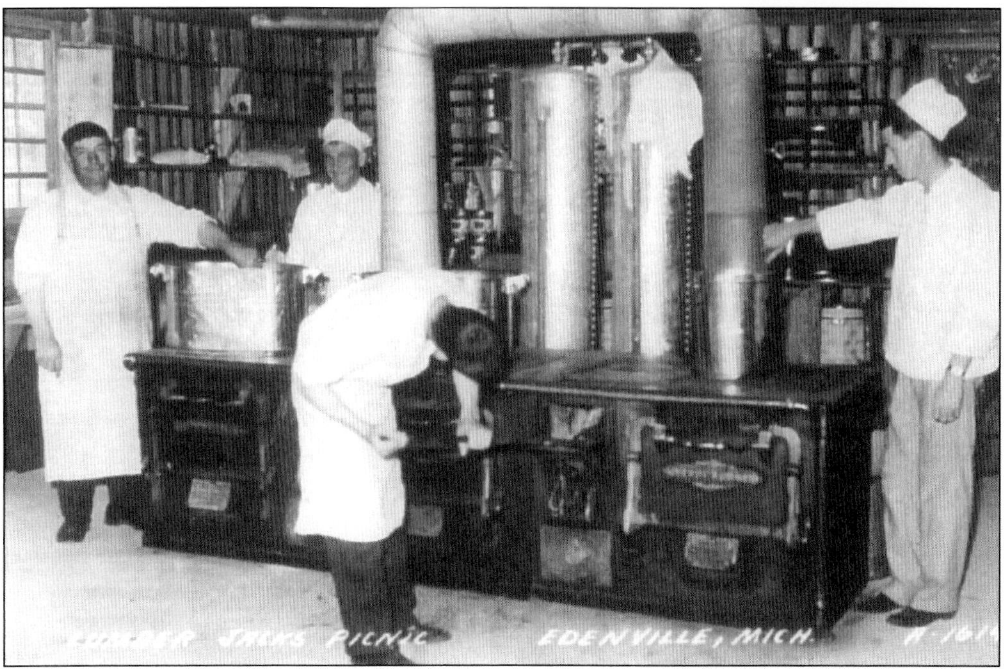

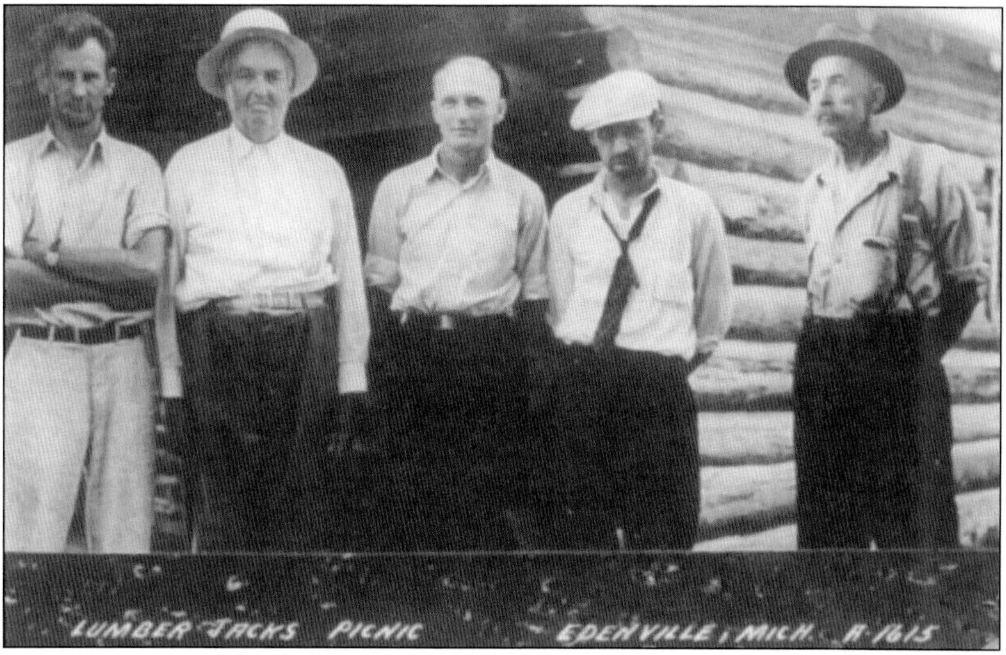

Frank Wixom. This is Frank Wixom, second from the left, with some of the men who helped him make the Lumberjack Picnics famous. People came from all over to stroll the 75 acres that were set aside on the Hayhurst farm on the high west bank of the Tittabawassee River for the occasion.

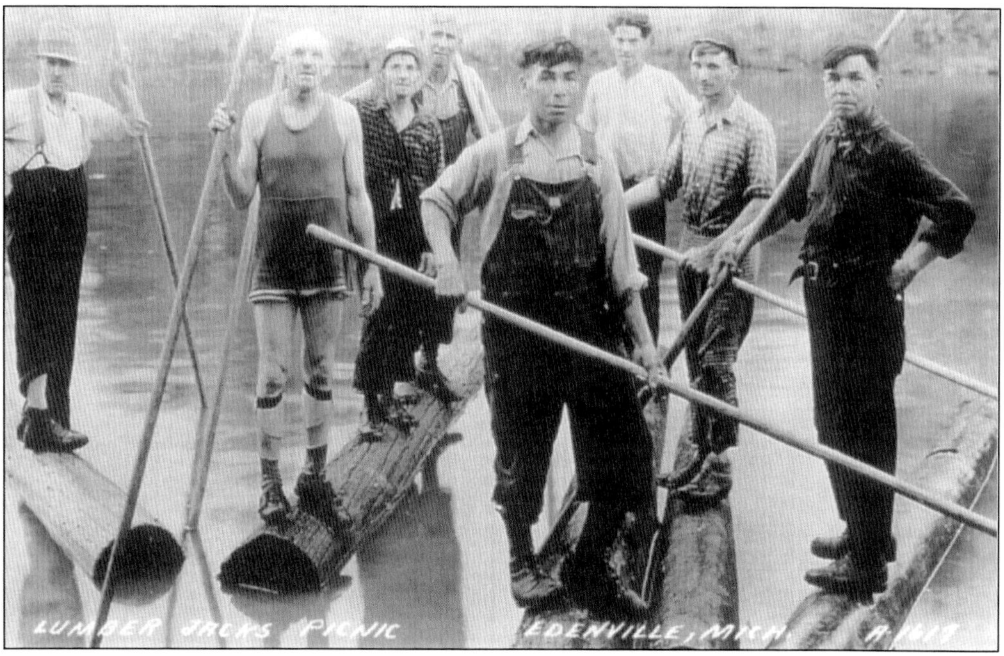

Lumberjack Contests. Wixom re-created the lumberjack days as much as possible. One entertainment was the log birling contests where men vied to see who could stay on a spinning log the longest while knocking their opponent into the river.

Six

MAKING OF A CITY

Praising what is lost makes the remembrance dear.

—Shakespeare

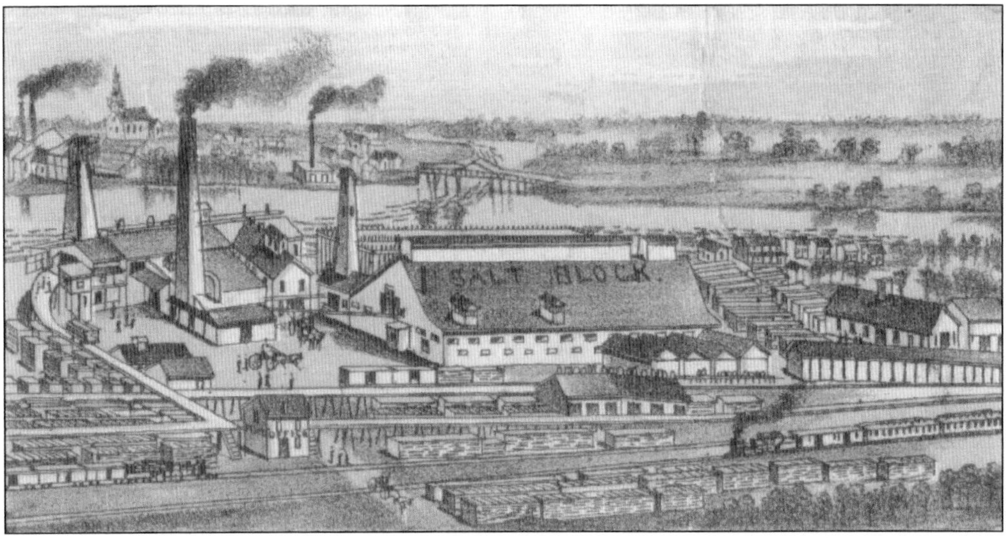

They were men of different backgrounds, different temperaments, different religions. Still they had certain things in common. They all came to the small town of Midland, Michigan to seek their fortune. They believed that much could be done if enough effort was put forth. And they all left an indelible mark on the city that has transcended their lifetimes.

John Wyman in 1837 began the immigration of settlers and pioneers to what was first called The Forks, followed by the Cronkright, Gordon, Fitzhugh, Townsend, Whitman, Vance, Ashmun, Kent, Nehil, Bailey, Dougherty, and Miller families. They were the first wave of people to come to the Village of Midland.

The second wave to come here brought names like Bradley, Arbury, Dow, Griswold, Gerstacker, Doan, Vogelsang, Collings, Stanford, Towsley, McCandless, and Cassidy. By now the town had become simply Midland, and while farming was important still, manufacturing and business overshadowed the early agrarian history of our small town. The following pages will show some of the men and women who turned a trading post in the wilderness into the city of Midland, Michigan.

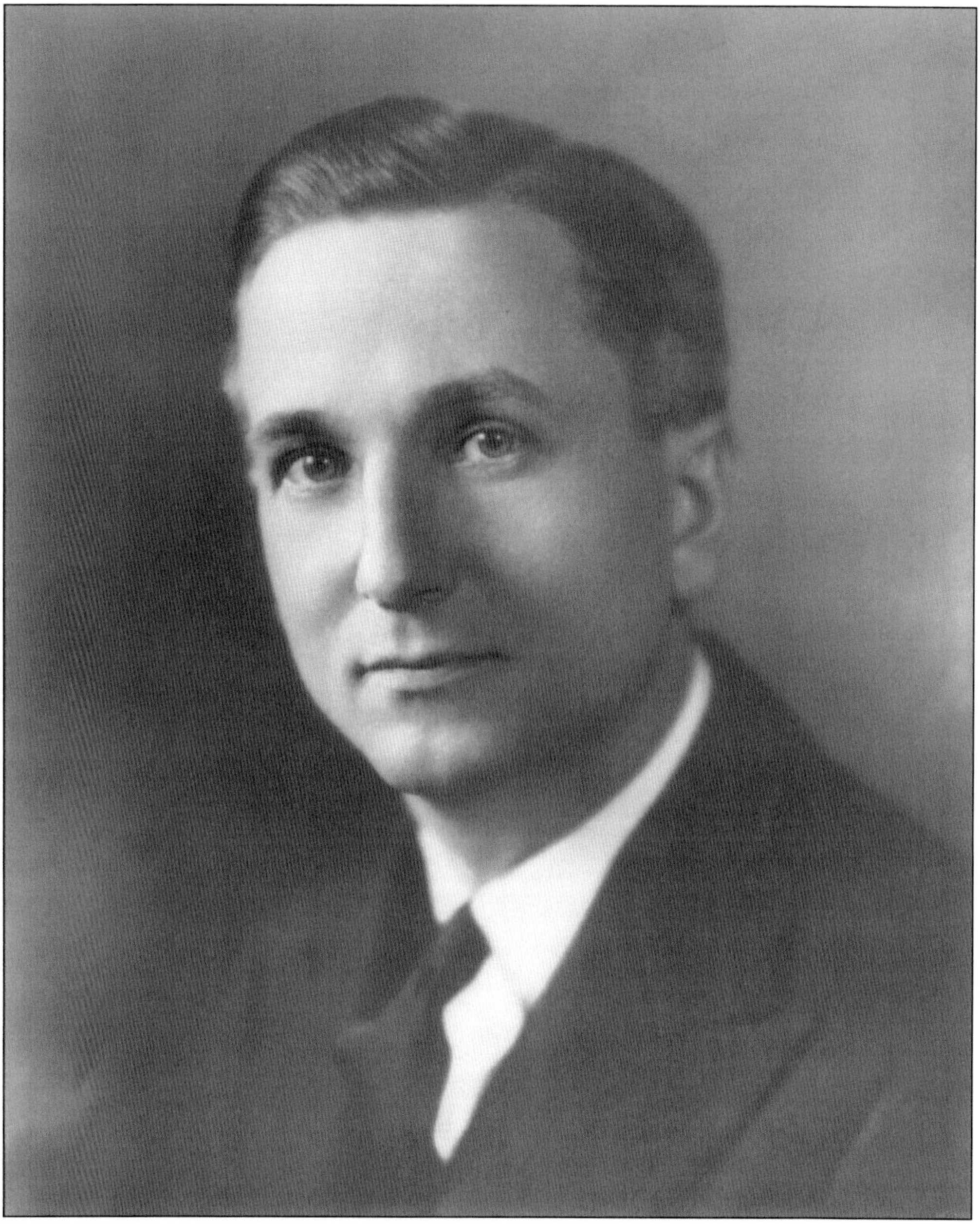

WILLARD DOW. Willard Dow was the third child and first son born to Herbert Henry Dow and Grace Ball Dow in 1897. He grew up in the small town of Midland and married a local girl, Martha Pratt, and in 1930 assumed the presidency of The Dow Chemical Company when his father died at the Mayo Clinic. Willard and Martha had two children, Helen and Herbert Henry II. Only 33 at the time that he took over the presidency of the chemical company in 1930, he guided it through the Thirties during the Great Depression and then through the traumatic years of World War II. Tragically, his life ended much too soon when he and his wife, Martha, were killed in a plane crash in 1949. (Photo courtesy of Post Street Archives)

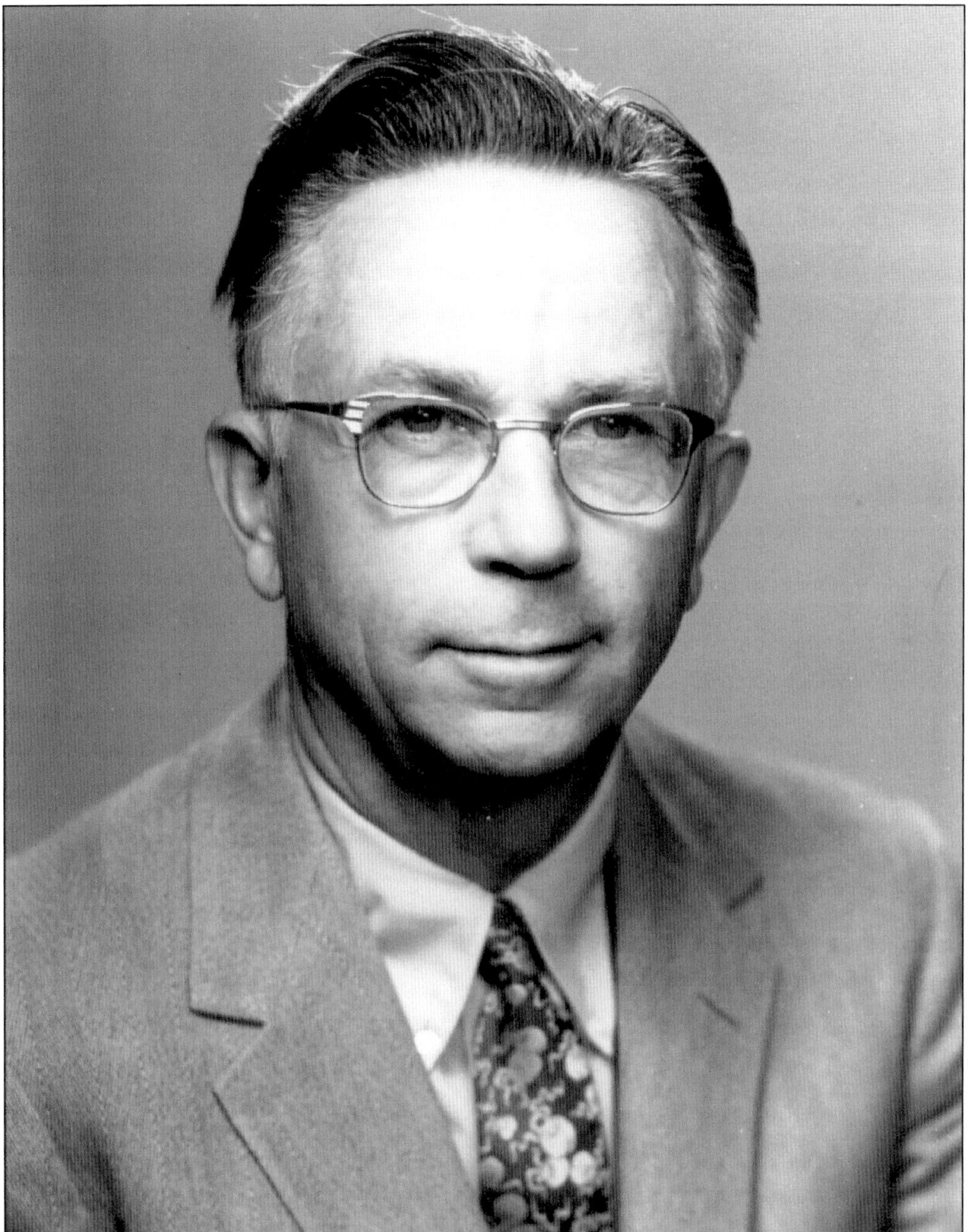

ALDEN DOW. Alden Dow was the fifth child born to Herbert and Grace Dow. Graduating from Midland High School in 1922, he visited Japan with his mother and father and fell in love with architecture. He dutifully went to college to become a chemical engineer but after three years he told his father that he wanted to be an architect and transferred to Columbia University to get his degree in that field. His work lives on in Midland landmarks including the Country Club, the Midland Center for the Arts, the Grace A. Dow Memorial Library, the Midland Community Center, and his home and studio located on Post Street in Midland. Alden Dow died in 1983. (Photo courtesy of Post Street Archives)

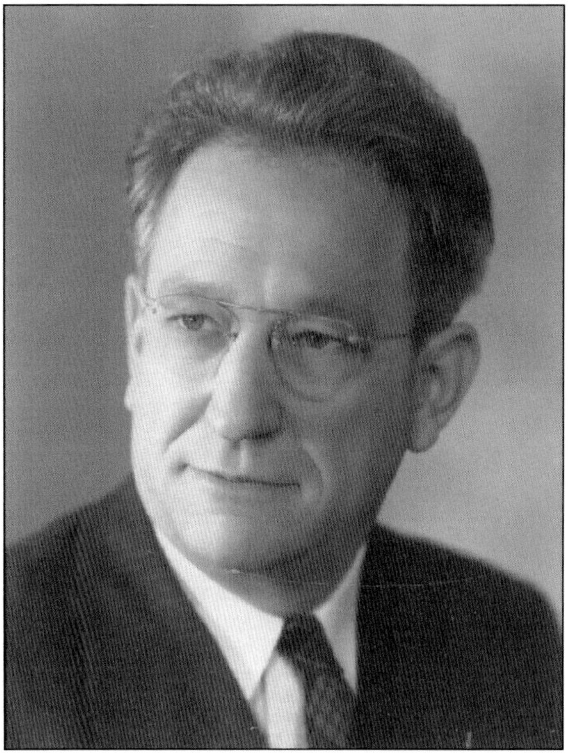

Phil Rich. Active in numerous aspects of civic accomplishments in Midland, Phil Rich was editor and publisher of the *Midland Daily News* and owner of the first radio station in Midland. He died on December 4, 1973, but the things he worked for live on. (Photo courtesy of *Midland Daily News*)

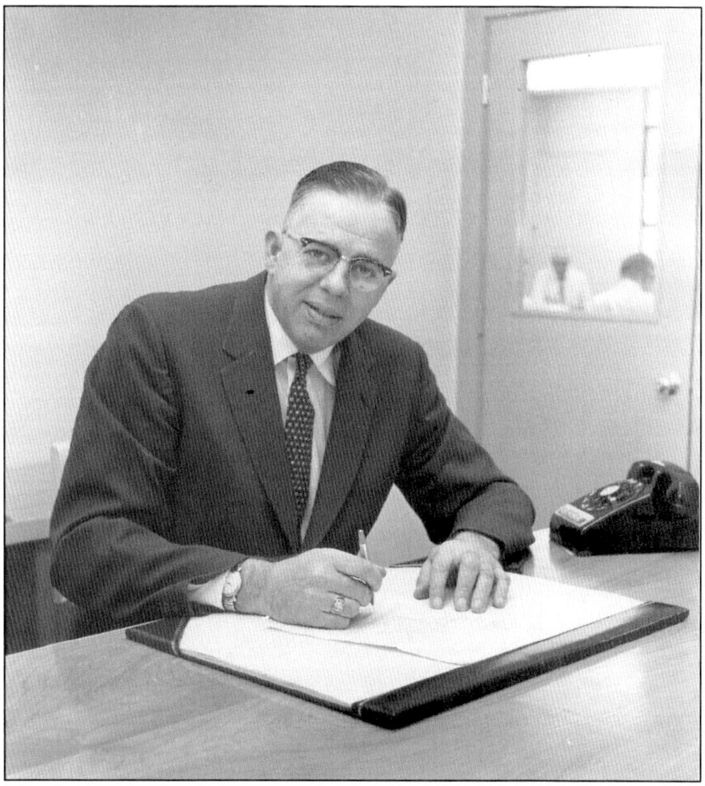

Norman Rumple. Norman Rumple worked his way up from wire editor to be named publisher emeritus of the *Midland Daily News*. When asked how he could turn out editorials day after day, year after year, he replied, "Well, you apply the seat of your pants to the seat of your chair." Slim died in 1996, leaving a legacy to be remembered. (Photo courtesy of *Midland Daily News*)

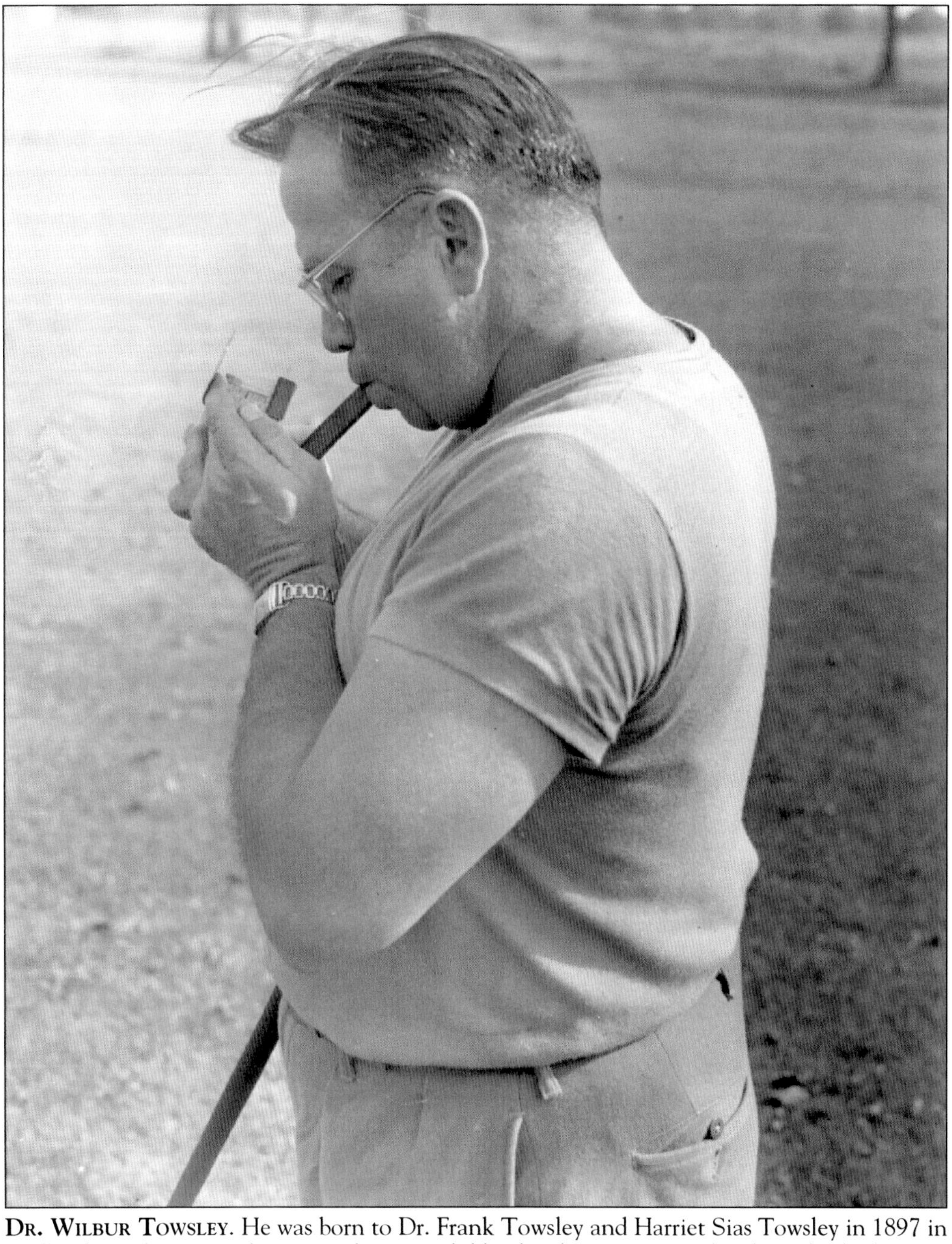

Dr. Wilbur Towsley. He was born to Dr. Frank Towsley and Harriet Sias Towsley in 1897 in Midland, Michigan. He became a doctor as did his brother Harry. His brother Charles became a dentist. Kind, compassionate, caring, he was the very best of what one envisions a doctor to be. He died in 1971 leaving a void that will never be filled. (Photo courtesy of Midland Daily News)

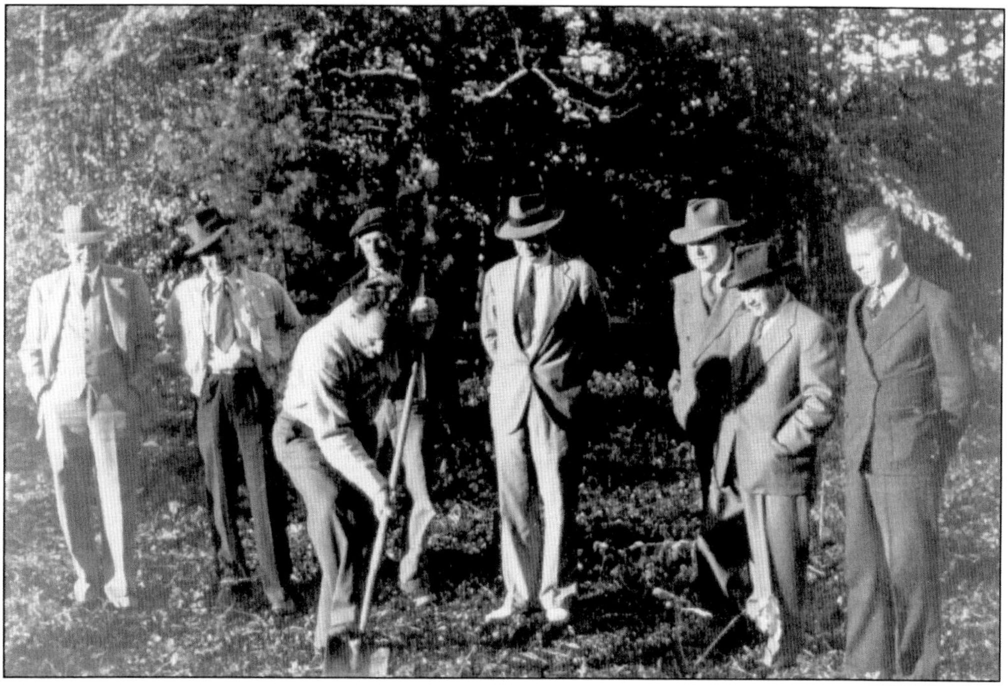

Hospital Groundbreaking. Groundbreaking for the new Midland Hospital took place in 1942 with Phil Rich, President of the Hospital Association, digging the first ceremonial shovel of dirt. In the picture, left to right, are: E.F. Holser, Martin Maxwell, Jacob Michel, Wayne McCandless, Aaron T. Bliss, Karl Sipple and Ralph Murray.

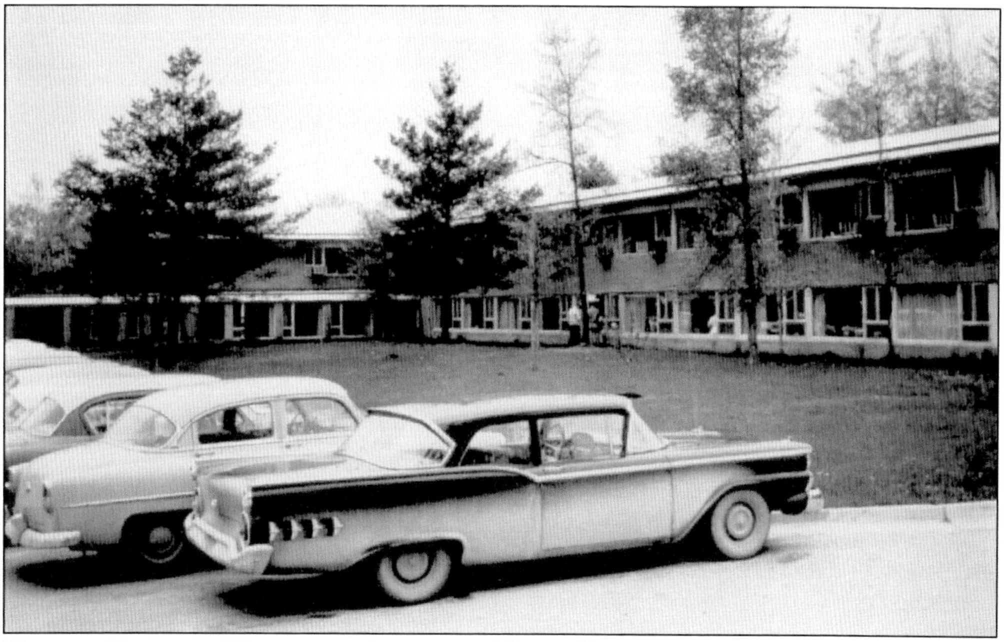

Hospital Exterior. This is an early picture of the Midland Hospital designed by Alden Dow. Room for 35 surgical-medical beds and 15 obstetrical beds was considered sufficient with the idea that expansion was possible.

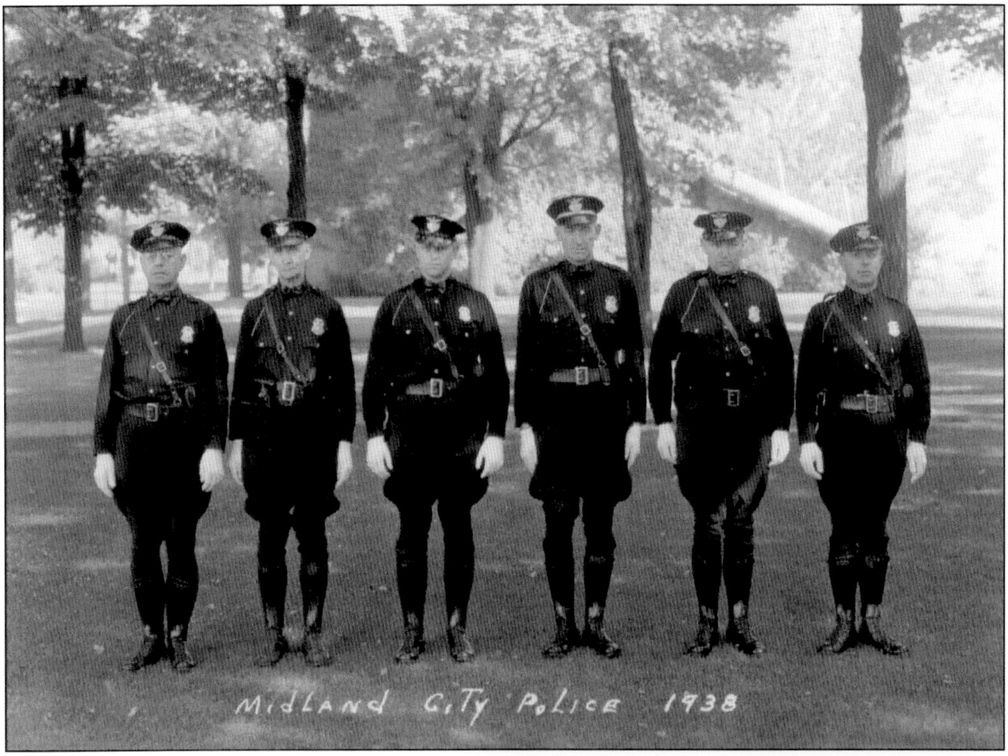

POLICE DEPARTMENT 1938. This is the Midland City Police force as it looked in 1938. Left to right are Fred Sayles, Sherman Howe, Ben Penner, Stanley Sage, Arthur Segerlund and Henry Ross.

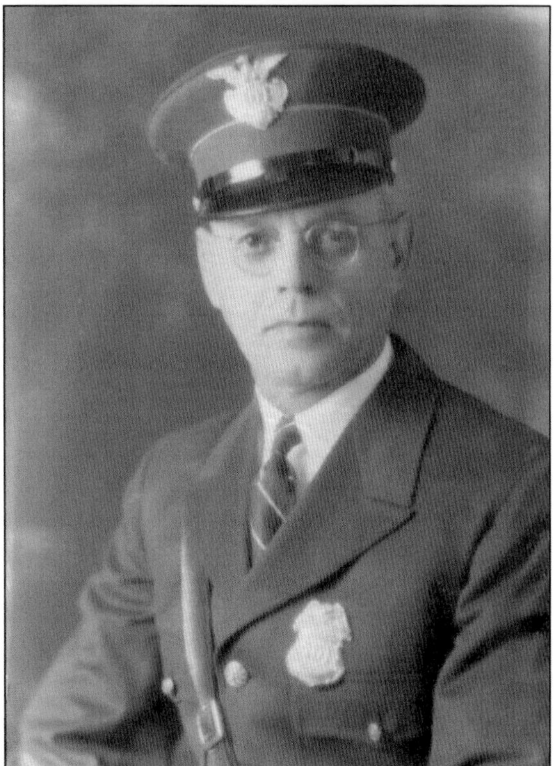

FRED SAYLES. Fred Sayles came to Midland in 1902, and for the next 60 years he was a major contributor to the community that he had adopted as his home. In May of 1921 he became the first chief of police in Midland, a position he held for the next 23 years.

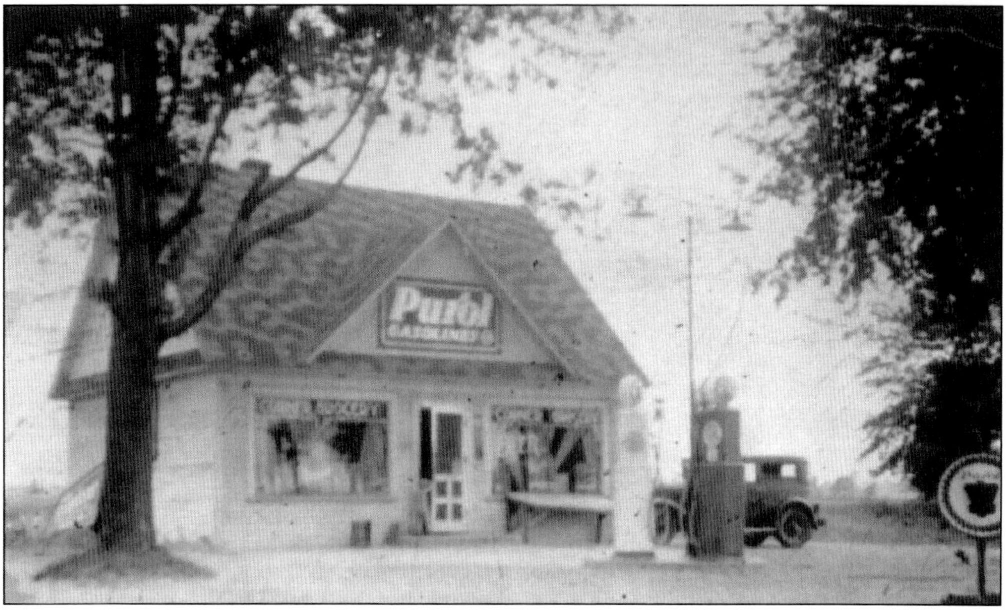

Solosky Store on the Circle. In 1932 the Solosky brothers had the first store located on what would become the Circle in Midland. Leo ran the grocery store and Frank took care of the two-pump gasoline station. Along with your gas purchase, the oil, battery, and tires were checked and the windshield was wiped clean. It was a full-service station. Frank aimed to please.

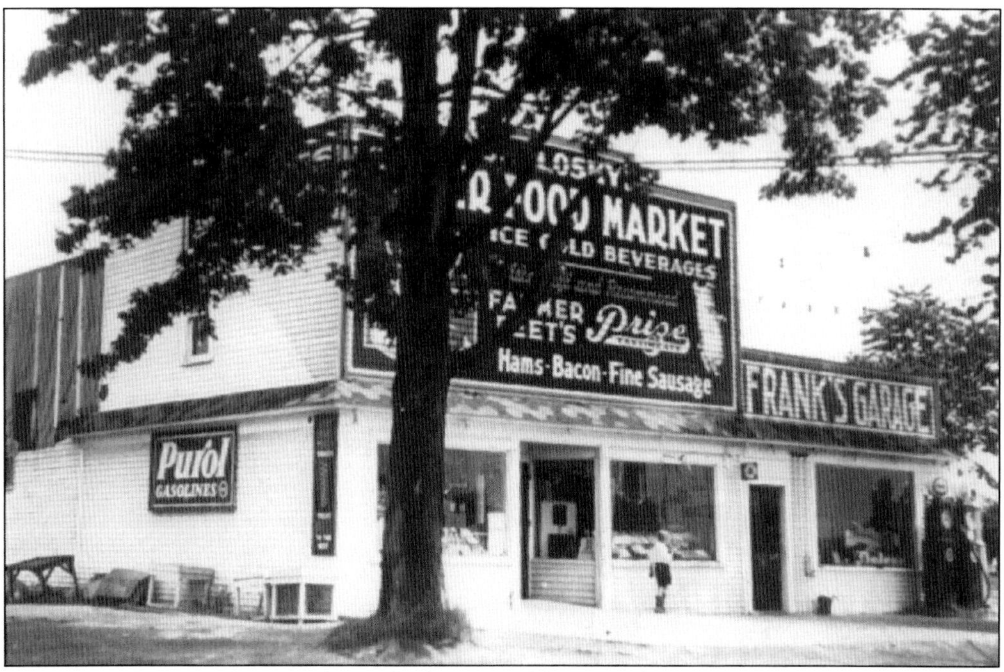

Remodeled Solosky Store. This is the bigger and better Solosky grocery store and gas station on the Circle. Leo put in a donut machine in the newly remodeled store where a customer could put a nickel in a slot, watch a blob of dough drop into a vat of hot oil and in a couple of minutes have a hot doughnut to eat.

PHELPS VOGELSANG. Phelps Vogelsang began his career in Midland as a forester for Dow, became mayor in 1944, got Lake Huron water into Midland, and designed the Veterans' Memorial Park in Sanford. When he died in 1970, Mayor Julius Blasy said in a memorial to the Vogelsang family, "He was the right man at the right time."

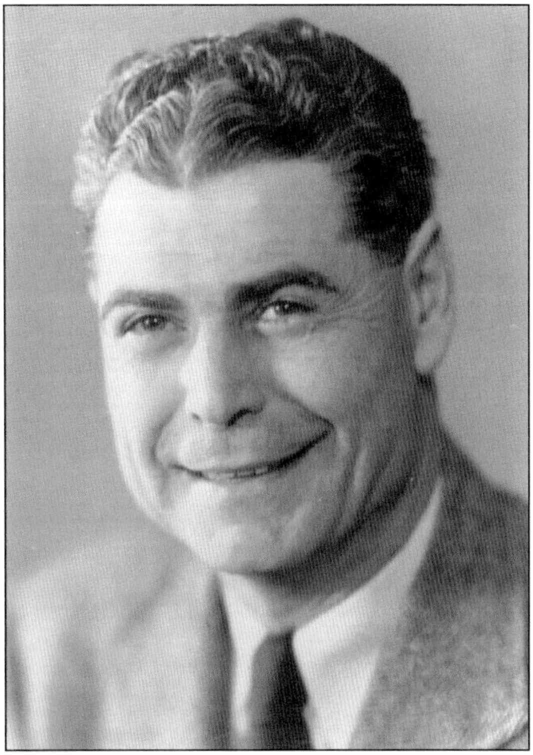

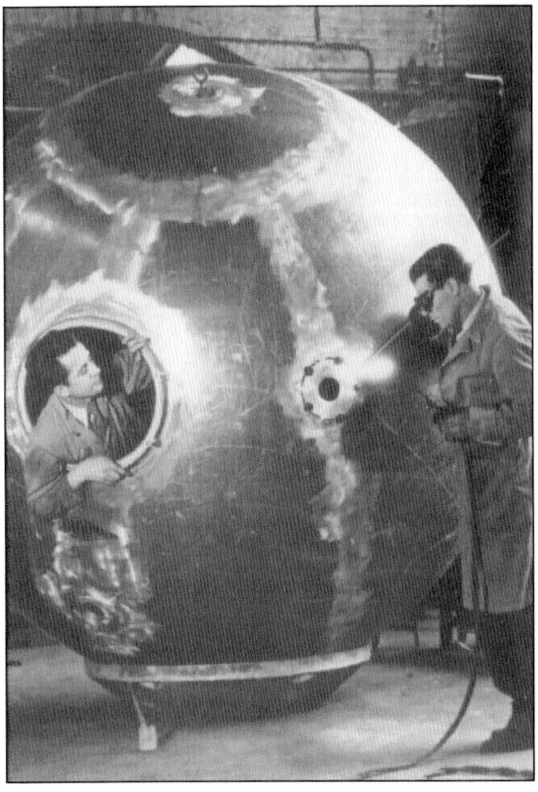

TOM MONTGOMERY. Dow was involved with the space race in the 1930s and the only man who could do the intricate welding on the gondolos was Tom Montgomery. But after three attempts, the project faltered. War threatened in Europe and the National Geographic Society decided there was no future in manned ballooning. Tom Montgomery is on the right. The man on the left is unidentified.

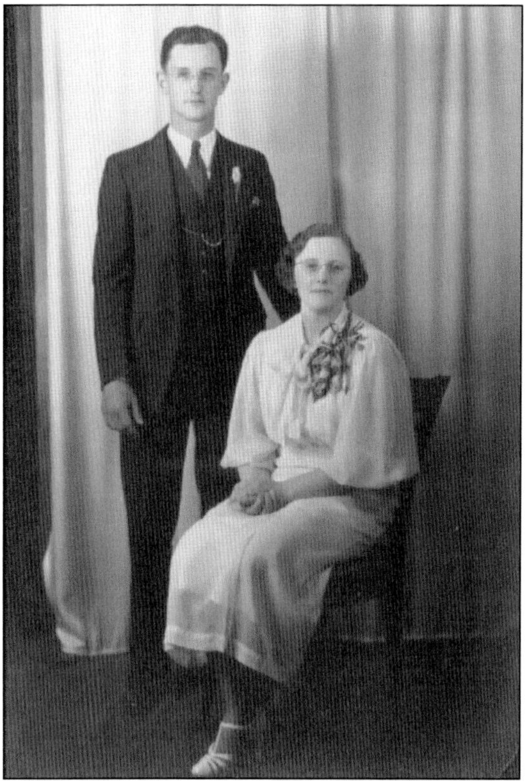

Lester and Marville Kent. This is the wedding picture of Lester and Marville Carey Kent married in 1934. When Midland faced a housing shortage, they went into the construction business building 1,000 pre-fab and "stick" homes with down payments as low as $300. Five decades later the houses are still a part of Midland.

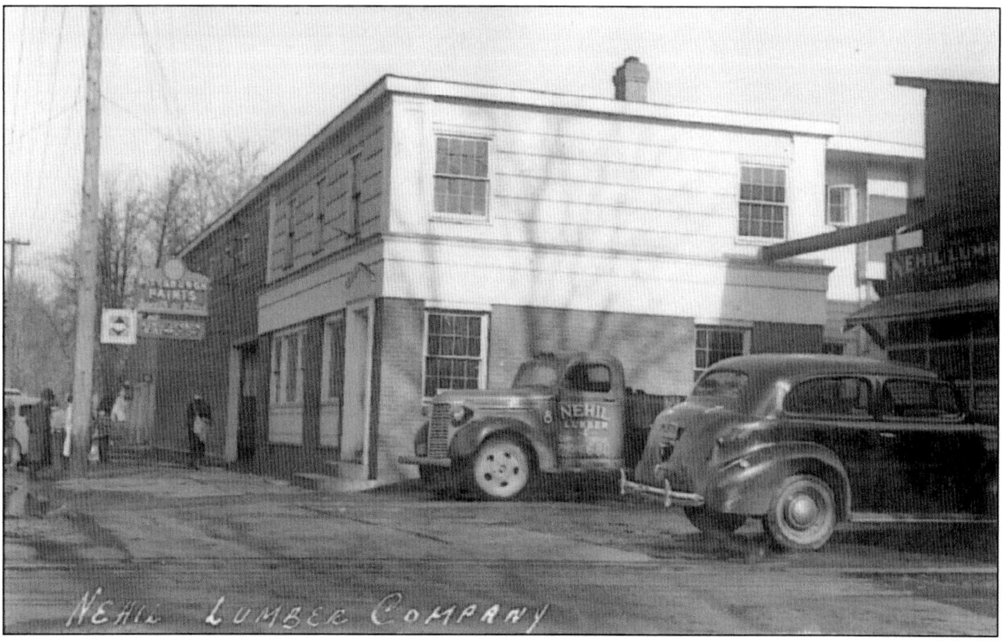

Nehil Lumber Company. Charlie Short came to Midland to work at The Dow Chemical Company, married Katherine Nehil and shortly found himself running the Nehil Lumber Company on Ashman in Midland, Michigan. Literally hundreds of young couples got their first homes due to Charlie Short's unflagging faith in human nature.

LELAND I. DOAN. Leland I. Doan became president of The Dow Chemical Company when a plane crash took the life of his brother-in-law and sister-in-law Willard and Martha Dow in March of 1949. He served in that position until 1962 when his son, Ted, assumed the mantle of president.

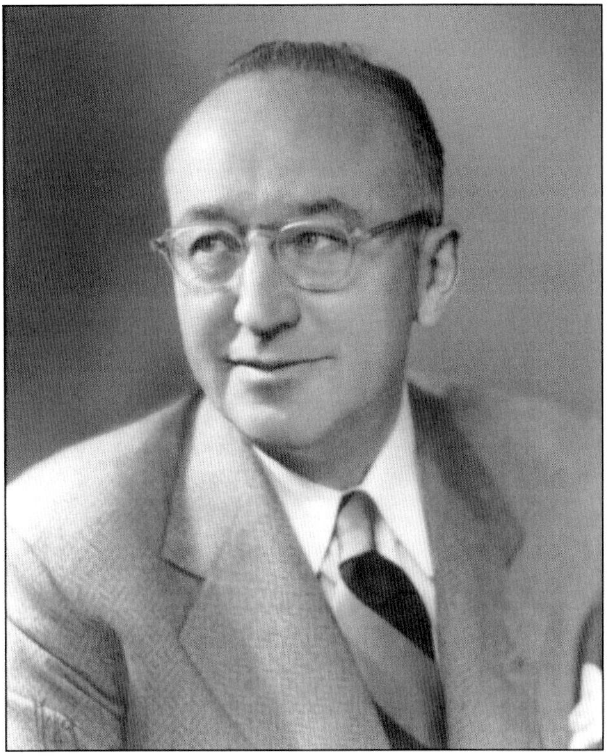

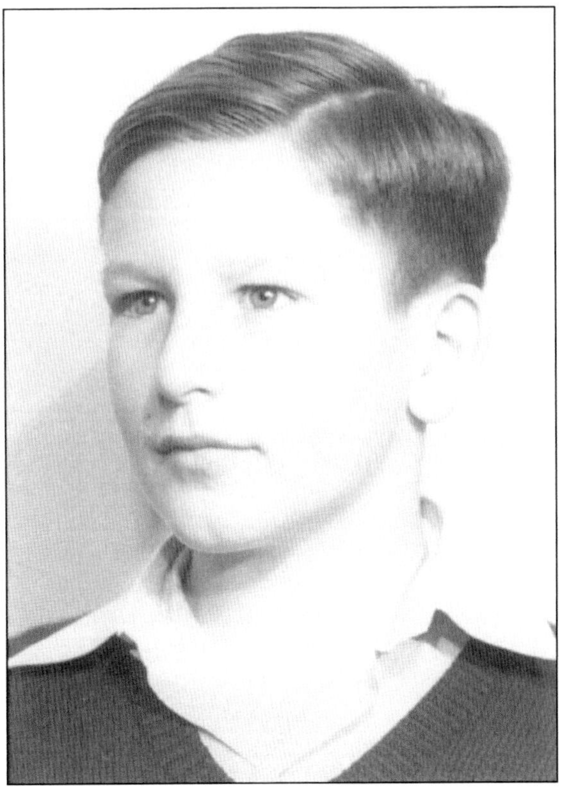

TED DOAN. This is Ted Doan as he looked in 1934, long before he became president and CEO of The Dow Chemical Company in Midland, Michigan. Born to Leland Ira Doan and Ruth Alden Dow, Ted was the last of their three children. The grandson of Herbert Henry Dow, he bears an uncanny likeness in spirit and enthusiasm to his grandfather.

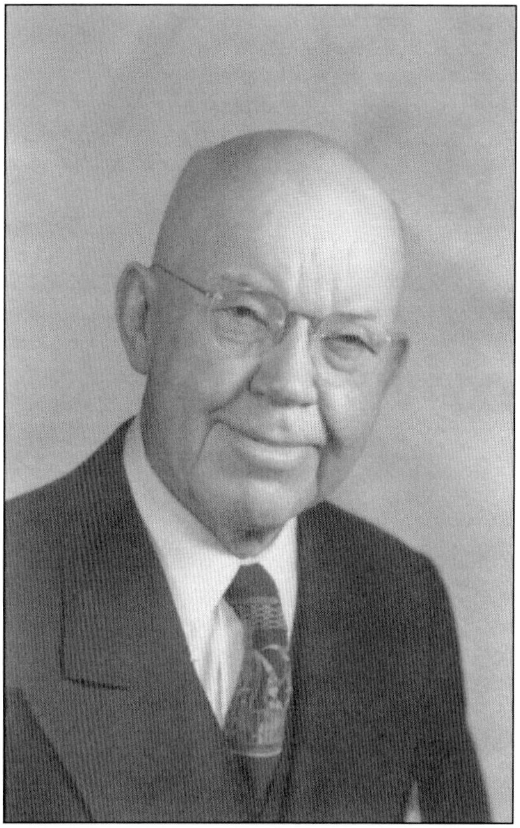

Gilbert Currie. Gilbert Currie was born in 1882 on a farm located at the Bluffs. Among his many contributions to the City of Midland were the development of Emerson Park and Currie Stadium, the war memorial by the court house, Currie-Bennett Park, and his dedication in establishing the Midland Country Club and its golf course. In 1952 he gave the city its first municipal golf course. (Courtesy of Midland Historical Society)

Ted Vosburgh. In the mid 1930s The Dow Chemical Company brought Dr. Theodore Vosburgh to Midland to head up their Dow music program. The Dow Male Chorus began in 1936 and were regular performers in music productions. This photo shows Dr. Vosburgh with the Dow Girls' Chorus before a performance in 1946. The Music Department eventually became a separate entity as the Midland Music Society.

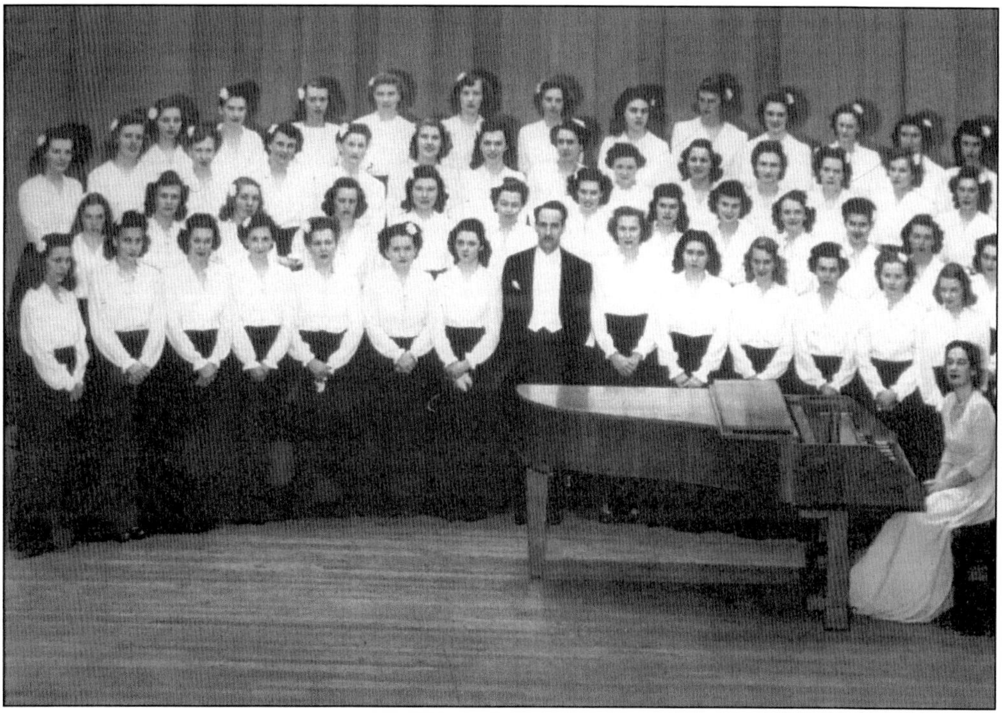

A.S. Arbury. Born in 1865, Andrew Stephen Arbury came to Midland in 1888 to work in a bank. His marriage to May Bradley ended with her death in 1895 following the birth of their second child. In 1903 he married Pearl Anderson. He died in 1949. She died in 1976 at the age of 92. She remained the family's matriarch to the end. (Photo courtesy of Midland Historical Society.)

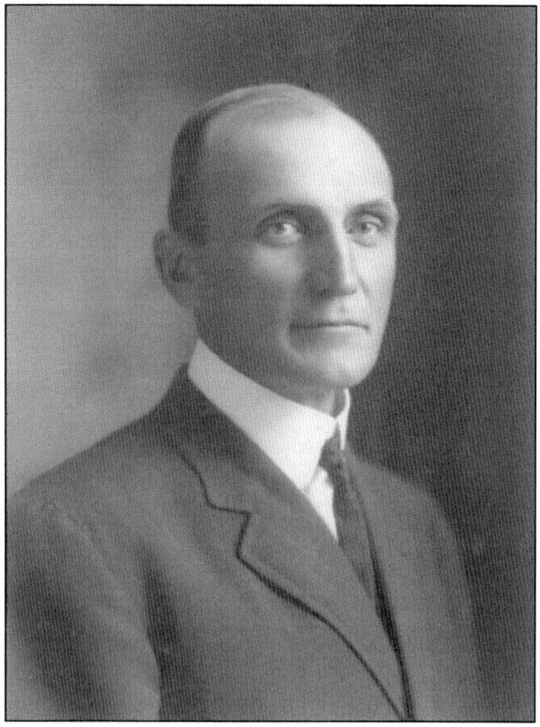

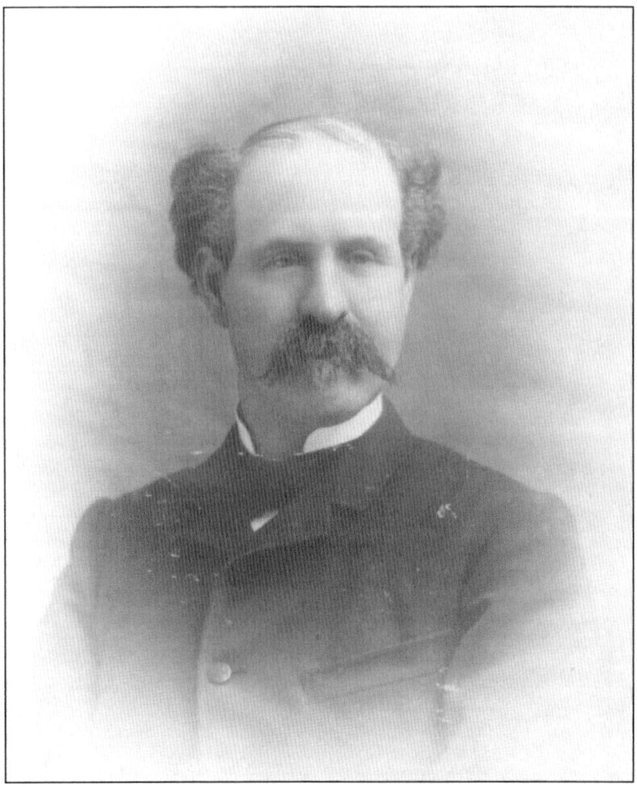

Benjamin F. Bradley. Benjamin F. Bradley became a mentor and life-time friend as well as a father-in-law to A.S. Arbury. While they launched various businesses, the most successful was their insurance business which continues today as A.S. Arbury Insurance. In 1874 Benjamin Bradley built the home which later became a part of the Historical Society's buildings on Cook Road. (Photo courtesy of Midland Historical Society.)

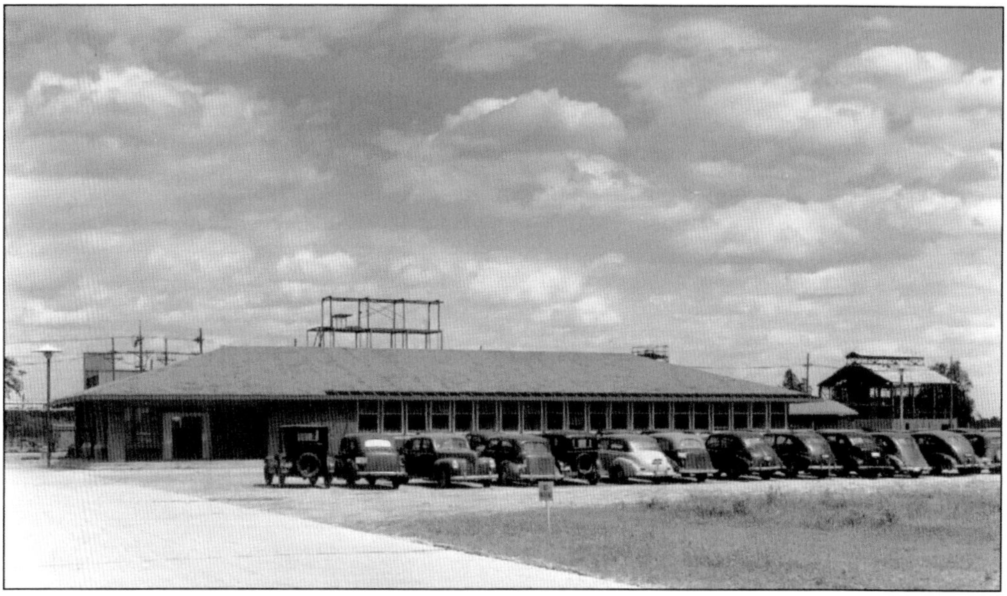

Dow Corning. In the early 1940s Corning Glass of New York and The Dow Chemical Company of Midland formed a new company they named Dow Corning. Built outside of Midland on the way to Freeland, it started out small but today is a huge conglomerate. This is the first office building that held the sales office, the bookkeeping department, the telephone switchboard, the timeclocks, and payroll department. (Photo courtesy of Dow Corning.)

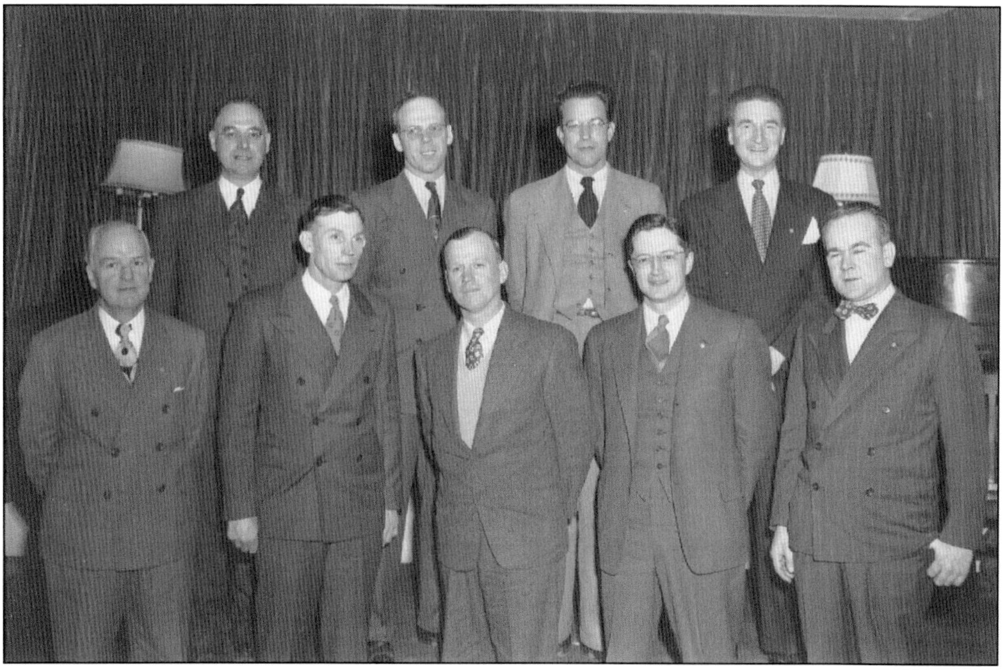

Dow Corning Men. Early Dow Corning Service Award Recipients, late 1949. Those honored are, from left to right: Dr. William R. Collings (president), Earl Roberts, Howard Cameron, Ollie Blessing, and Charlie Sanford; (back row) Al Smith, Bill Cron, Dr. Shailer Bass and Howard Fenn. (Photo courtesy of Dow Corning.)

Seven

Churches and Schools
The First 100 Years

Every day is a little life and our whole life is but a day repeated. Therefore, live every day as if it would be the last. Those that lose a day are prodigal. Those that save a day have saved a little piece of eternity for themselves.

—Bishop Hall

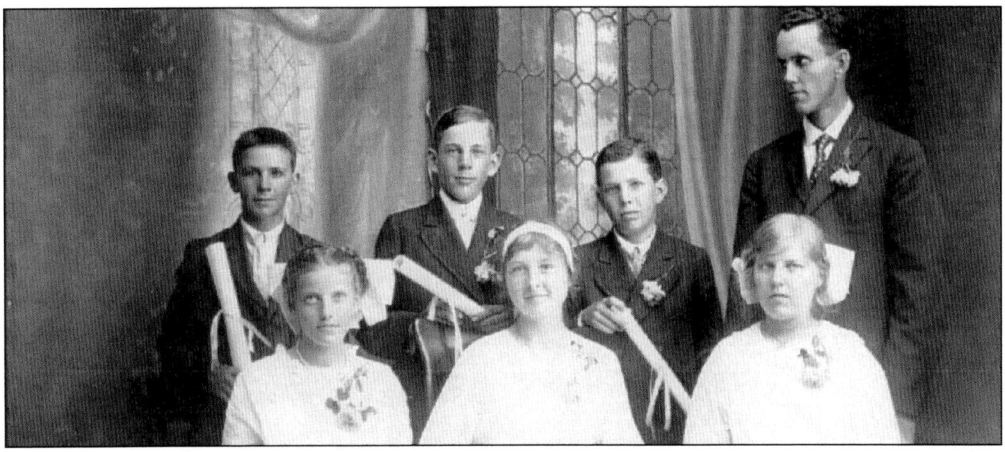

From the very beginning, settlers and pioneers in Midland County built schools and churches to accommodate educating their children and to have a place to worship. Schools were small one-room log cabins in the beginning with one teacher and children all the way from the age of 5 to 16. In 1872 the Union School was built on Grove Street with room for 200 children and it contained classrooms, a gymnasium, showers, an auditorium and a chemistry lab. As Midland continued to grow, so did its educational system.

The first church organized in Midland was the Methodist Church in September of 1857. On September 4, 1867, the First Presbyterian Church was organized. October of 1867 saw the Episcopal Church come into existence in the Village of Midland City. And on June 2, 1869, the First Baptist Church of Midland City was organized. Early Catholic families gathered at the William Keeley residence in Paddy's Hollow to recite the Rosary. In 1870 the first Mass was celebrated at the Keeley residence and in 1871 the first St. Brigid's Catholic Church was completed. St. John's Lutheran was originally known as the German Lutheran Church and had its beginning on June 14, 1884, at the Karl Haefka home in Midland. Eventually Midland became known as the "City of Beautiful Churches."

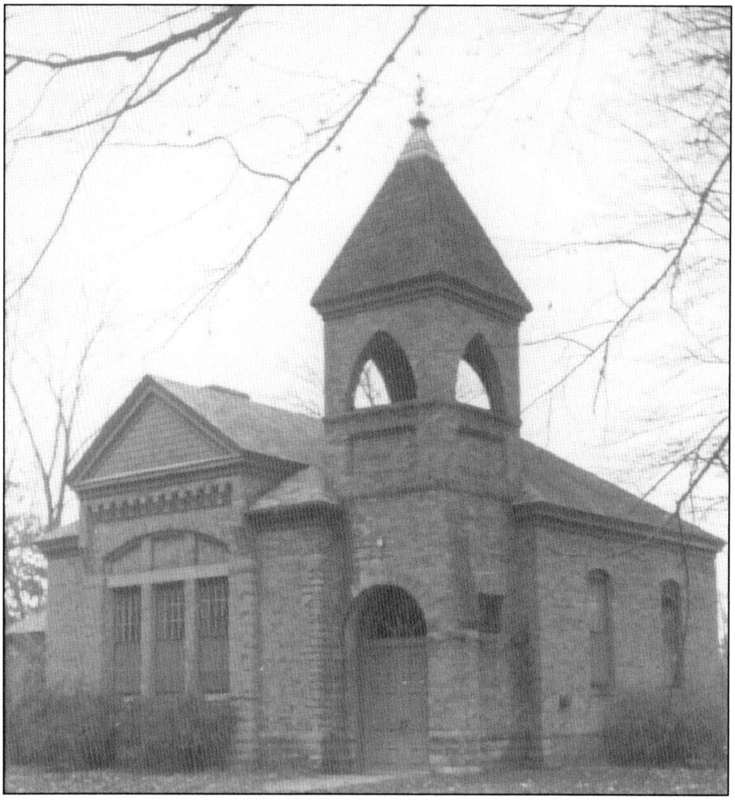

Post Street School. Built in 1876 on Post Street, it was appropriately named the Post Street School, teaching Beginners through the third grade. Later it was the home of the County Normal and then it was the Post Street Playhouse, the Post Street Workshop, and today it is the site of the Post Street Archives where Ned Brandt, company historian for The Dow Chemical Company, heads an archival staff.

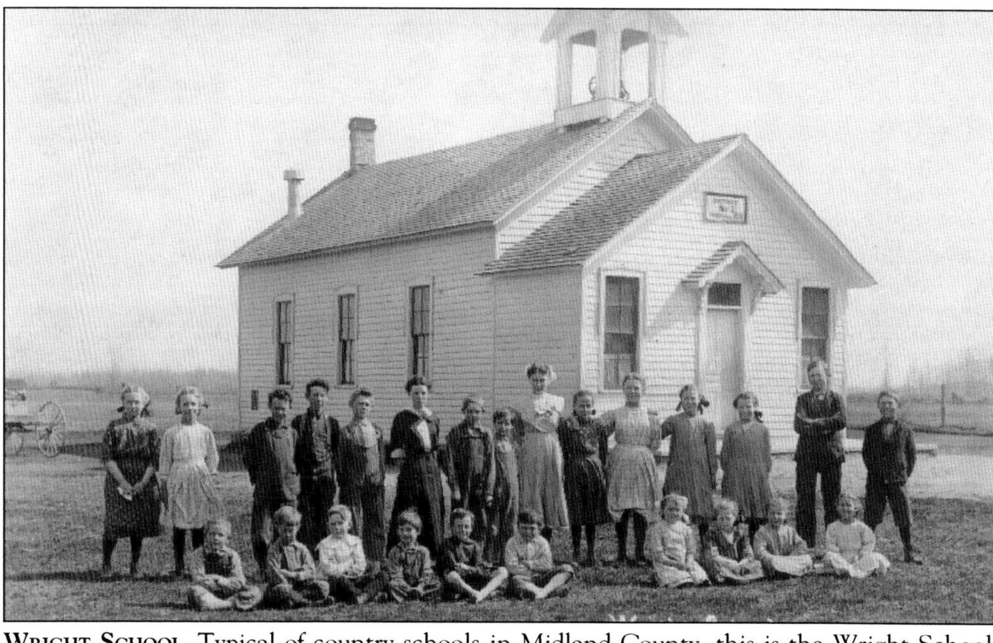

Wright School. Typical of country schools in Midland County, this is the Wright School, located on LaPorte Road in Ingersoll Township, shortly after it was built in 1882–1883. It was in operation until 1958. Someone once wrote: "Twas a little school. but there are those who loved her." Those words could have been written about the little Wright School.

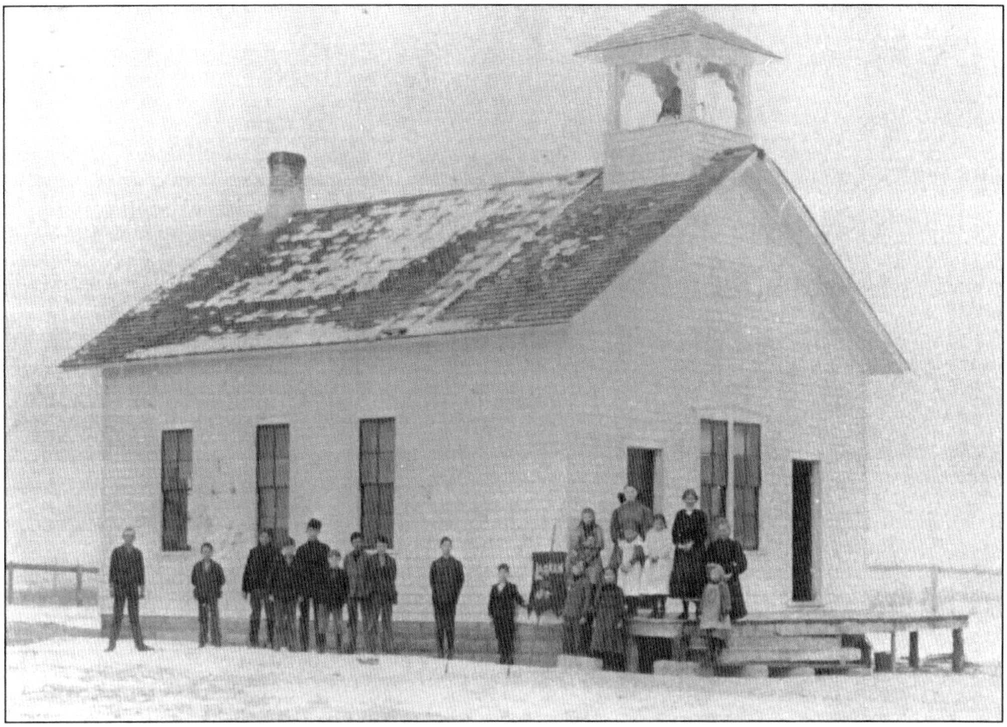

CADY SCHOOL. This is the Cady School on Sturgeon Road in 1907. Kids walked to school regardless of weather conditions. Lunches were carried in syrup pails or brown paper bags. A flowing well in the schoolyard provided water. Children ages 5 to 16 spent 7 hours a day, 5 days a week together with one teacher doing just about everything, including the janitor work.

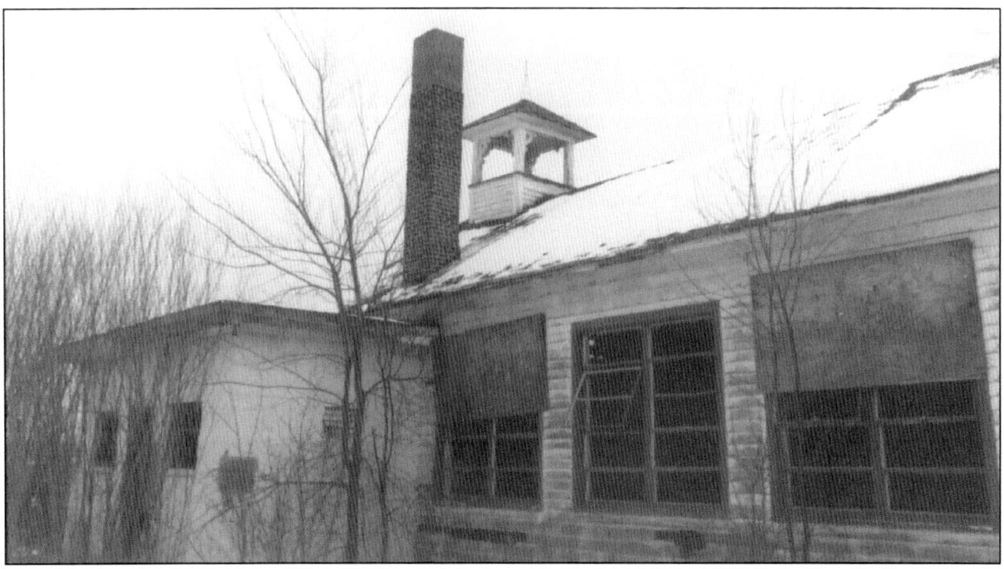

CADY SCHOOL. This is the Cady School, boarded up and ready for demolition. Note that at some point in time the belfry was moved to the back of the school. Wooden desks were nailed to the floor. Blackboards went across the front of the room. And pictures of George Washington and Abraham Lincoln scowled down at us from September to May.

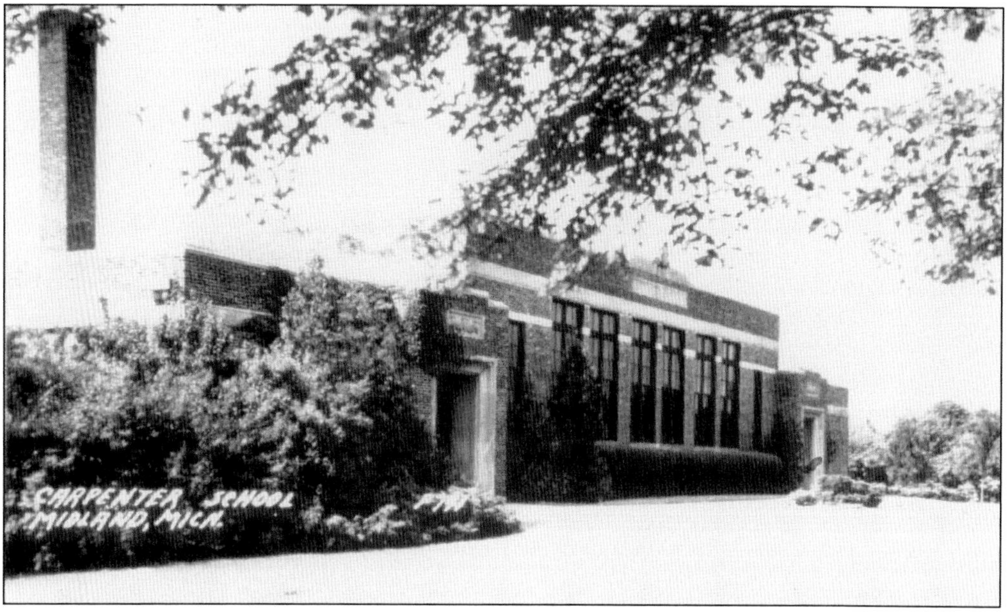

CARPENTER STREET SCHOOL. This is the new Carpenter Street School on Carpenter Street. The first classes were held there on January 31, 1927. Viola Perdue was principal from 1937 to 1965. Mary Claire Nims took over that position in 1965, and today John Blahunka is principal.

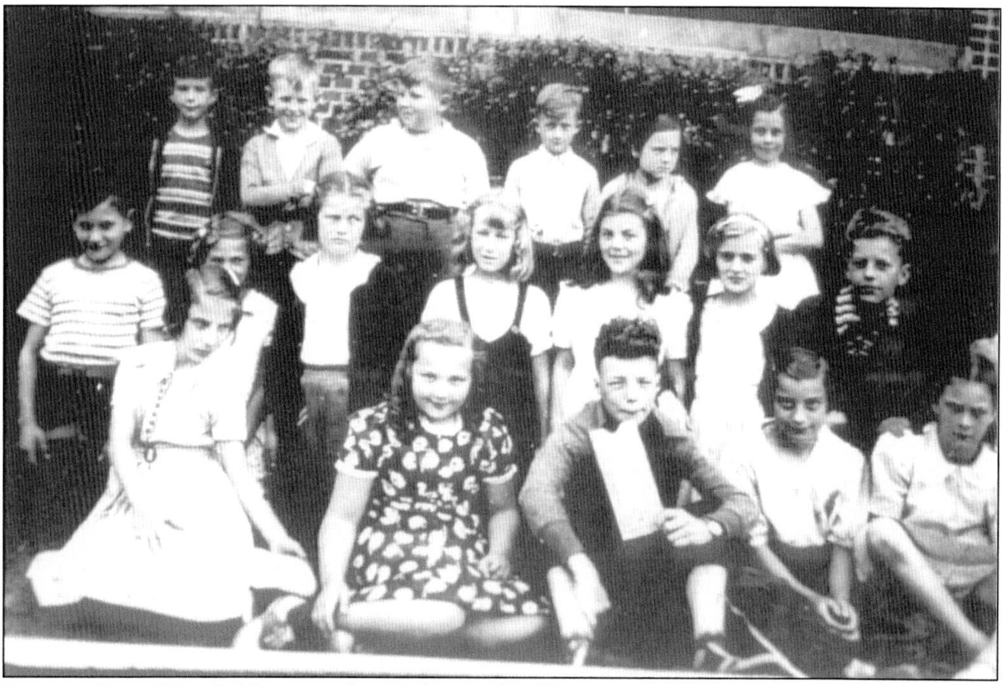

PICTURE DAY. The children are, from left to right: (front row) Lois Dingman, Jean McCreadie, Kent Snow, Hazel Brown, and Betty June Slater; (middle row) Bill Schartow, June Lightfoot, Elaine Brown, Mary Alice Beshgetoor, Dorothy Brown, Nancy Fullen, and Miles Cook; (back row) Bob Schwartz, Bob Betron, Clayton Heppner, Edsel Yaxley, Delores Klumpp, and Frances Eshelman. The picture is dated 1938, fourth grade, Carpenter.

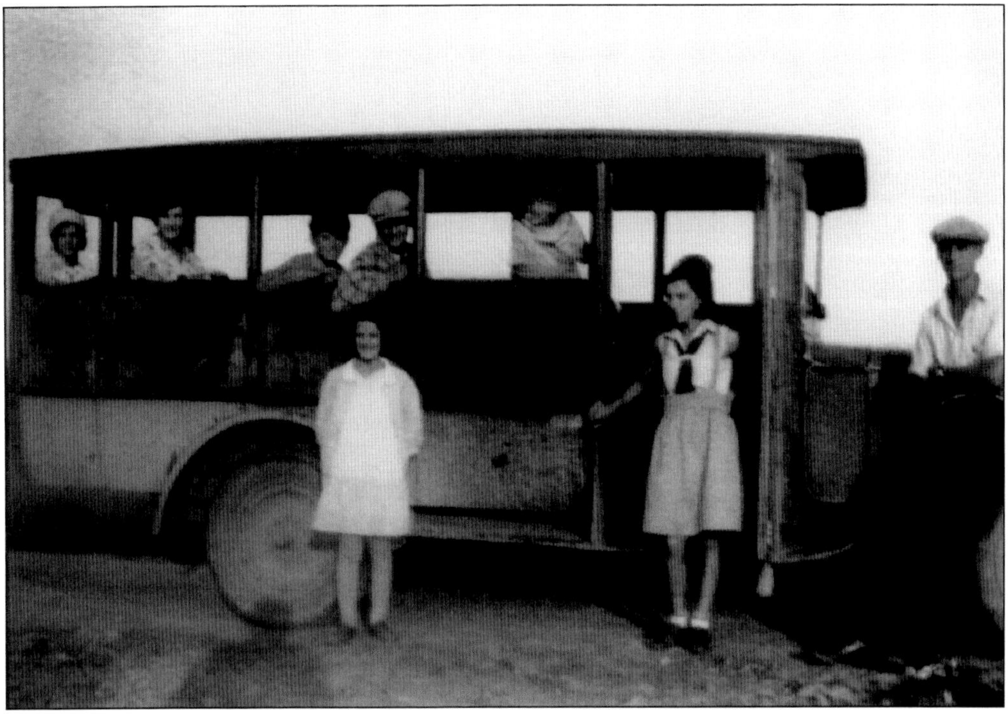

School Bus. Yes, there were school buses in the 1920s, at least in the Coleman, Michigan area. Here six students and their bus driver pose for a picture. Note that there is no glass in the windows in the bus.

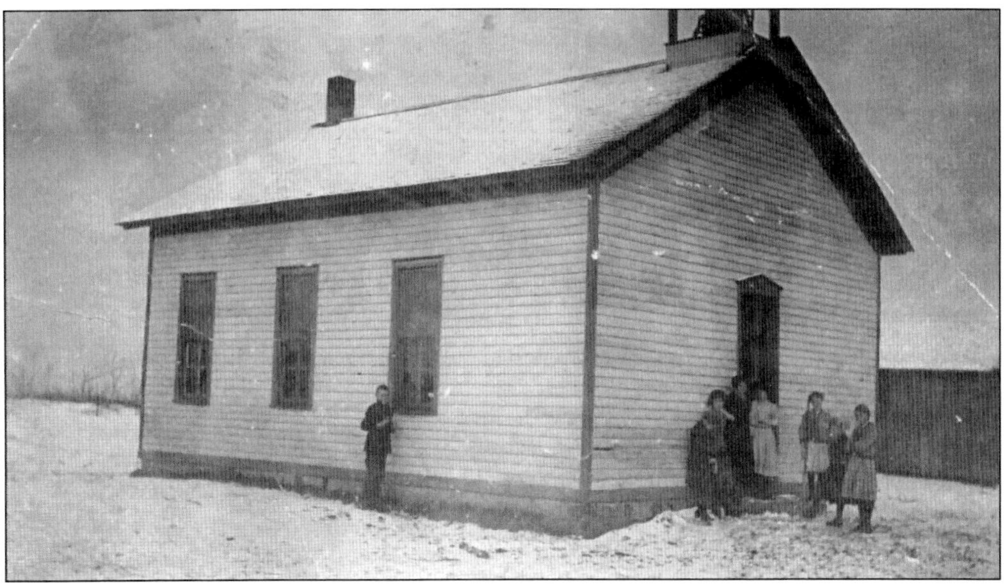

The First McGill School. Built in 1876 on Waldo Road, the McGill School was the typical one-room country school. A four-room school was built in 1939 and a two-room building was built "sometime in between." Only an empty field marks the site of the McGill School today.

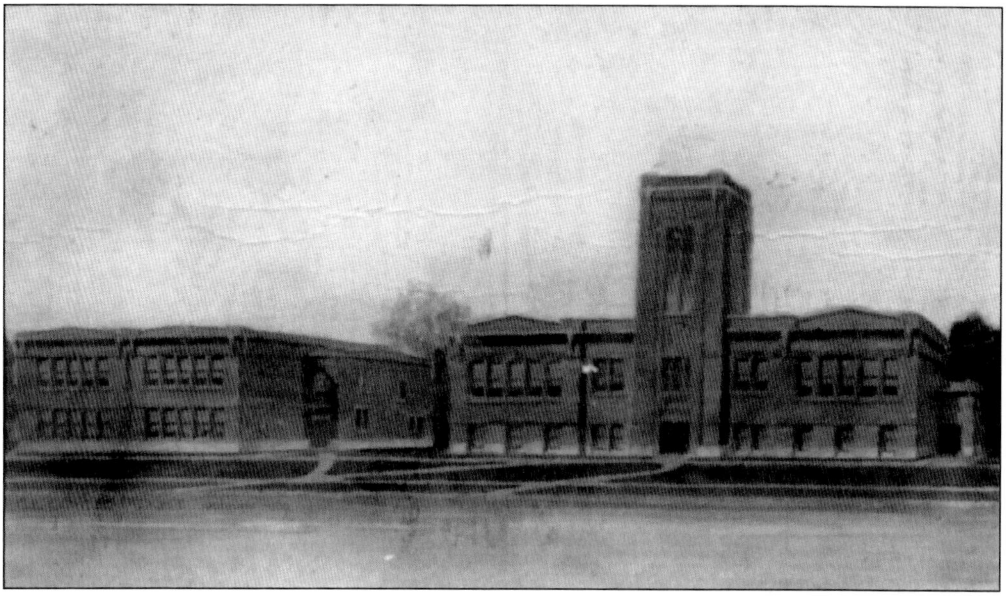

Senior High 1909. After the Union School burned in 1908, new buildings were constructed on Grove Street to house the senior high, junior high, and elementary school children. This picture is dated 1910 and was photographed by Will Evens.

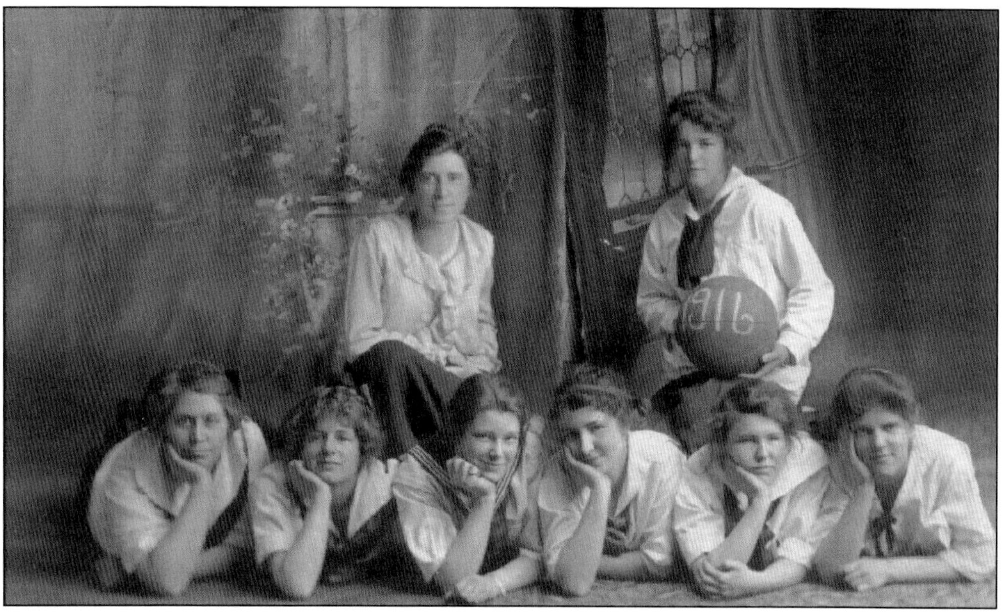

Girls' Basketball Team. Yes, girls played basketball even in 1916 in Senior High. Here the girls pose with their gym teacher who is on the left in the back row. The only one identified is Mary Weaver in the front row, second from the right.

JACK CLINE. He was football coach, track coach, and Director of Athletics at Midland Senior High from 1928 to 1938. A star athlete at Central Michigan College of Education in Mt. Pleasant, Michigan, he was headed for the 1928 Olympics when he hurt his leg and had to bow out.

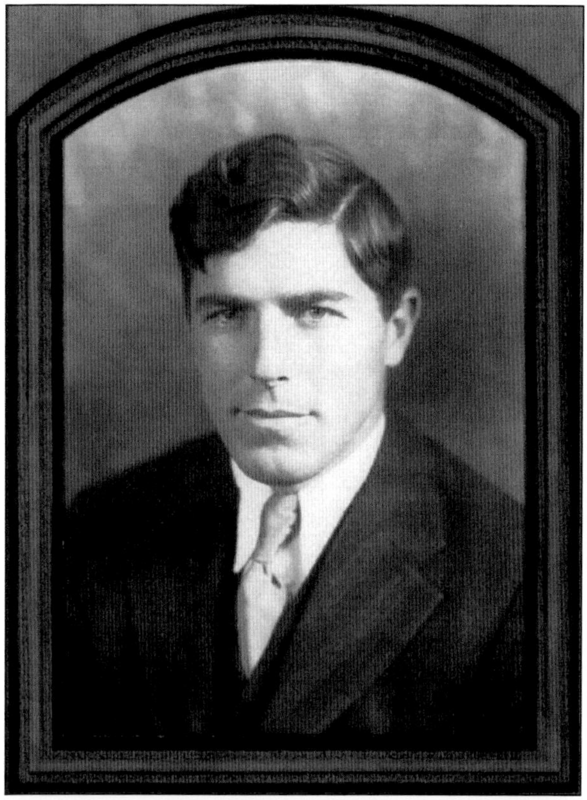

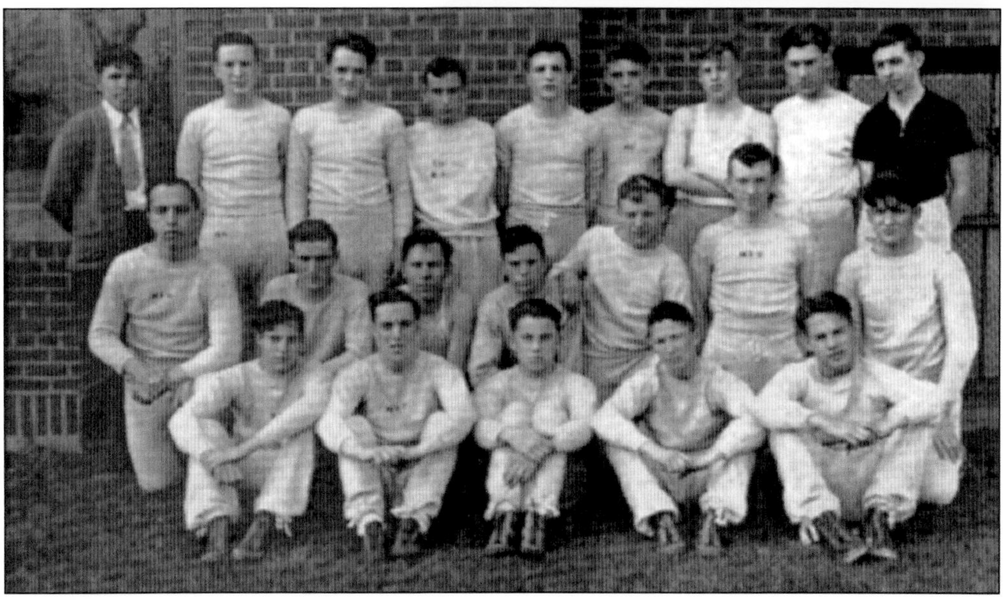

TRACK TEAM. The team, from left to right, is: (front row) Morris Marshall, Clifford Freeman, James Thomas, Warren Virgil, and Jerry North; (middle row) Bill Poulos, Bill Grebe, George Thomas, Don Quehl, Bob Wall, Elmer Anderson, and Carroll Taylor; (back row) Coach Jack Cline, S.T. Crampton, Lawrence Maxwell, Harry Scott, Ted McCann, Bill Fisher, Don Beckwith, Ralph Lewis, and Bob Cook.

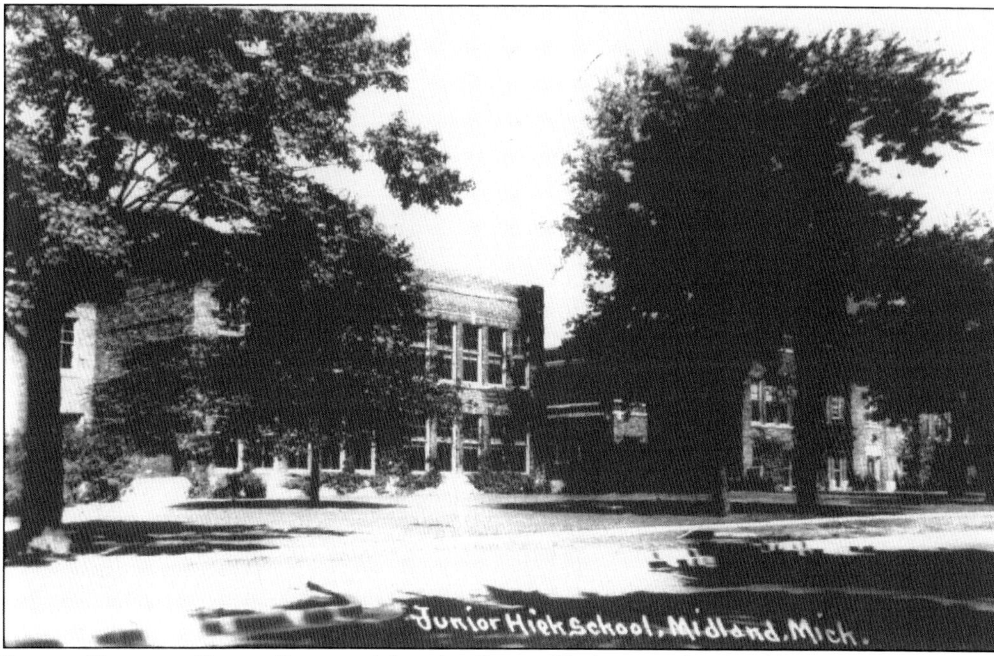

JUNIOR HIGH ON GROVE STREET. After the Senior High moved to Rodd Street, this was the Junior High school in Midland housing the seventh and eighth grades. In 1957 it was razed and today Grove Park occupies the space.

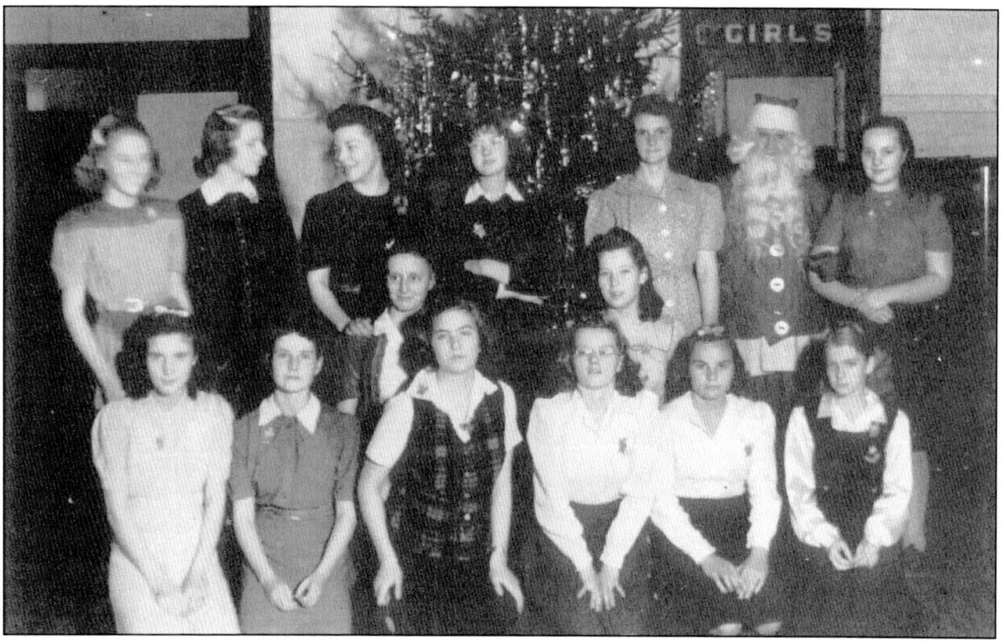

CHRISTMAS PARTY IN JUNIOR HIGH. Teachers were role models and none better than Jane Anderson who taught Home Economics at Junior High. Her students, from left to right, are: (front row) Leona Clark, Dorothy Wiltsie, Frances Milks, Anna Lee Stanford, Charlotte Fenske, and Virginia Merritt; (middle row) Harriet Cook and Nora Supinger; (back row) Pat Barr, Delores Howard, Jane Anderson, Bonnie Craig, Betty June Slater, Santa Claus, and Jean McCreadie.

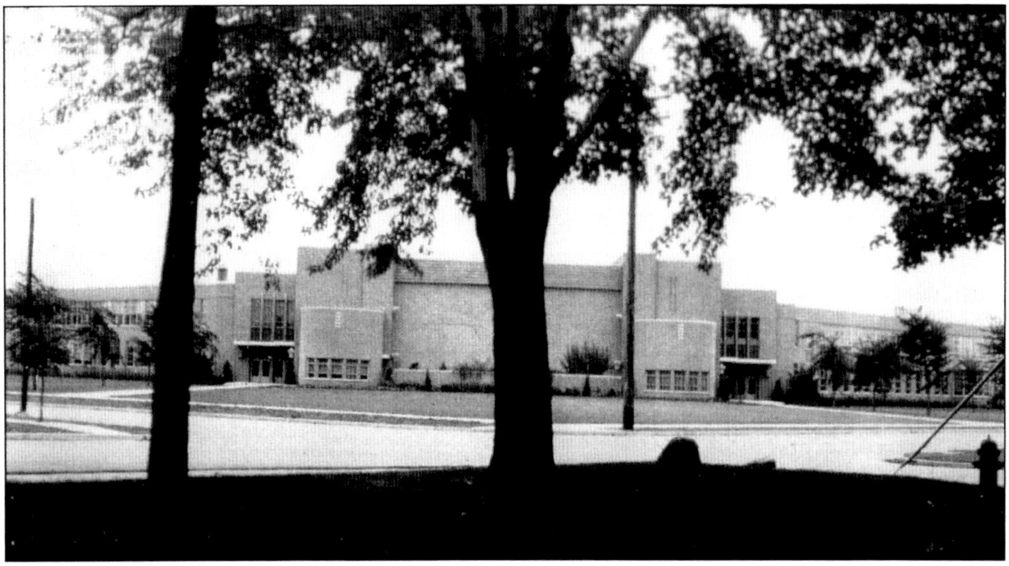

Senior High on Rodd. In 1937 the new Senior High on Rodd Street was ready for occupancy and the class of 1938 was the first to graduate from there. Built to house 1,200 students by 1955–1956 it was so crowded that half-days were instituted. September 4, 1956, the new Senior High on Eastlawn opened.

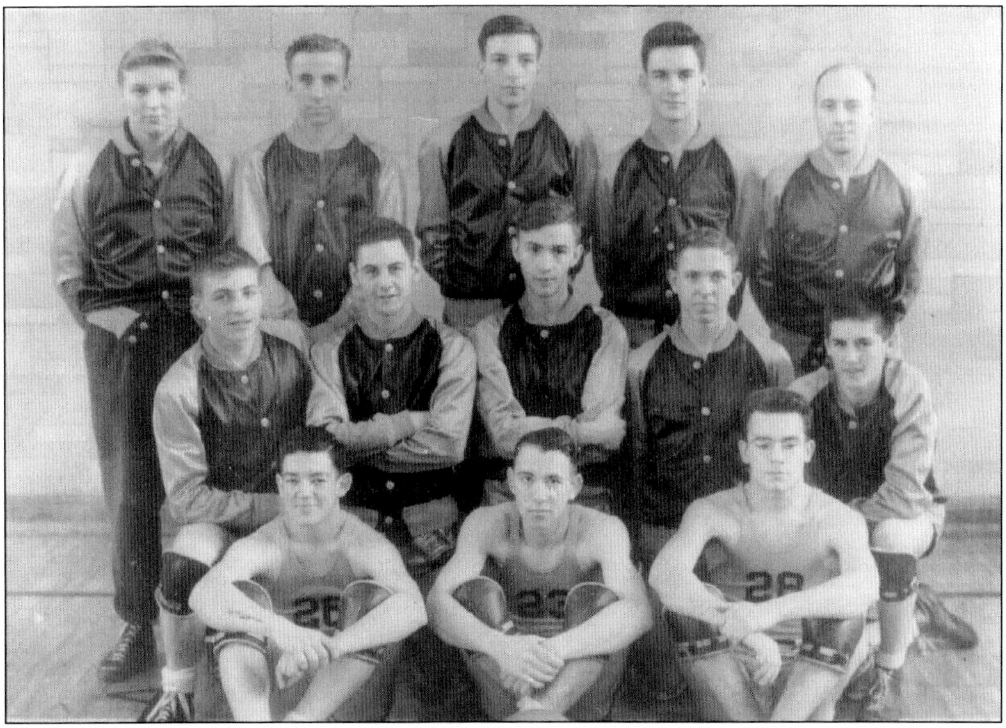

Basketball Team. Sports were big in high school even in 1945. The players, from left to right, are: (front row) Jack Lee, Bill Bridge, and Jake Vitkuske; (middle row) Norris Manley, Tom Sinclair, Lovell Sovereen, Cecil Rogers, and Ed Cookson; (back row) Paul Reiger, Jerry Trombley, Ken Youngs, Jim Smith, and Coach Bob Stoppert.

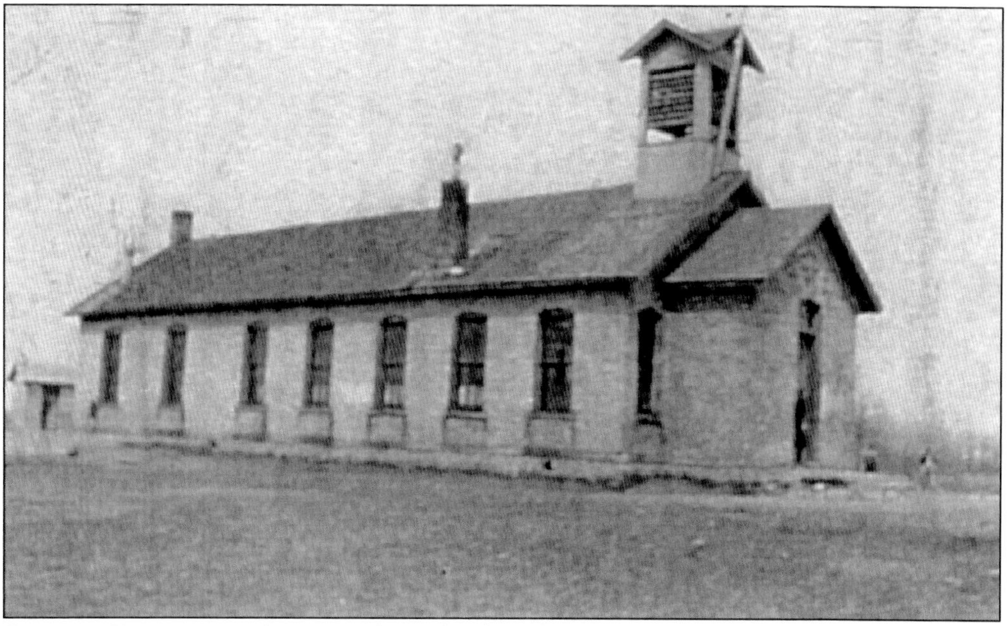

ORIGINAL PHETTEPLACE SCHOOL. This is the first Phetteplace School located on Brooks Drain Road in Ingersoll Township, Midland County. Named for William Phetteplace, he established it as a separate entity from the Bluff School District in 1865 with the first teacher being Emma Blodgett. It burned to the ground on October 7, 1930.

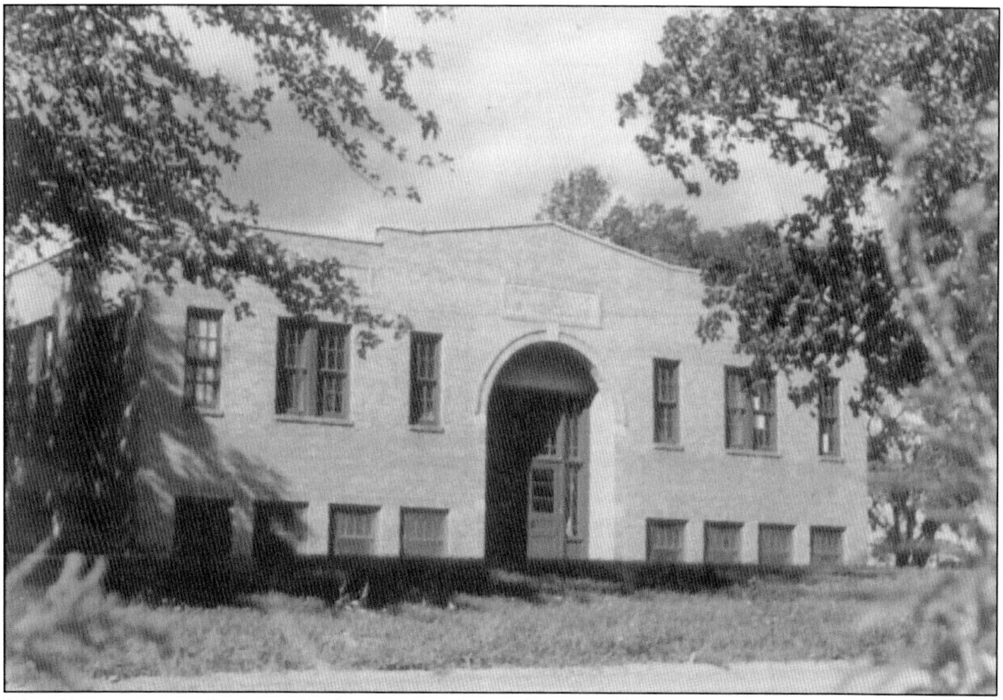

NEW PHETTEPLACE SCHOOL. Built in 1931, this is the new Phetteplace School. Costing $15,000 the new school consisted of classrooms, a library, a full basement, indoor flush toilets and an auditorium. It was considered equal to any city elementary school.

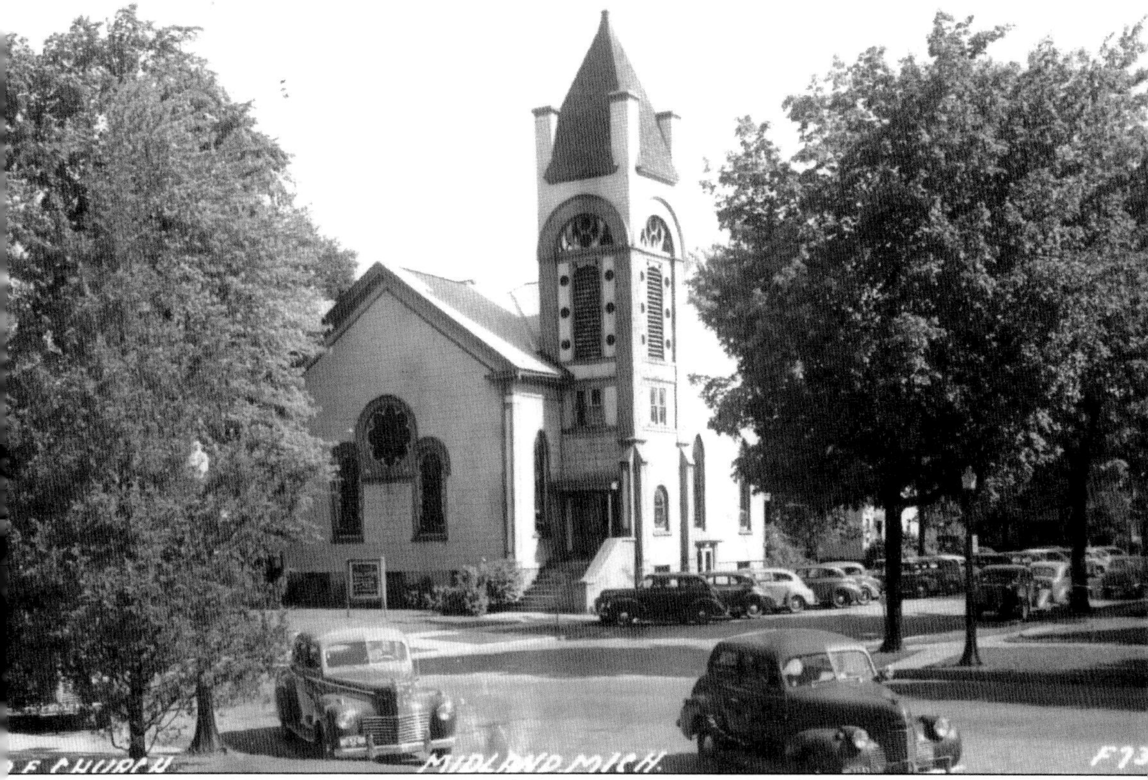

First Methodist Church. The *Portrait and Biographical Album of Midland County*, published in 1884 reported, "The first meeting house erected in Midland county was built one mile south of Midland City by the Methodist fraternity who were then doing missionary work among the Indians that lived on the south bank of the river opposite the village of Midland." A circuit was organized bearing the name of "Midland" at the session of the Detroit Annual Conference in Port Huron in September 1857. It was composed of the Village of Midland City, the Bluffs, King's (later the Freeland circuit), Higgins', Swan Creek, Shield's and Crook's. The first church building was completed in 1869 on the corner of Gordon and Main streets but was moved in 1883 to Main and Fitzhugh. Today the modern First Methodist Church is at the same location.

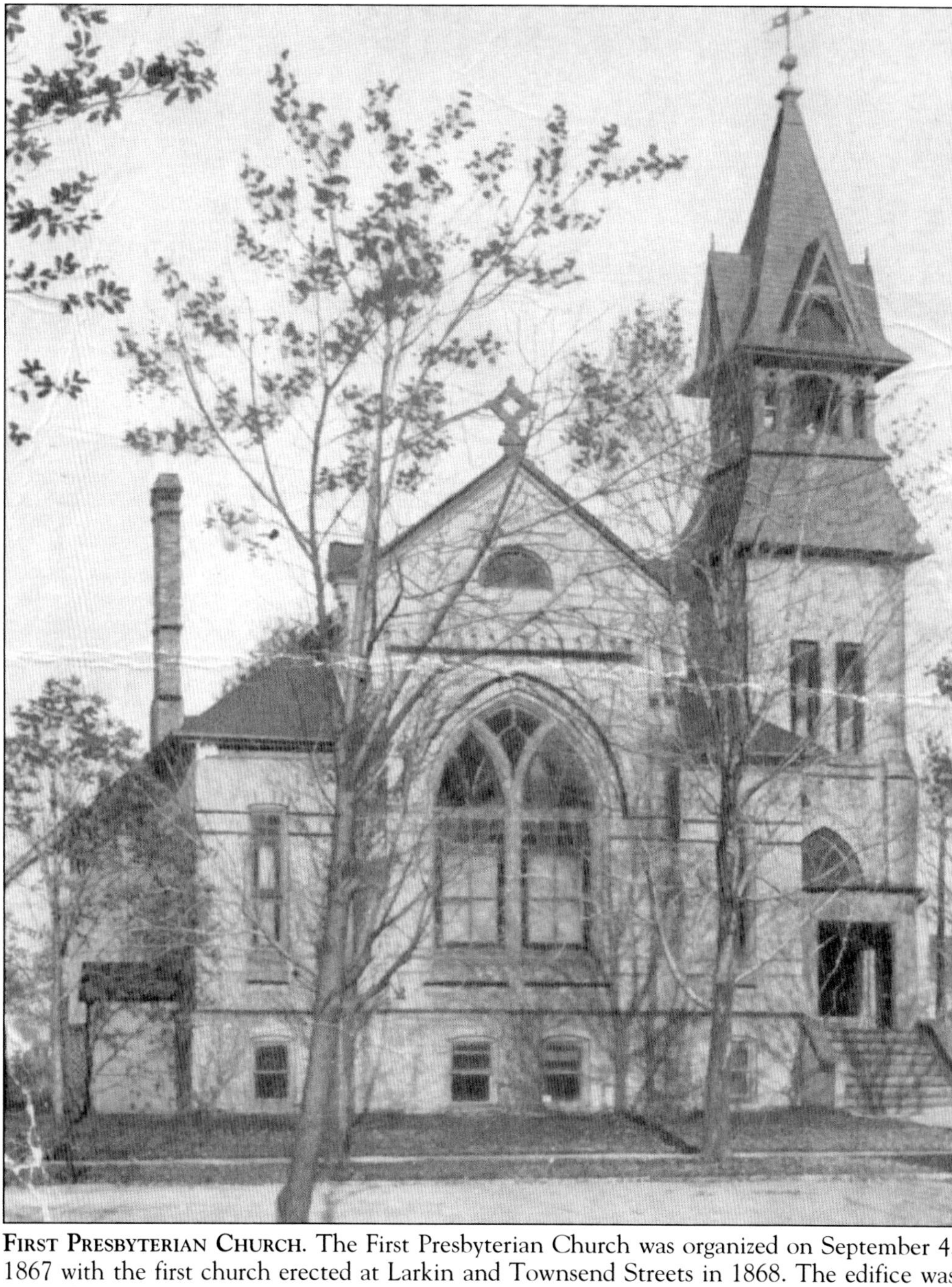

First Presbyterian Church. The First Presbyterian Church was organized on September 4, 1867 with the first church erected at Larkin and Townsend Streets in 1868. The edifice was erected and largely financed by Solomon Heald, a builder and contractor of that period. In 1876 the church burned to the ground in the fire that destroyed 52 buildings in the Main Street area. In 1880 Reverend P.S. Davies came to minister to the little church and by 1882 a new church was built on the same corner. The Methodist and Baptist churches omitted their own services so their members could also attend the ceremonies. As churches moved out of the Main Street area into the residential areas, it is now known as the Memorial Presbyterian Church and is located at 1310 Ashman Street.

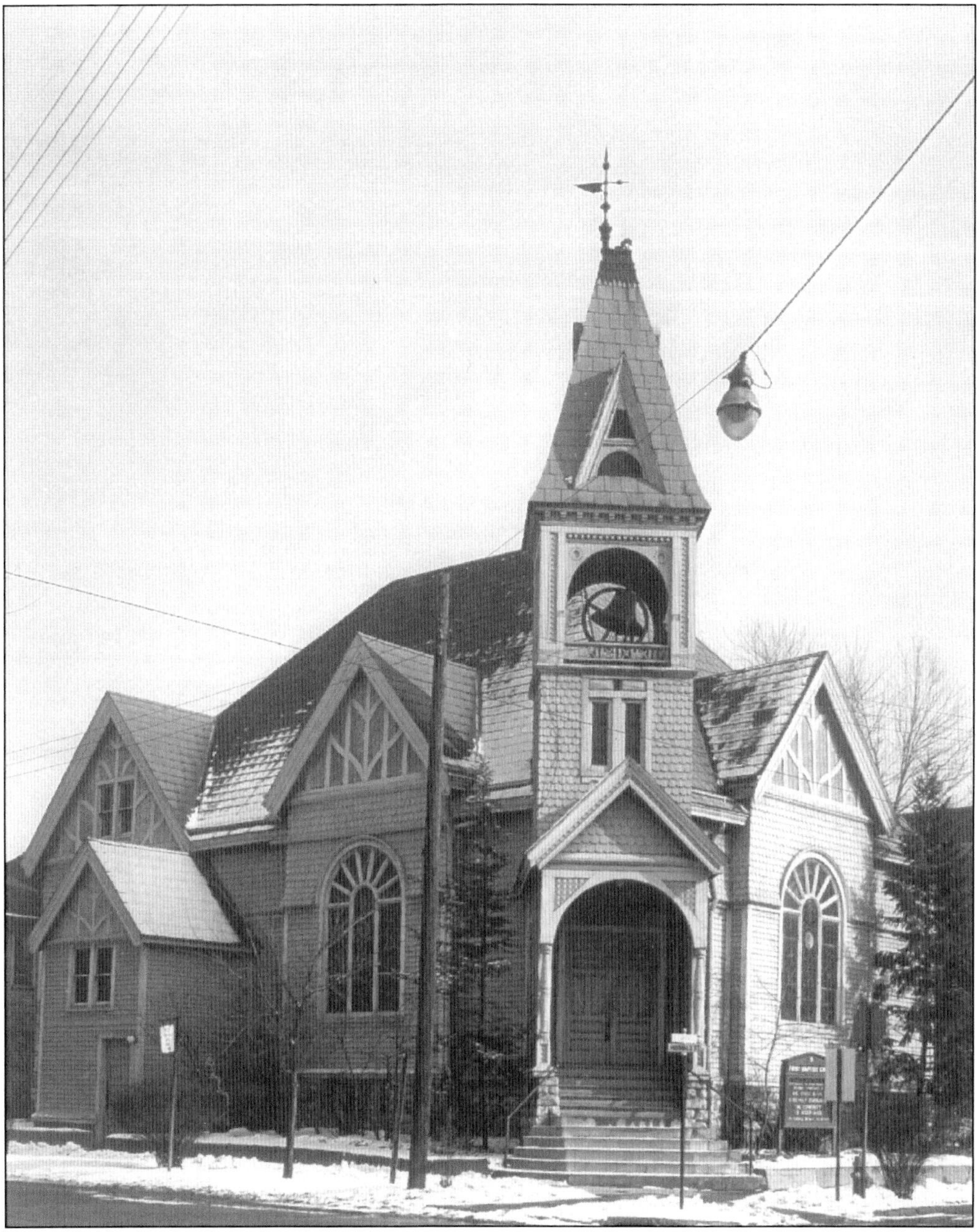

FIRST BAPTIST CHURCH. On June 2, 1869 a meeting was held in the Presbyterian Church to organize a Baptist church and was given the name of First Baptist Church of Midland City. The first worship service was held on January 15, 1870, and a small church was built on the west side of the Tittabawassee. After a spring flood which floated the organ over the backs of the pews the Baptists were convinced it was time to move and erected their new church on the corner of Larkin and McDonald.

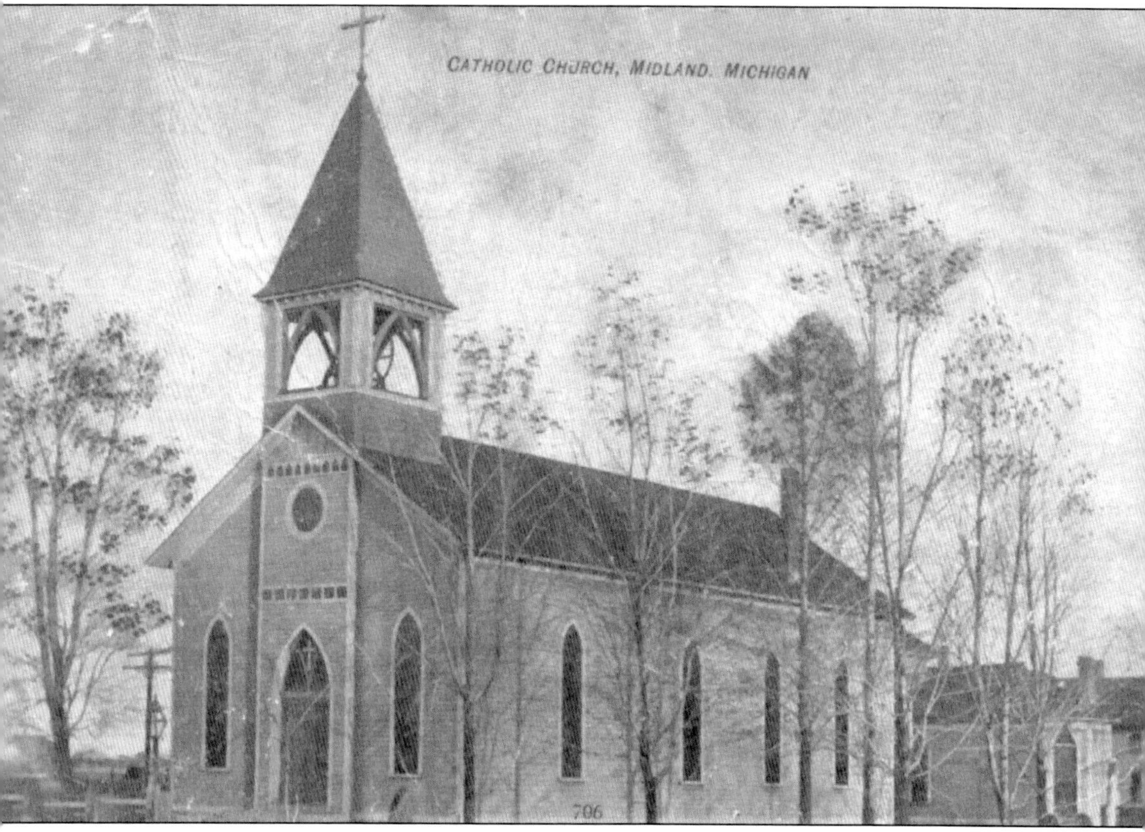

ST BRIGID'S CATHOLIC CHURCH. Early Catholic families gathered at the William Keeley residence in Paddy's Hollow to recite the rosary. In 1870 the first Mass was celebrated at the Keeley residence, and in 1871 the first St. Bridget's Catholic Church was completed at a cost of $1,800 on the corner of Indian and Haley. Soon after, the church was christened "St. Bridget" in honor of the fifth century Irish saint. In 1918 it was discovered that St. Bridget was a Swedish saint and steps were taken to rename the church with the proper Irish spelling "Brigid." In 1908 the church building was moved to the corner of Larkin and Ashman streets. In addition to St. Brigid's, today there are two other major Catholic churches in the Midland area: Blessed Sacrament and Assumption Catholic Church.

Eight

They Served...

In great deeds something abides. On great fields something stays. Forms change and pass; bodies disappear; but spirits linger, to consecrate ground for the vision-place of souls. And reverent men and women from afar, and generations that know us not and that we know not of, heart-drawn to see where and by whom great things were suffered and done for them, shall come to this deathless field, to ponder and dream, and lo! the shadow of a mighty presence shall wrap them in its bosom, and the power of the vision pass into their souls.

—General Joshua Lawrence Chamberlain
Gettysburg, October 3, 1889

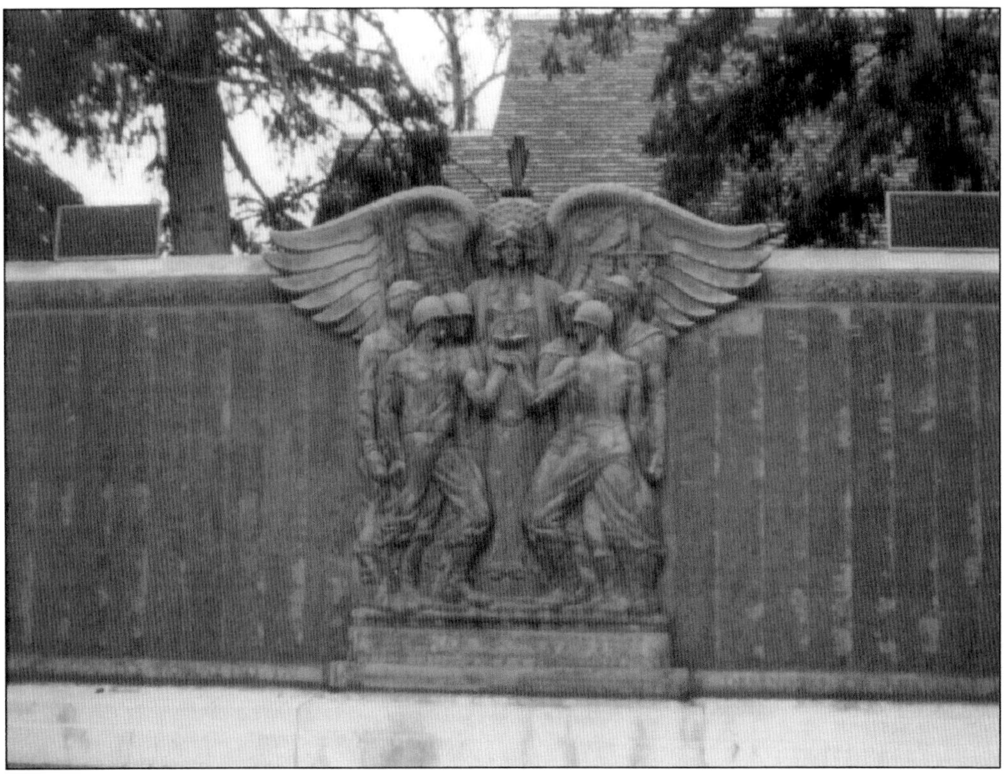

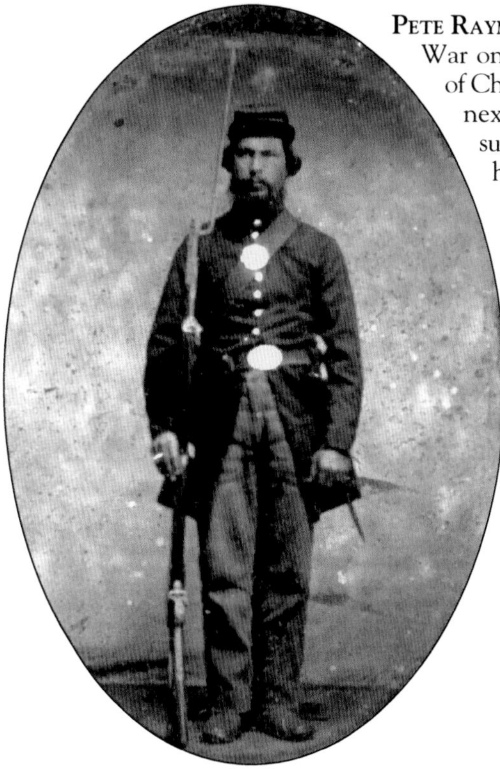

Pete Raymond. John Peter Raymond enlisted in the Civil War on July 18, 1862. Taken prisoner after the Battle of Chickamauga on September 20, 1863, he spent the next 18 months in various Confederate prisons. He survived the horrors of Andersonville to return home to Hope, Michigan where he spent the rest of his life living the quiet life that he had fought so valiantly for.

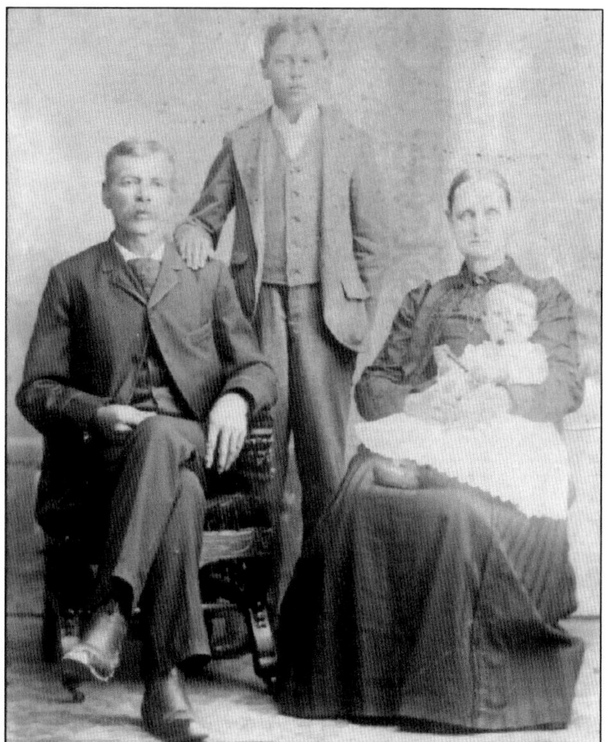

Israel Sayles. Israel Sayles enlisted in the Civil War in New York State, and was captured in 1863 at the Battle of Culpepper, Virginia by the Confederates. Discharged on June 22, 1865, he married, raised a family and in 1879 moved to Michigan. Left to right: Israel, Gilbert, Nancy, and Fred. Fred came to Midland in 1902 and stayed.

CHARLES WILLIAM SINCLAIR. Charles William Sinclair served in the War Between The States (Civil War). He was a private in the W.H. Gremison Company E of the First Michigan Lancers.

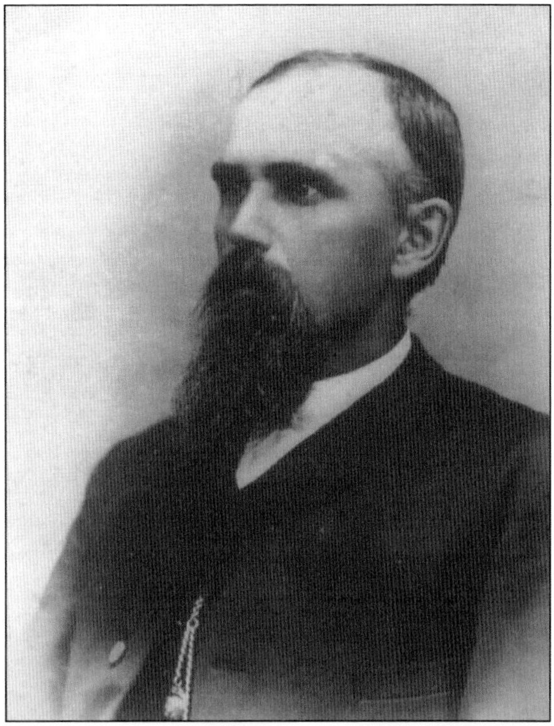

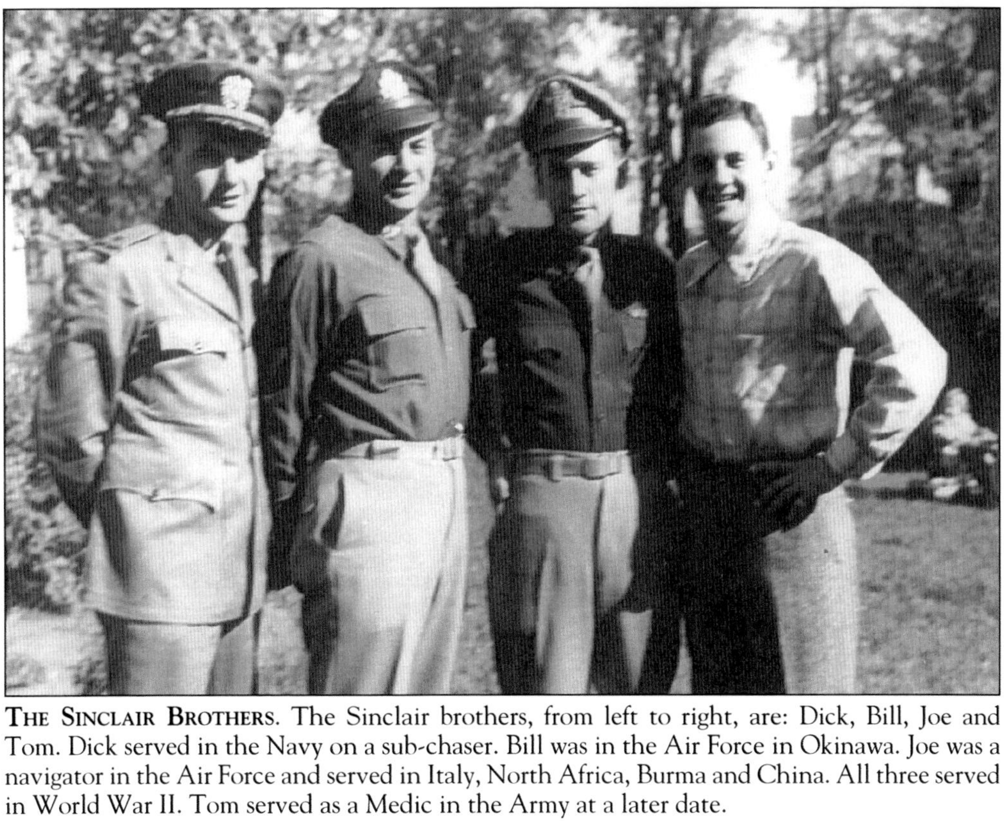

THE SINCLAIR BROTHERS. The Sinclair brothers, from left to right, are: Dick, Bill, Joe and Tom. Dick served in the Navy on a sub-chaser. Bill was in the Air Force in Okinawa. Joe was a navigator in the Air Force and served in Italy, North Africa, Burma and China. All three served in World War II. Tom served as a Medic in the Army at a later date.

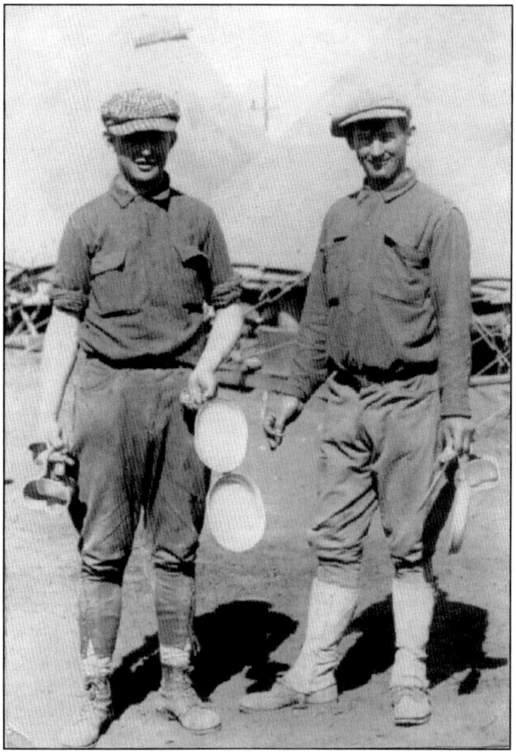

JOSEPH DEMSKI. Joseph Demski, a son of Stanislaus and Mary Demski, died in the battle of St. Mihiel Salient in France on September 1, 1918, ten weeks before the end of World War I. It was four years before his body was shipped back to Midland for burial. Joseph is on the right in the photo. The other man is unidentified.

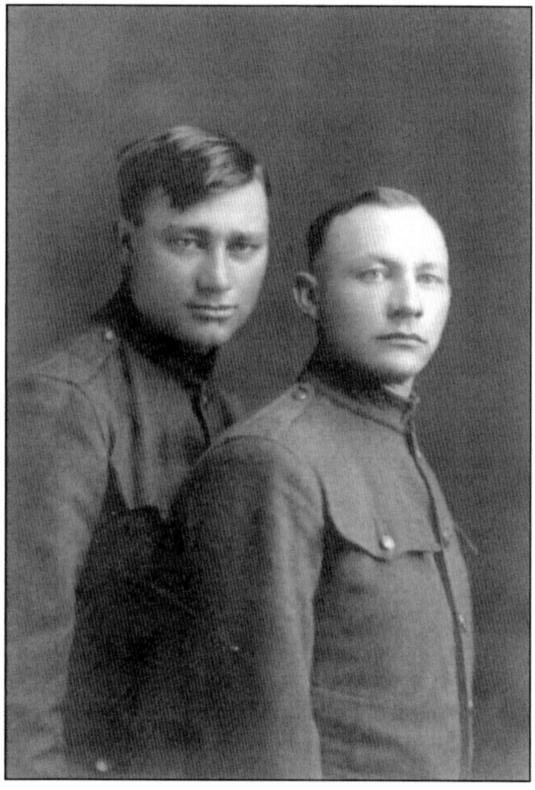

WALTER AND FRED GERSTACKER. Walter Gerstacker, on the left, is 25 years old in this photo, and his brother Fred is 21. Sons of Conrad and Katherine Gerstacker, both fought in World War I. And both returned to Larkin Township, Midland County, to marry and raise families.

John Roberts. John Roberts served in the Marines from 1943 until his honorable discharge on May 7, 1946. He served in Guam, was wounded on Iwo Jima and then did a tour of duty in occupied Japan. In 1946 he returned to Midland, Michigan to marry a local girl, Delores Klumpp.

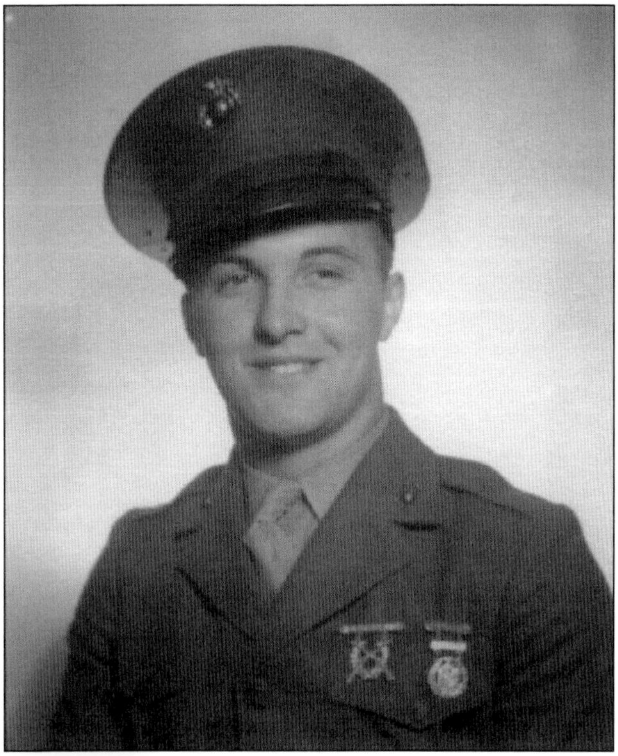

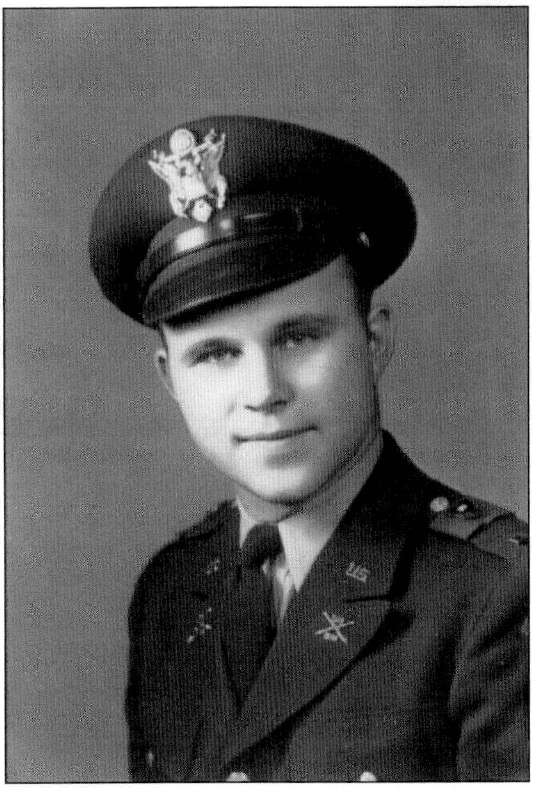

Jack McCandless. Jack McCandless went into the service in February, 1951 as a Second Lieutenant and was shipped to Germany. The Korean War was in progress but Germany was also having trouble with both American and Russian troops occupying parts of it. He served 19 months, came out a First Lieutenant, and returned to his home town, Midland.

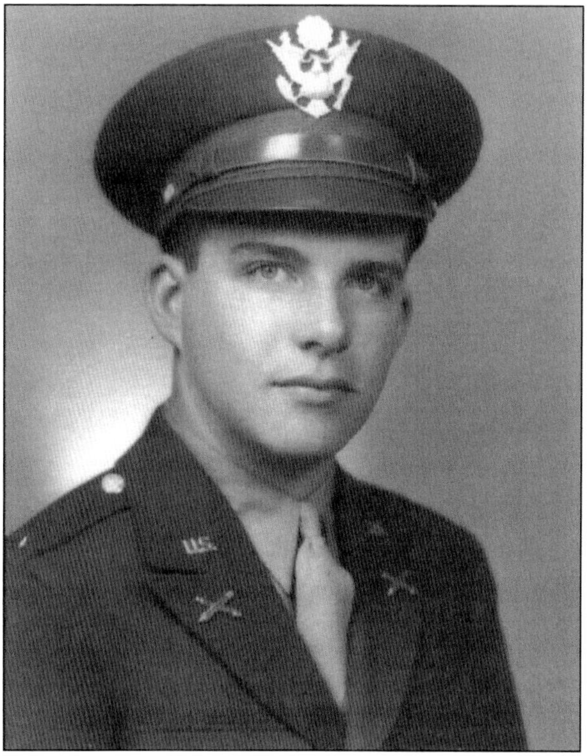

STUART BRANSON. Stuart Branson entered the service in August of 1942, attended Officer's Candidate School, and graduated as a Second Lieutenant in April of 1943. He was wounded in January, 1945, and again in March, 1945. He returned home to Midland on June 1, 1945, to his wife Kay and young son Carl.

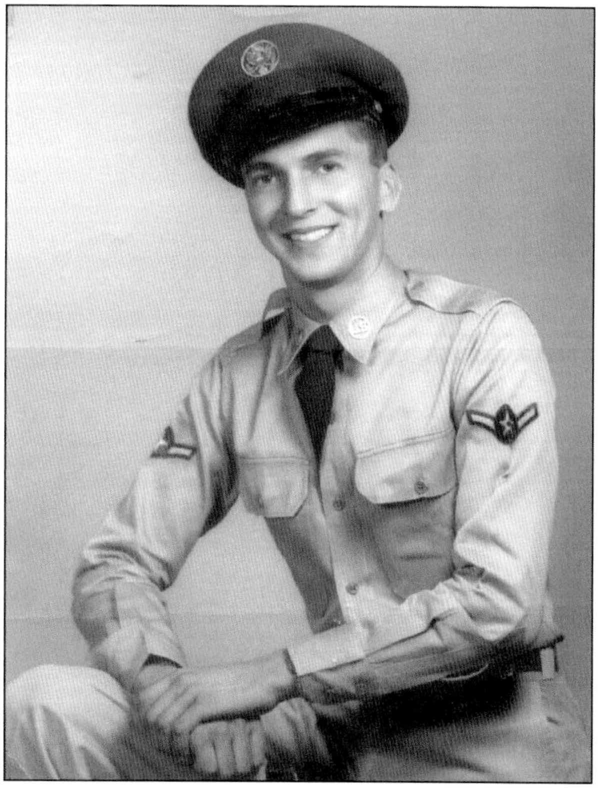

ED ZONDLAK. Ed Zondlak enlisted in the Air Force and spent three years in Korea. (The Korean War began on June 25, 1950 and ended on July 27, 1953.) Like many other young men, he had a sweetheart waiting for him to return, Jeanne Beson.

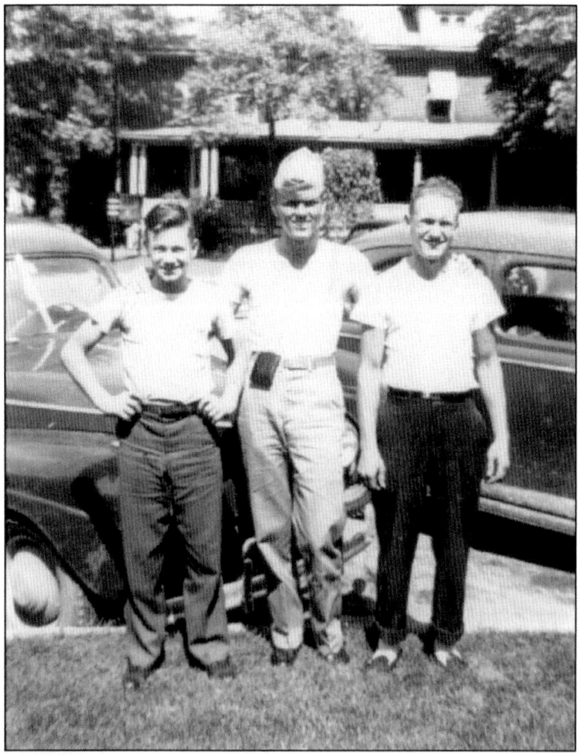

SPEAKER BOYS. Left to right are brothers Jack, Lorin and Lynn Speaker. Both Jack and Lynn were in the Navy Sea Bees. Lorin was in the Army during World War II in France and received a Purple Heart, the Bronze, Gold, and Silver Stars.

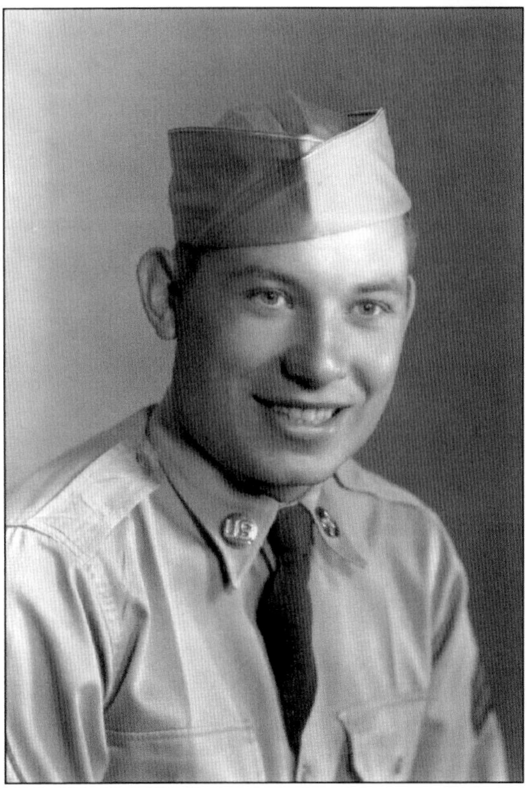

EARL HOON. Earl Hoon was in the service during the Korean War. He went into the Army in 1951, was shipped to the Panama Canal Zone first, spent three months in Greenland and Iceland, and then it was back to Panama until he was discharged on January 8, 1953, and he married Alma Stevens on January 30, 1953.

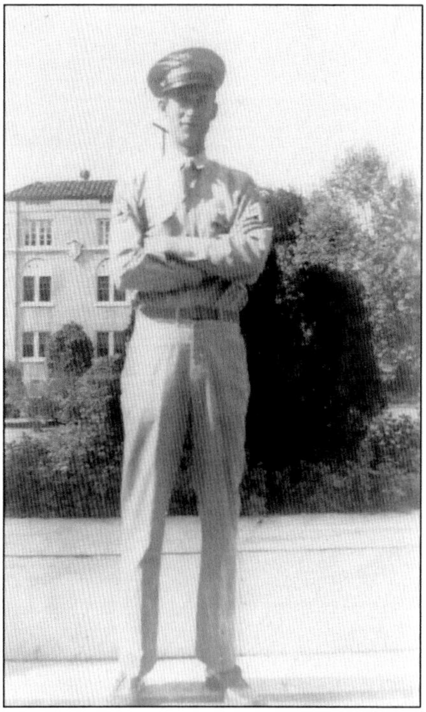

Robert Sinclair. Robert David Sinclair was in the Army Air Force and served overseas in World War II.

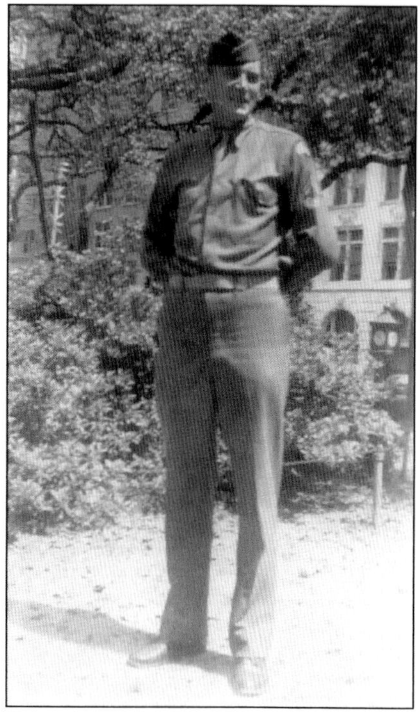

Don Sinclair. Harry Donald Sinclair was in the Army on a tank destroyer in World War II.

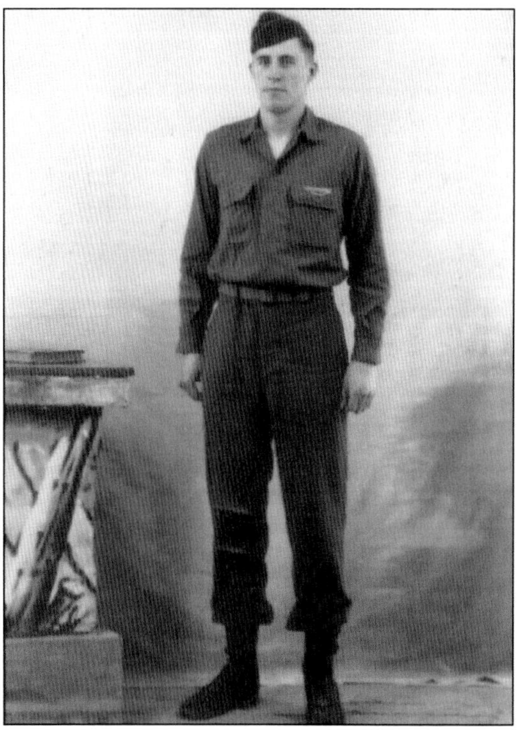

Jack Sinclair. Jack William Sinclair was in the Army Infantry overseas in World War II. Bob, Don and Jack Sinclair were all sons of Harry and Stella Sinclair.

EUGENE SMITH. Eugene Smith was with the U.S. Army and served in Germany following World War II.

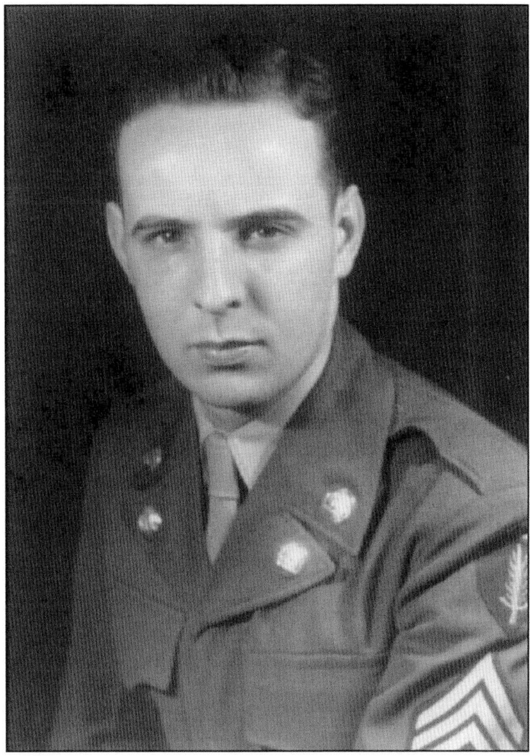

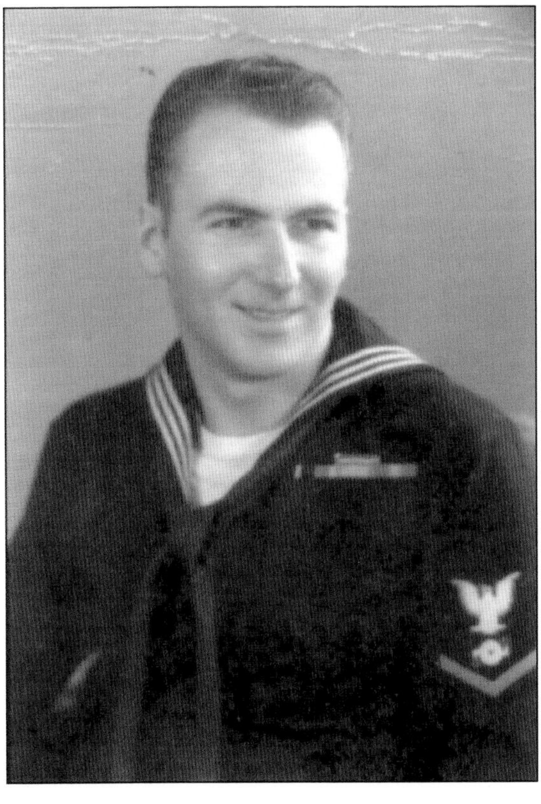

DICK SMITH. Dick Smith was in the U.S. Navy and served on the USS *Hornet* during the Korean War, returning to his wife Colleen and son Dick, Jr.

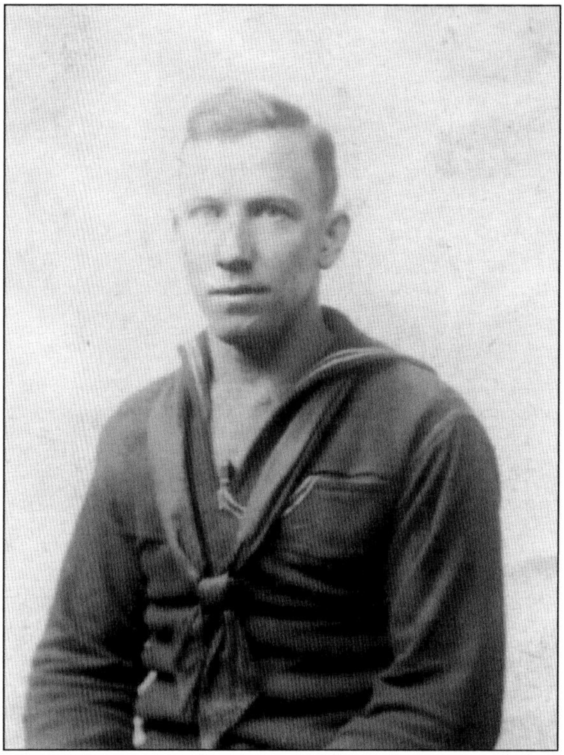

Roy Blake. Roy Blake joined the Merchant Marines in World War I. His future sister-in-law Henrietta Weaver wrote, "Oh, I hate to see Roy go away but yet I am proud of it. It will be so lonesome without him."

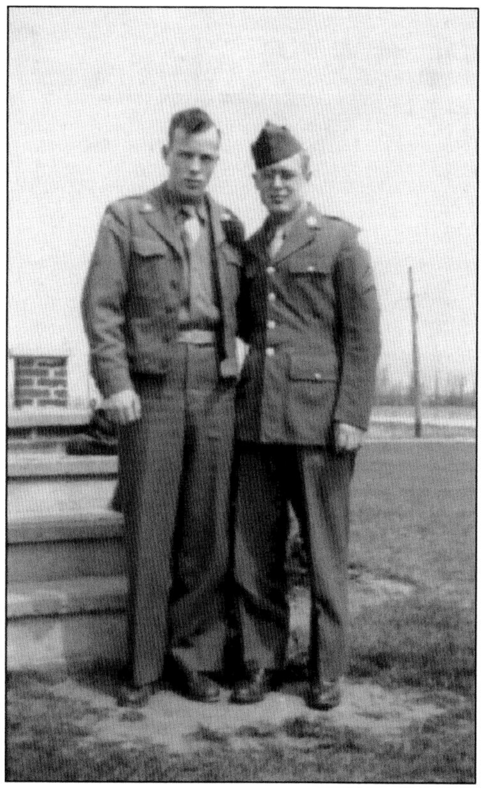

Richard Blake and Harold Gay. Richard Blake (son of Roy Blake) on the left and Harold Gay on the right served during World War II in the Army. Later they would become brothers-in-law when Richard married Harold's sister, June.

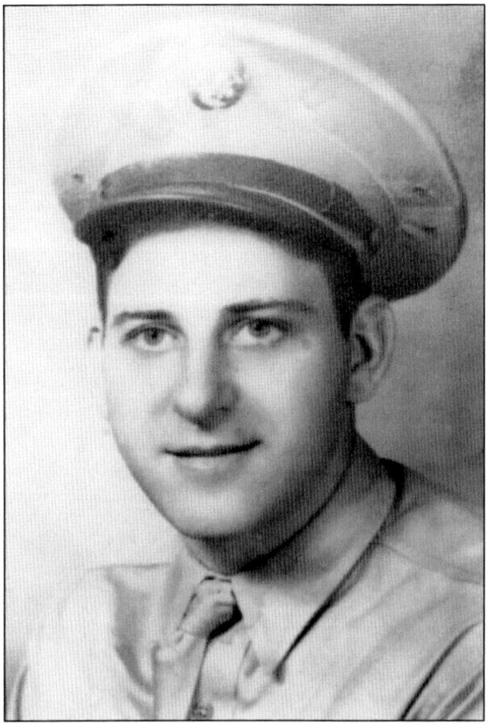

FRANK LEIGEB. After induction in the Army in World War II, Frank Leigeb saw action in North Africa and then Italy. He was discharged with the rank of sergeant.

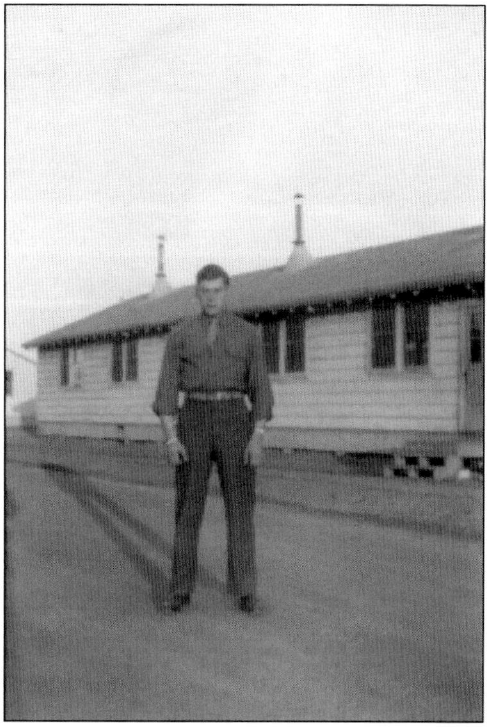

OLLIE LEIGEB. Ollie Leigeb was the fifth son of Michael and Mary Leigeb to serve his country. Ollie was in the Korean War and spent a year in Okinawa.

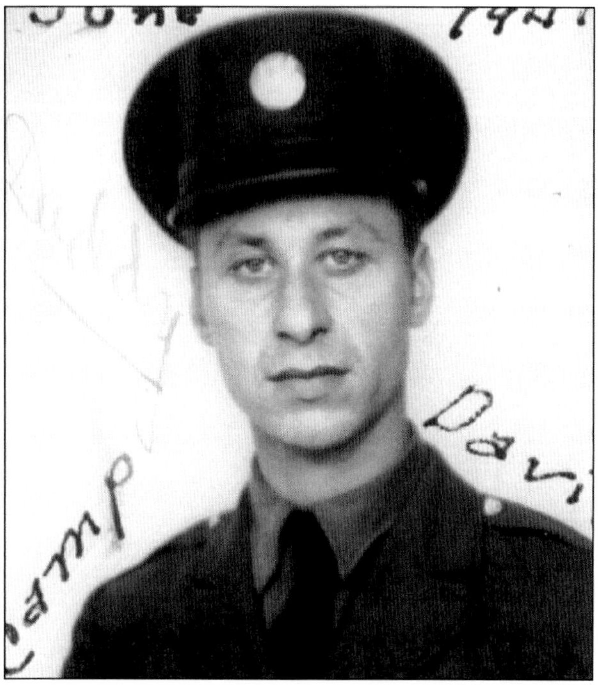

TONY LEIGEB. Tony Leigeb was inducted in the Army on May 7, 1941, and went for training to North Carolina. Illness caused his discharge and he returned home to Averill, Michigan.

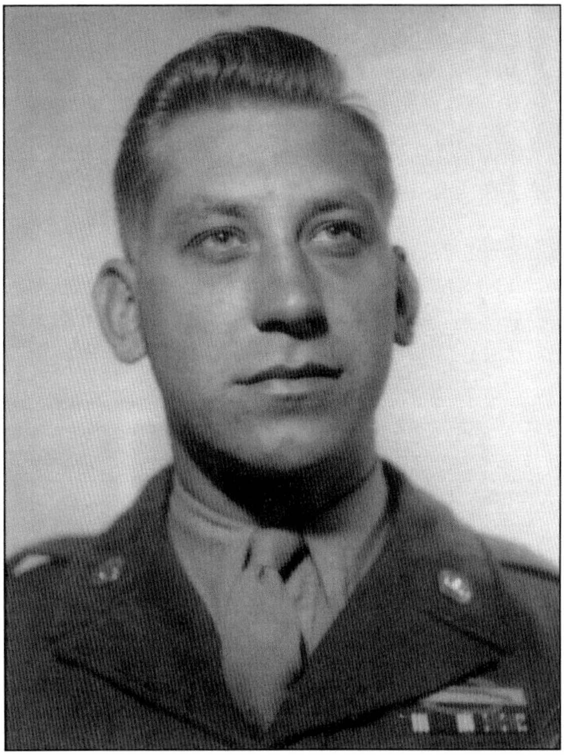

Ed Leigeb. Ed Leigeb, son of Michael and Mary Leigeb, went into the service December 17, 1942, and served during World War II in France, Germany, and Austria. Discharged in December 1945, he had the rank of staff sergeant.

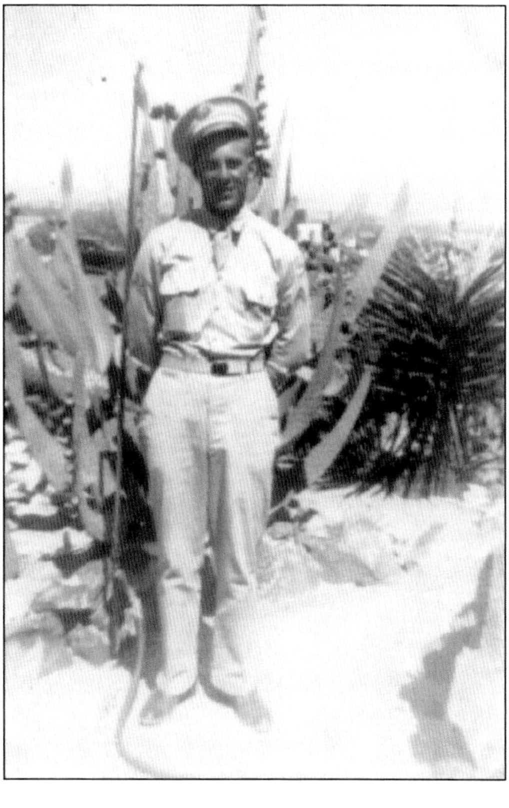

Elmer Leigeb. Elmer Leigeb, son of Michael and Mary Leigeb, was inducted in the Army on May 7, 1943, went overseas in 1944, and fought in France, Belgium, and Germany before being discharged February 19, 1946, as a sergeant.

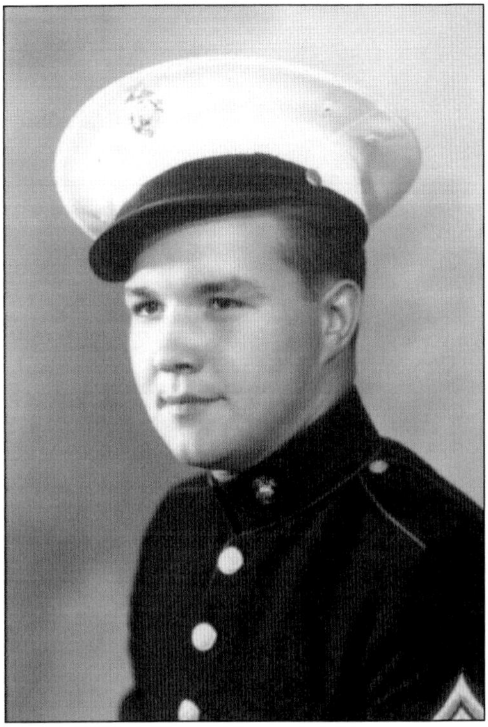

Dale Crampton. Dale Crampton served in the U.S. Marine Corps during World War II and was stationed in China.

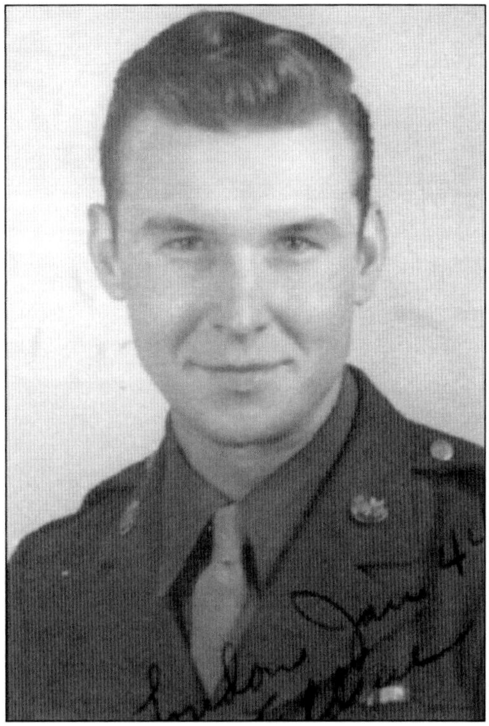

Eldene Crampton. Eldene Crampton served in the U.S. Army during World War II and was stationed in Europe.

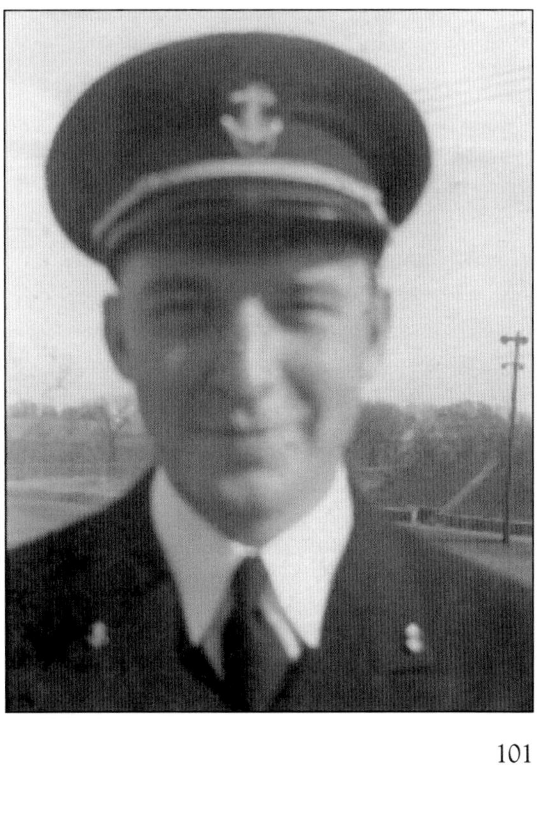

S.T. Crampton. S.T. Crampton served in the U.S. Navy Air Force in World War II.

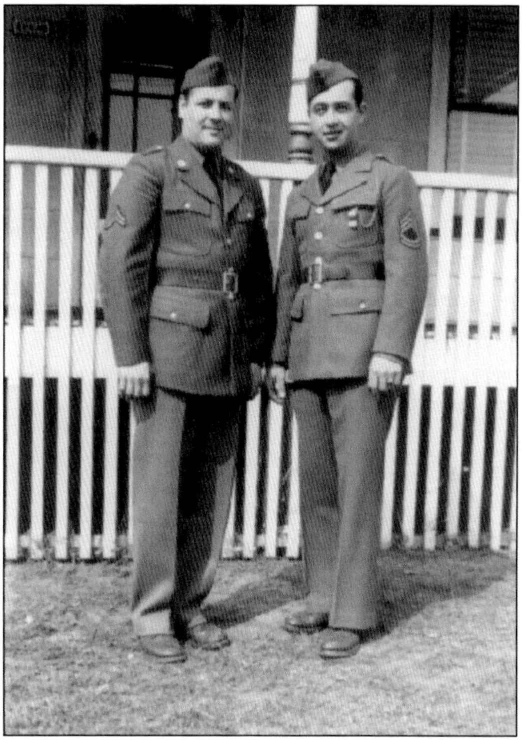

Howard Smith and Henry Yeakle. Howard Smith and Henry Yeakle both served in World War II and were in the historic Battle of the Bulge. Howard received a purple heart.

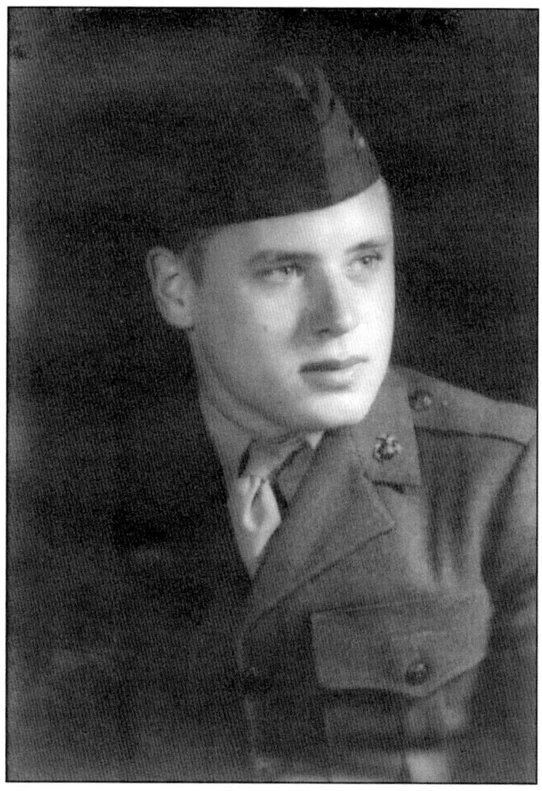

George Gay. George Gay was a U.S. Marine in the Korean War and was in Guam and Hawaii.

Nine

SETTLERS AND PIONEERS

The past never departs, no truth or goodness ever dies, all is still here, living and working through endless changes.

—*Carlyle*

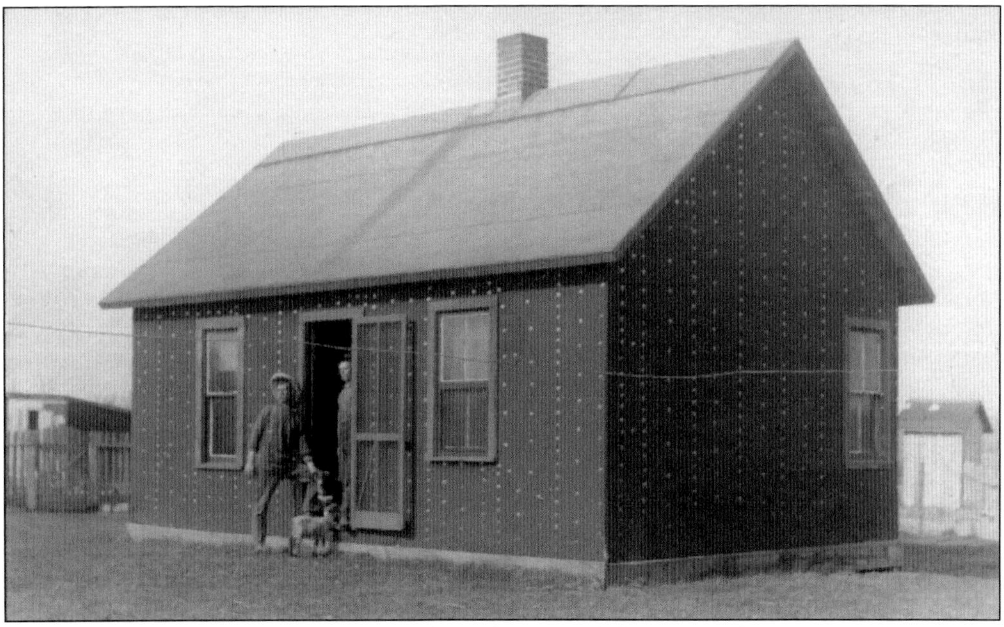

They came to the small town of Midland, Michigan, and the surrounding territory for a variety of reasons. They came to buy land. They came to work in the lumber camps. They came across the Atlantic Ocean seeking a safe haven for themselves and for their children. And once here, they made Midland their home.

Names like Varner, Draves, Yeakle, Gay, Weaver, Kelly, Madill, Finney, Dow, Gerstacker, Doan, Zondlak, Bartos, Bliss, Balcirak, Franklin, Sinclair, Sirrine, Allen, Speaker, Demski, Sayles, Raymond, Andrick, Clark, Hubble, Yager, Gransden, White, LaRue, Hebner, Fitzgibbons, and Hinds—all were immigrants in one way or another. All played a part in the history of Midland. Settling land that was barely a step away from wilderness, they overcame both obstacles and set-backs. On the following pages are just a few of those who came and settled Midland.

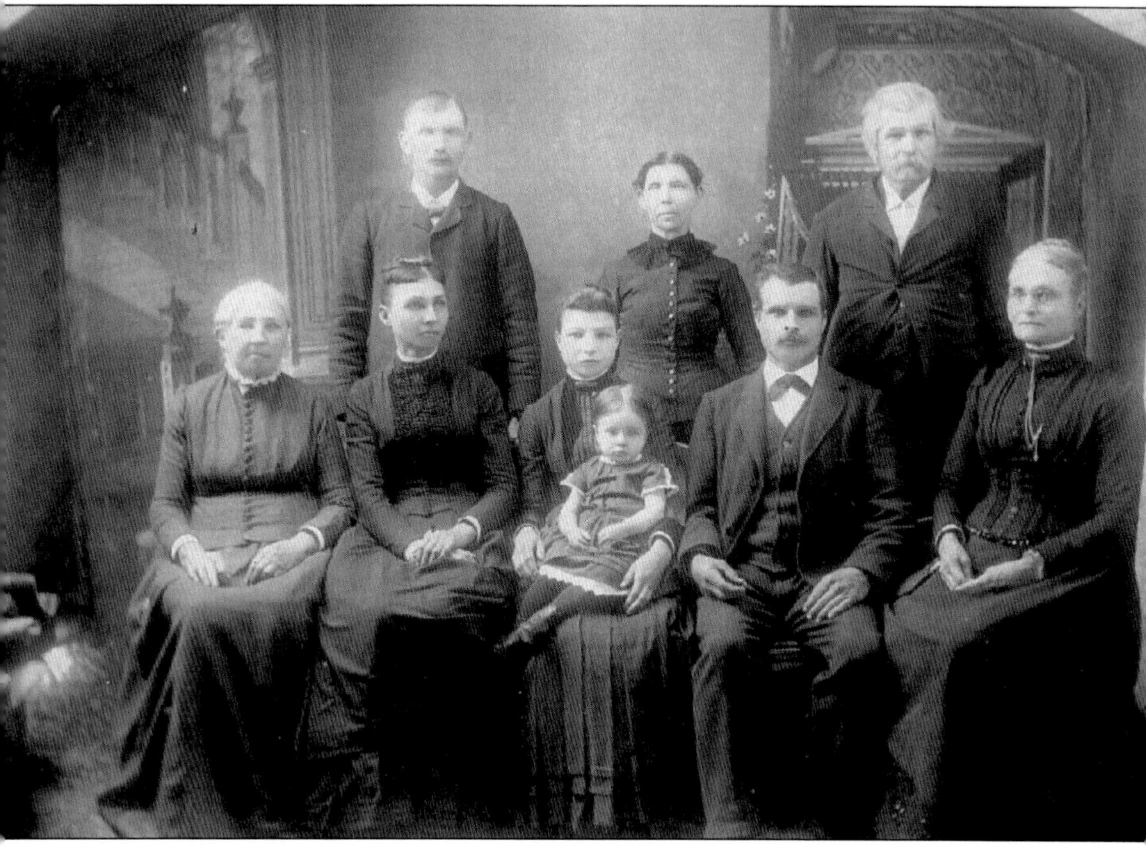

WELSH, CHASE, AND TIPPIN FAMILIES. In 1887 William James Tippin married Adella Alice Chase and in 1898 they moved to Porter Township on the corner of Nine Mile and Redstone. Will served for 18 years as Township Highway Commissioner. Their daughter Alma married Everett Foster and in 1931 she died at the age of 32 leaving six small children: Esther, Niki, Frances, Cecil, Arthur, and Robert, as well as her husband, Everett Foster. Niki and other descendants remain—the Northrup School is gone, the house and barn are gone, and the beloved snow apple tree was cut down—but memories remain of the farm that nourished William and Adella Tippin and their descendants. The family, from left to right, is: (front row) Lenora Gates Welsh, Clarissa's mother; Clarissa Welsh Chase, Adella's mother; Adella Chase Tippin holding Achsah Tippin; Burns Chase, Adella's father; and Lettice Fleming Chase, Burns' mother; (back row) W.J. Tippin, Adella's husband; Sarah Long Tippin, W.J.'s mother; George Tippin, W.J.'s father.

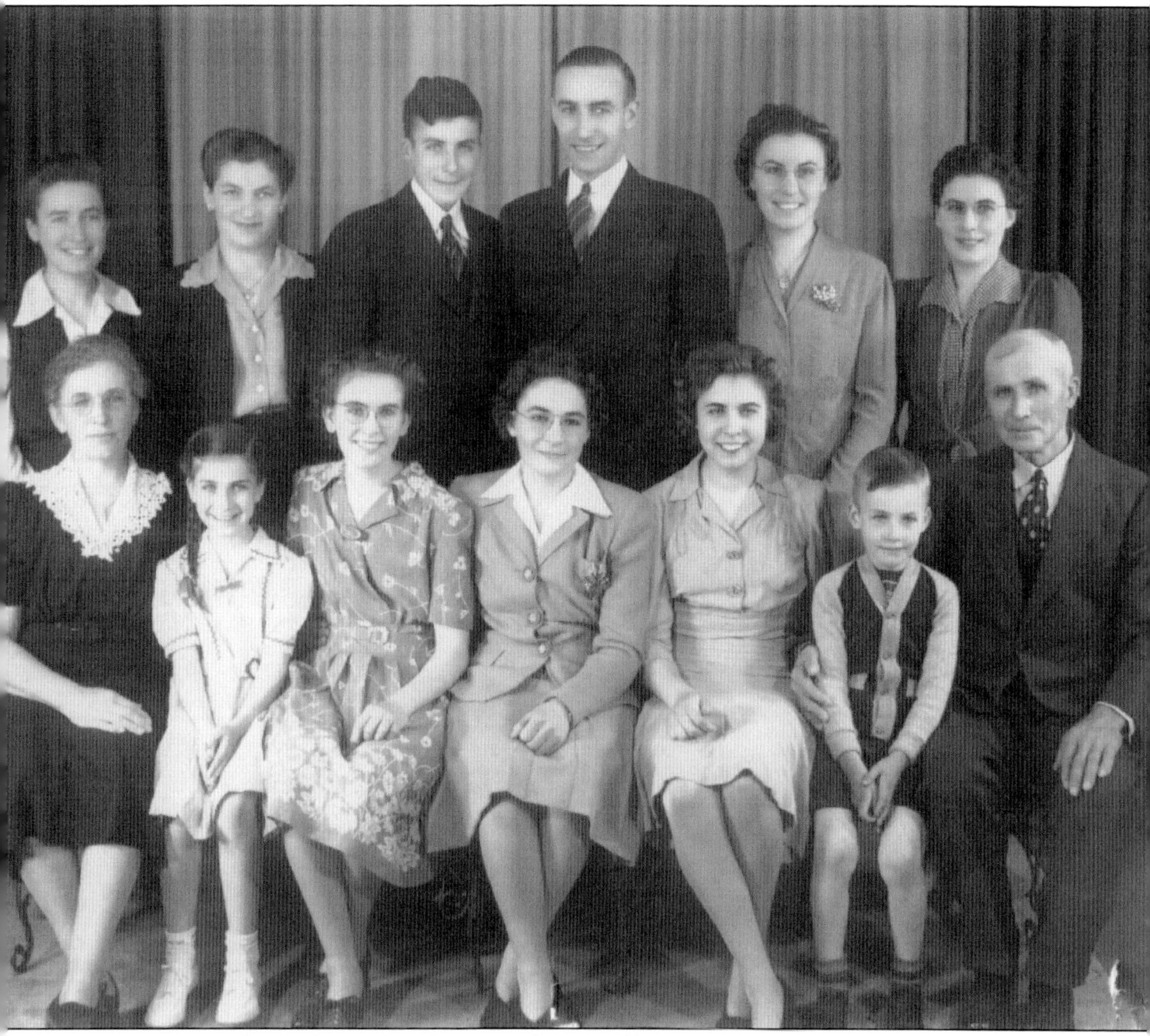

HEBNER FAMILY. Shown here, from left to right, are: (front row) Clara (Mortzfeldt) Hebner, Phyllis, Freda, Clara, Rowena, and Jim and Frank Hebner, father; (back row) Sophia, Anna, Bill, Franklin, Evelyn, and Martha. Frank, an immigrant from Germany, arrived in the small town of Curtice, near Coleman, Michigan, in 1895. He worked in the sawmill and lumber camp as well as in a blacksmith shop as he struggled to save money to buy land that was selling for $8 an acre. In 1909 he married Clara Mortzfeldt and they raised 11 children on their farm located on Bergman Road. Clara canned and preserved food in huge quantities. Meat was preserved in several ways. One way was to make salt brine to soak the meat in. When an egg could float in the brine it was considered salty enough to cure the meat. Today the youngest brother, James Hebner, owns the family homestead.

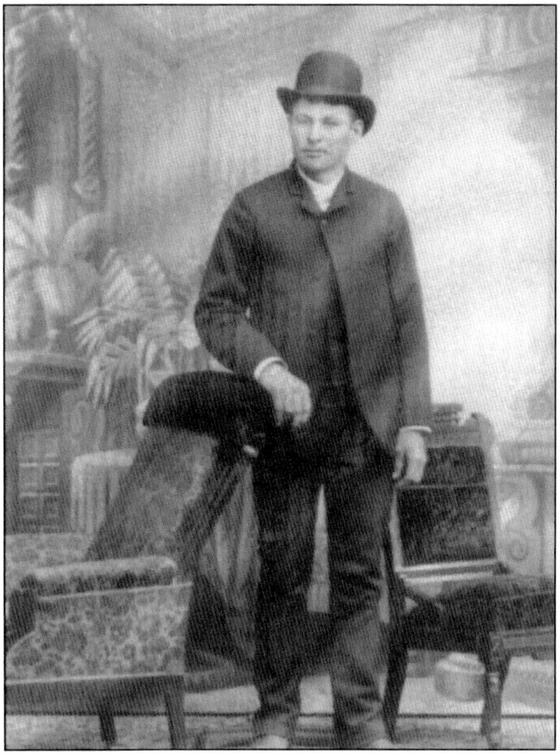

JOHN ANDRICK. The John and Anna Barbara Andregg family came to the United States from Oberbipp, Switzerland. The name was changed to Andrick in 1853. In 1885 their son John moved to Hope, Michigan, and lived with his uncle John Shearer while he began buying land and setting up a sawmill business. John moved his portable sawmill to the Maxwell Settlement. In 1902 he married Anna Boroff Stout.

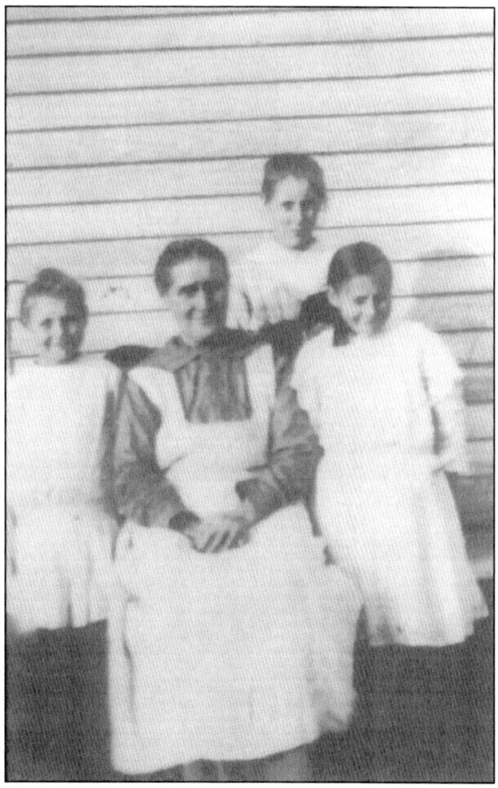

ANNA BOROFF STOUT ANDRICK. John and Anna Boroff Stout Andrick had eight children, six of which survived. In July of 1994 the Andrick home at 2035 East Baker Road became the first Centennial Farm in Mills Township. Today John's grandson, Jim, continues living there. From left to right, pictured are Grace Andrick Keber, Effie Andrick Hall, and Minnie Andrick Havens posing with their mother Anna Boroff Stout Andrick.

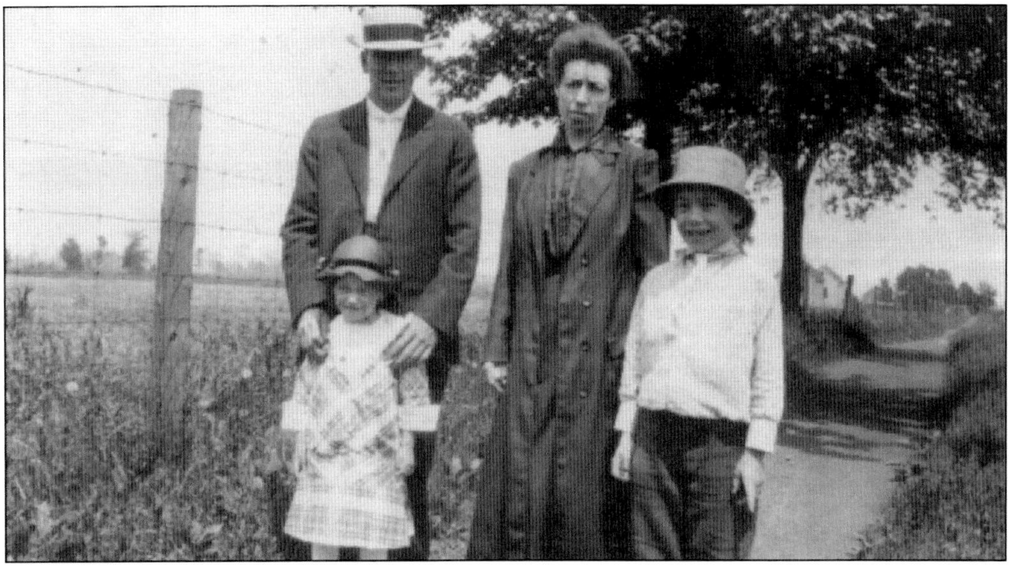

The Bloom Family. Adam and Mary Bloom pose with their children Bessie and Karl. They moved to the small town of Midland, Michigan, in 1919 where they purchased five lots in Crane's Addition and he built a new house on Adelaide Street. Adam became caretaker of the new Carpenter Street School building and grounds in 1927. He died unexpectedly in 1940. Karl married Martha Friedle in 1928.

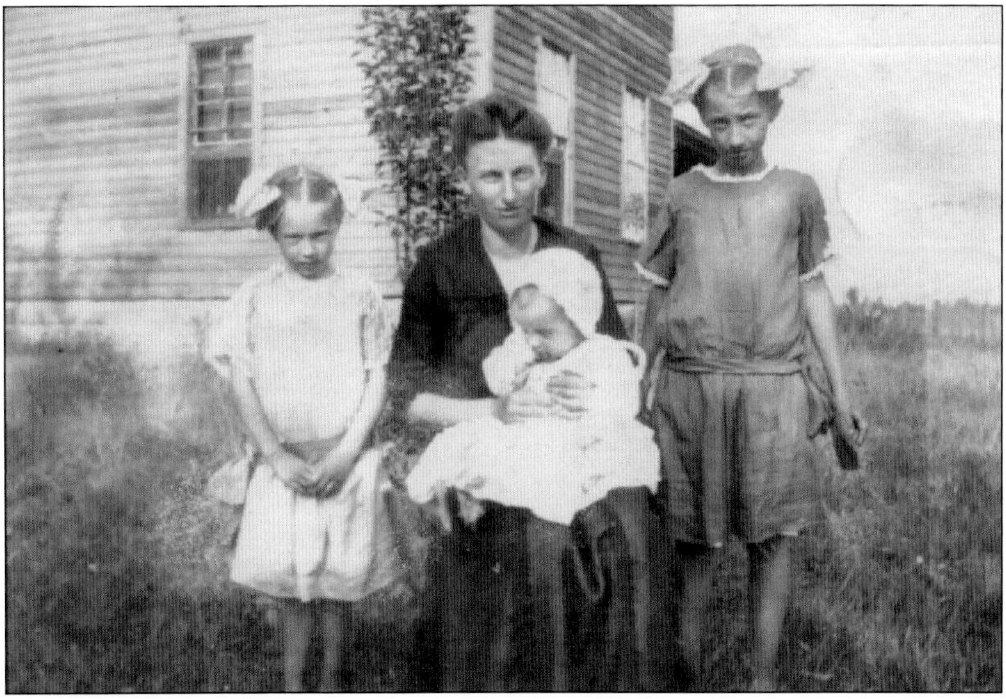

The Friedle Family. This picture is dated 1917 and Lucinda Grovey Friedle is holding Laurence. Helen is on the left and Martha is on the right. In the background is the home that Frank built for his family in Mills Township. Frank and Lucinda moved to Midland from Ohio about the same time that Adam Bloom moved his family to Midland. Frank and Lucinda had 11 children.

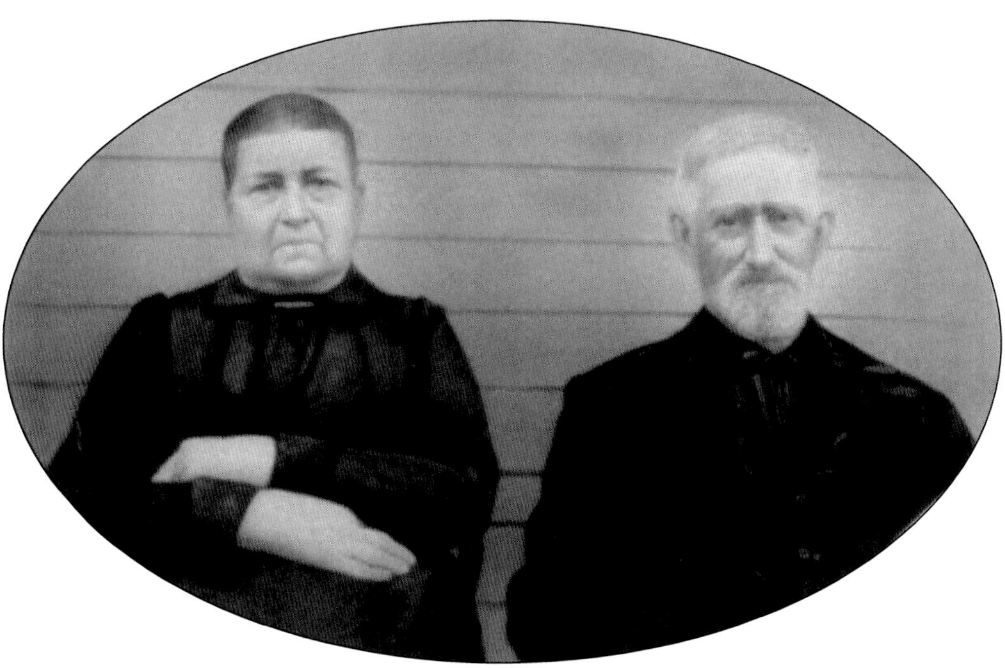

FIDELIA AND JAMES HOWE. When William Anderson Craig married Armena Adams on February 17, 1917, at the Baptist Church in Midland, they united five pioneer families from Midland County's history: the Gothams, the Andersons, the Howes, the Craigs, and the Adamses. Armena's grandmother Fidelia Gotham was born in 1831. In 1847 Fidelia married James Charles Howe. In 1870 they moved to Averill in Midland County, Michigan.

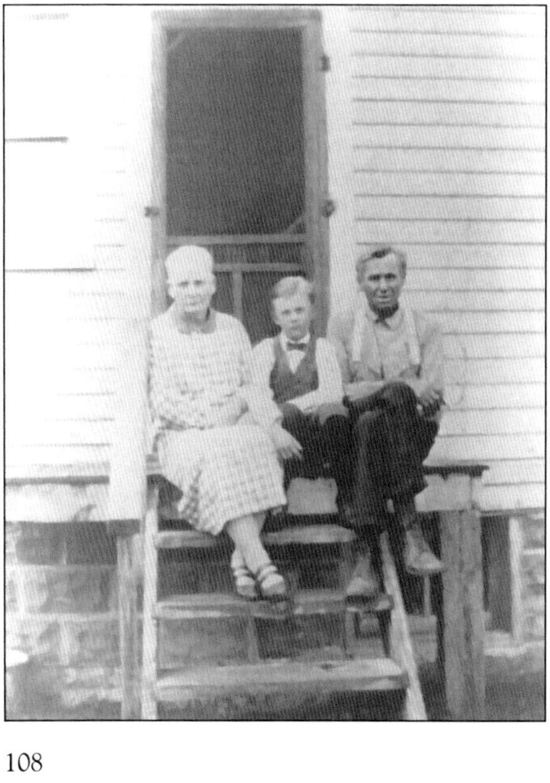

RACHEL AND WILL ADAMS. Rachel Howe Adams and her husband Will pose with their grandson Kenneth Craig on the back stoop of their porch on Sturgeon Road. Rachel and Will were married in 1892 in Midland County. They had five children but only Armena reached adulthood. In 1917 Armena Adams married William Craig. They had 11 children.

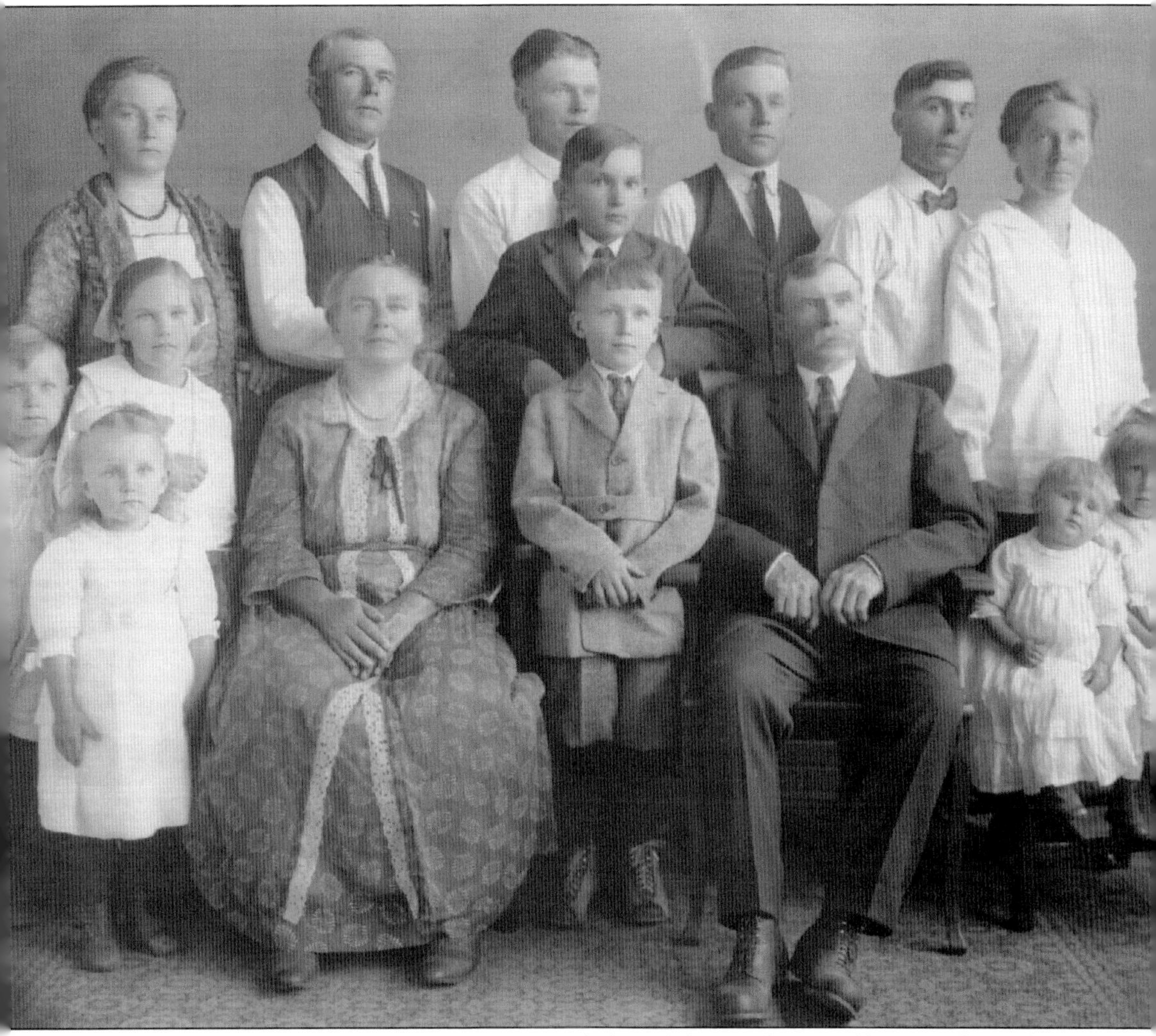

Caroline and Andrew Bartos Family. Pictured, from left to right, are: (front row) Frank, Anna, and Helen Skalnican, Caroline Bartos, Eddie Bartos, Andrew Bartos, and Anna and Lucille Zondlak; (back row) Jennie and George Skalnican, Henry Bartos, Steve Skalnican (in front of Henry), Frank Bartos, and James and Mary Zondlak. Caroline arrived in Midland, Michigan, in 1894 along with other members of the family and sent word for her husband, Andrew, to come from Pennsylvania to Michigan. Andrew and his brothers purchased land in Larkin Township from Cyrus Call.

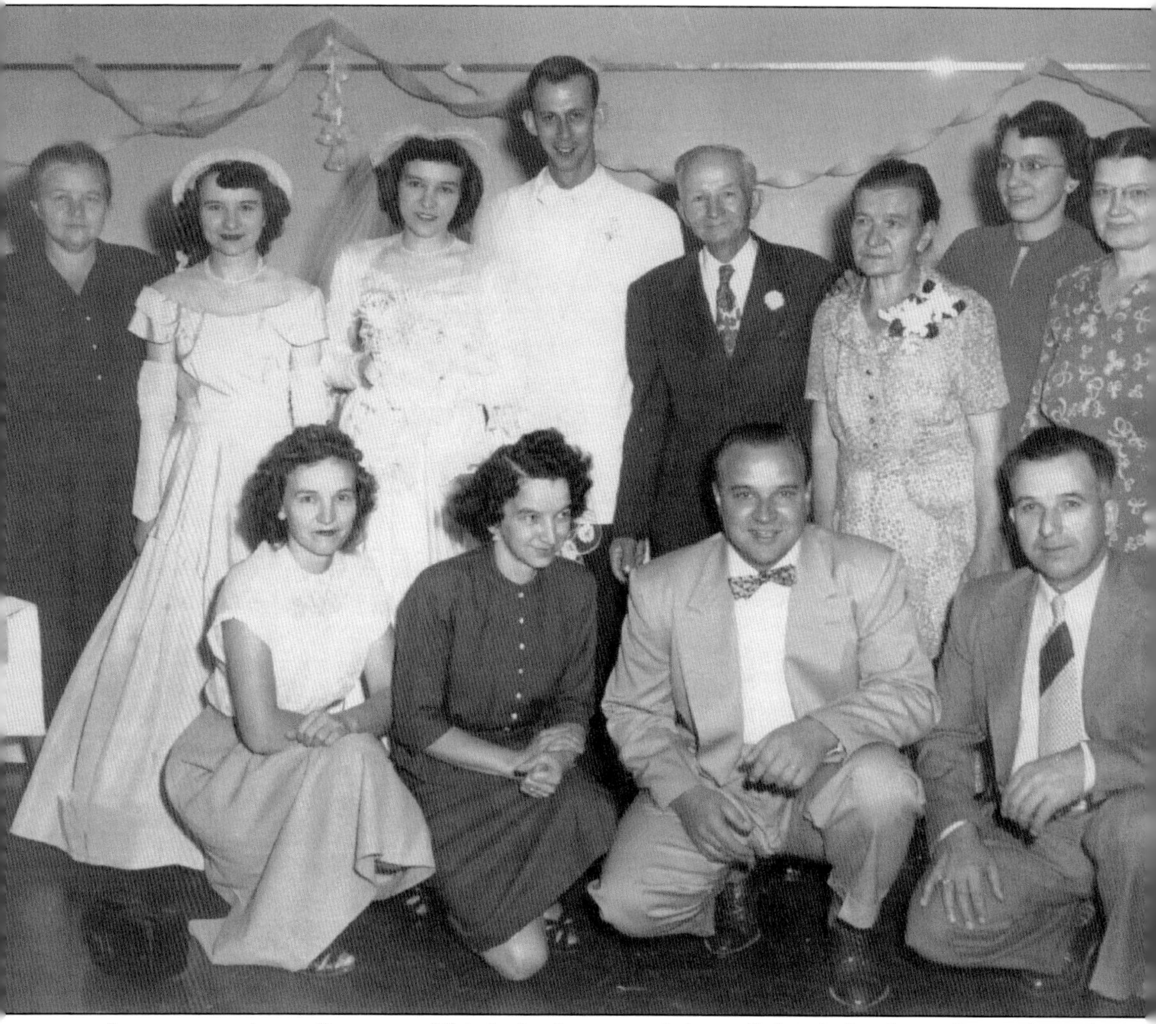

IGNACE AND ANNA BALCIRAK. This is the Ignace and Anna Balcirak family on September 15, 1951 on the day their daughter Eleanor married Ted Wejrowski. Celebrating in this picture, from left to right, are: (front row) Emily Balcirak Agostinelli, Helen Balcirak Modjesky, Steve and Frank Balcirak; (back row) Frances Balcirak Bartos, Lillian Balcirak Wejrowski, Eleanor and Ted Wejrowski, parents Ignace and Anna Balcirak, Ann Balcirak Hanson, and Rose Balcirak Bartos. Ignace emigrated from the village of Pielkielnik to Chicago in about 1895. Anna Buron emigrated from the same village to Chicago in 1903. Ignace and Anna (Buron) Balcirak were married November 7, 1906, in Illinois. They moved to Larkin township in 1910. They lived in a log home first and then built their own home around 1925 on Sturgeon Road.

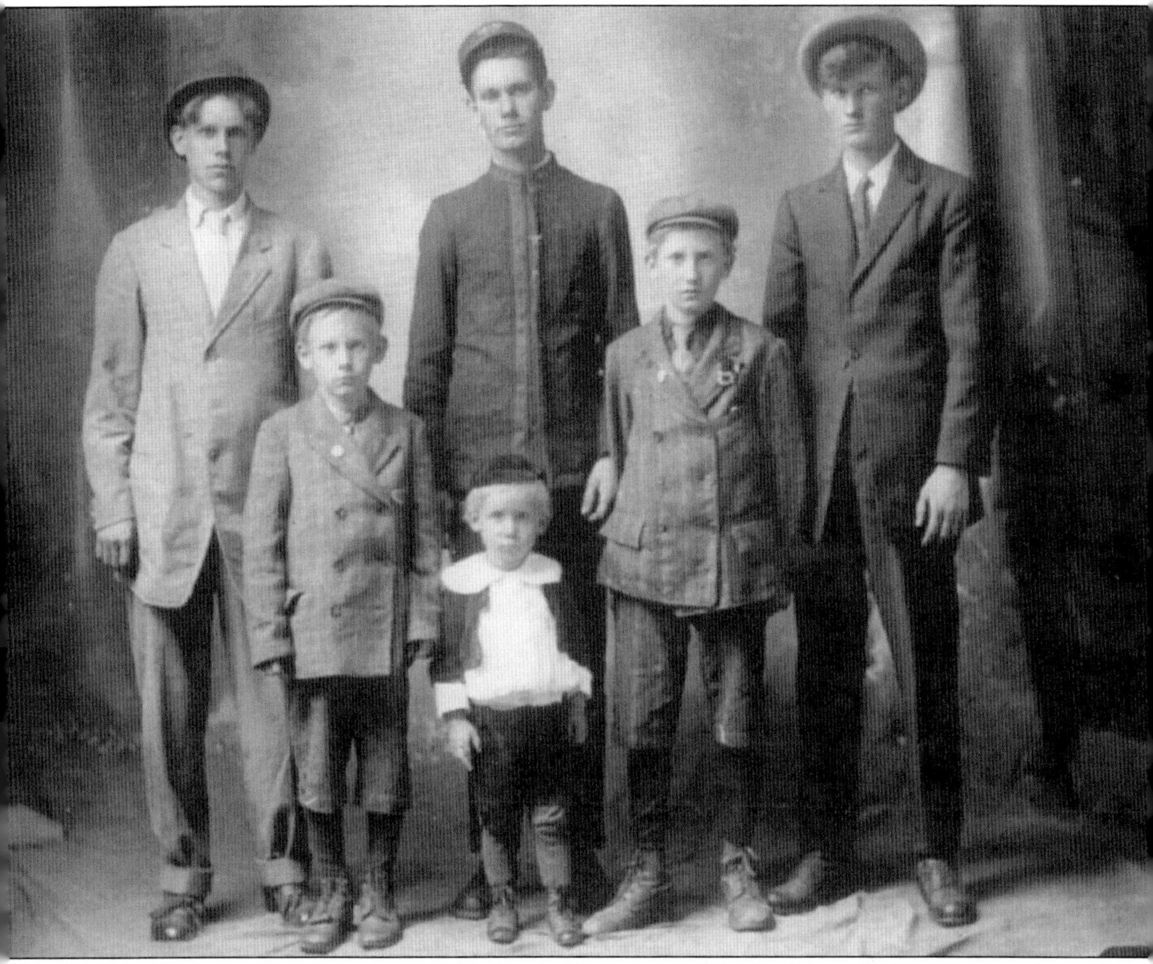

The Eastman Family in Midland. The first trading post at The Forks on the Tittabawassee River was opened by James Eastman. And today the Eastman family can boast of a minister, a lawyer and 15 businesses owned and operated by family members. This 1911 photo was taken at the photo booth at the Midland County Fair. From left to right, these Eastmen family members are: (in front) Elmer, Orville, and Harry; (in back) George, Frank, and James. Church life played an active role in the Eastman family with Frances Eastman setting the pace when she became a minister of the Floyd Church of God in a day and age when women seldom ventured into a church's pulpit.

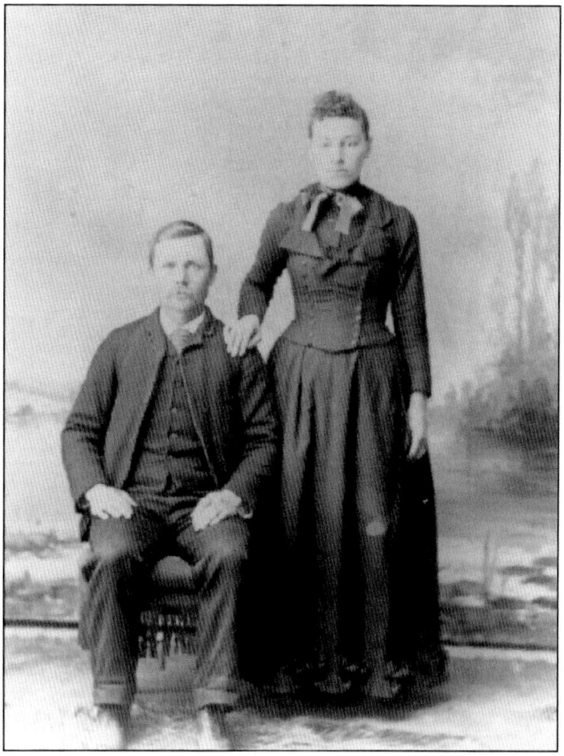

Sarah and William Yeakle. Sarah and William Yeakle with their five children moved to Ingersoll Township in 1909 from Adams County, Indiana. Sarah, who wrote a weekly letter back to the *Geneva Herald* in Geneva, Indiana has supplied her descendants with a cherished diary of the life that she and her husband lived for years in Midland County.

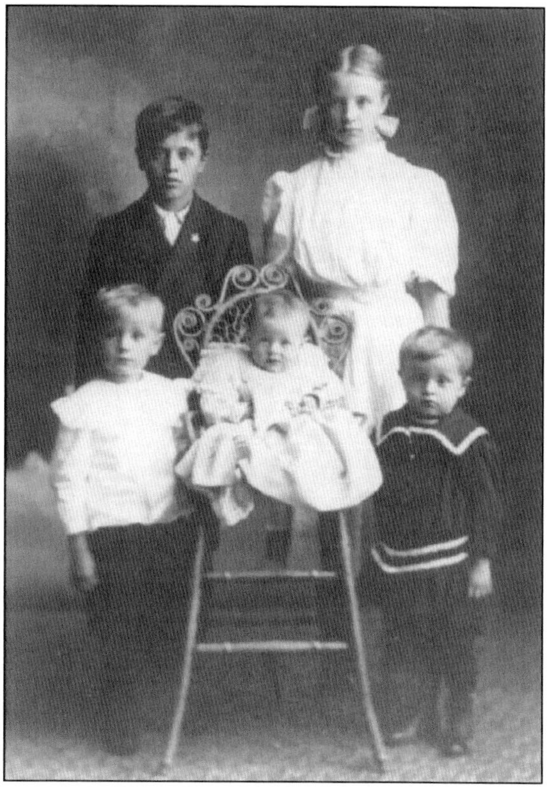

Yeakle Children. Front left to right are Merrill in the white blouse, Coy is the baby, and George is in the sailor suit. Behind them are Roy and Lexie. George and Coy were killed in a tragic train-car accident in 1924. The marriages and children of the three remaining Yeakle children carry on the heritage of Sarah and William Yeakle.

Ignace and Mary Zondlak. Mary Bartos was born 1896 to Andrew and Caroline Bartos in Midland County. Ignace (Jim) emigrated in 1912 from Piekielnik, the Province of Slovakia, Austria-Hungary. They married September 19, 1918, in St. Brigid Catholic Church in Midland, Michigan. They had nine children: Lucille, Anna, Mary, Loretta, Joanne, Donald, Dorothy, Edward, and Therese.

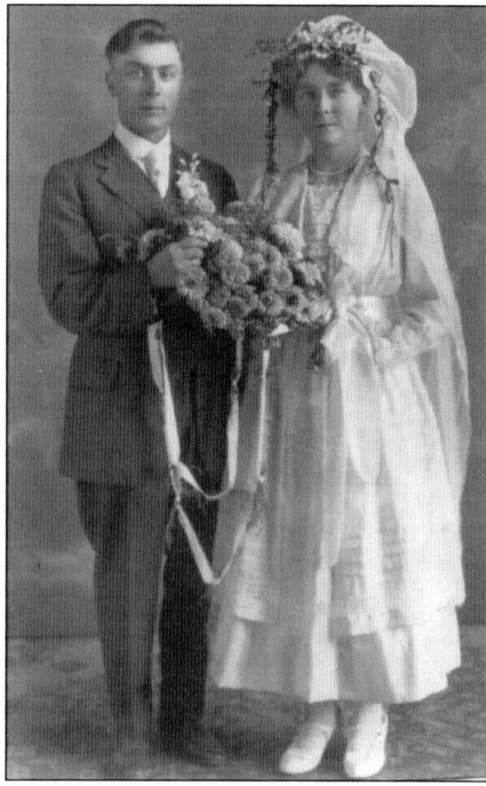

Hoon Family. In 1924 Elna Hoon homesteaded 120 acres of land on the corner of Eleven Mile and M-20. For years this intersection was called Hoon's Corners. While building their home, the Hoons lived in lumbermen's shanties on their property. Pictured, left to right, are: (front) Vernie May, Bernice (mother), Eva, and Roy; (back) Nina, Lloyd, Elna (father), Avis, and Etta. Earl and Norma weren't born yet.

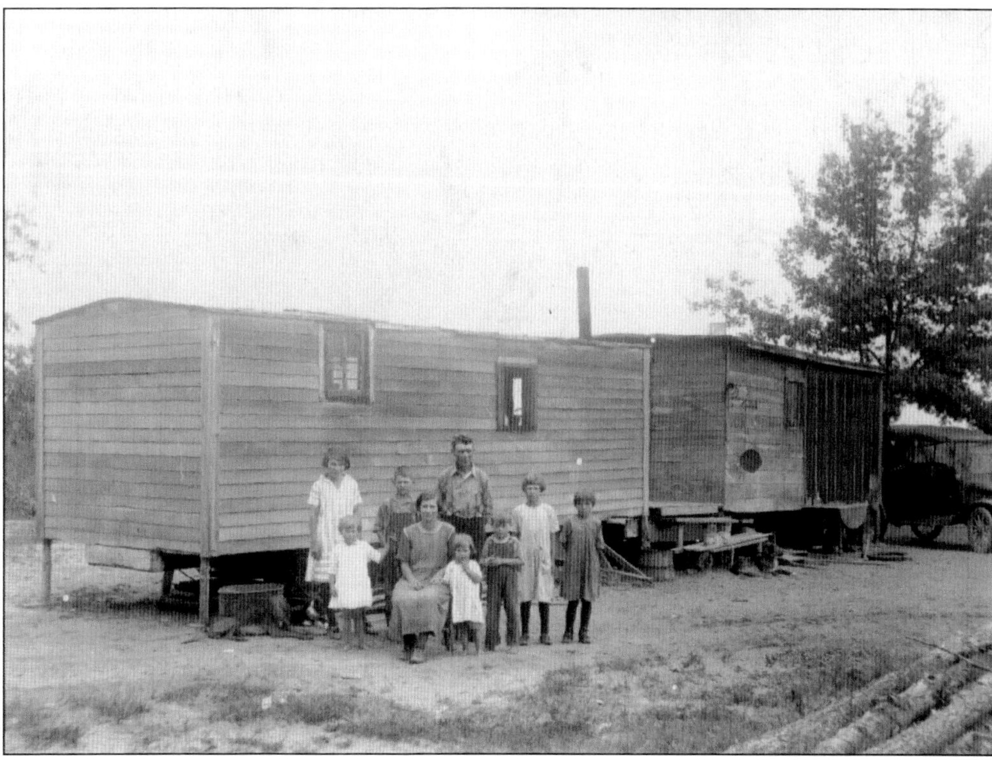

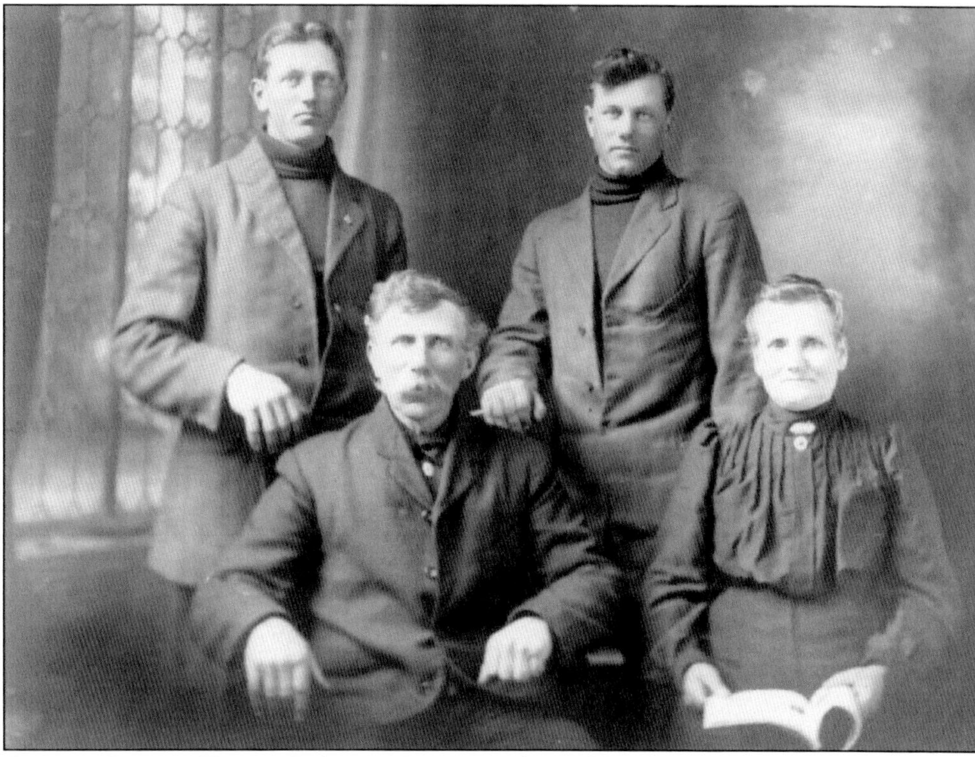

Charles Speaker Family. Left to right, pictured are: (front) Charles, Henrietta (Prochnow) Speaker; and (back) William and John Speaker. John Speaker's son, John E., and his wife Cheryl still reside on the Speaker farm on Sturgeon Road which is now a Michigan Centennial Farm.

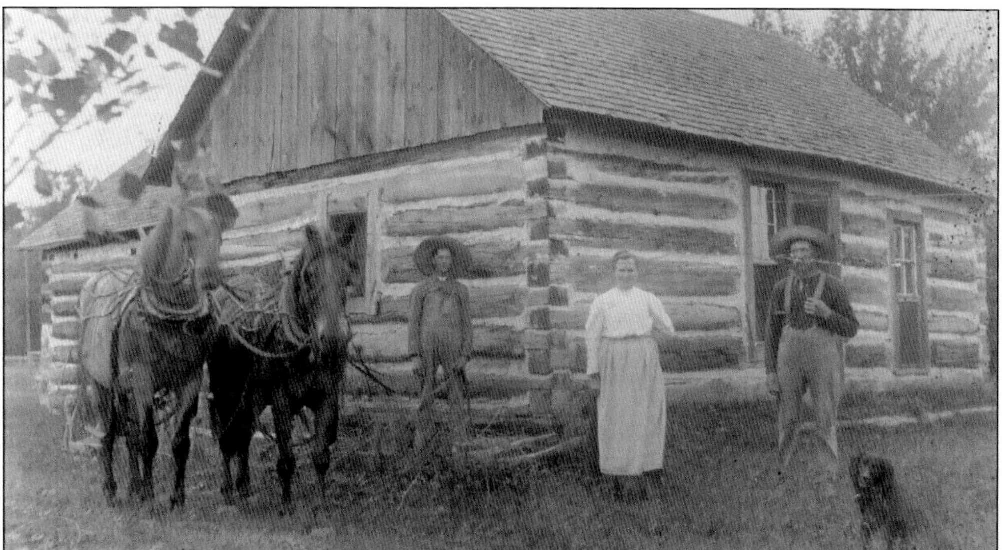

Log House. This is the log farm house on the original property purchased by Charles Speaker in 1887. In the photo from left to right are William, Henrietta, and Charles Speaker. Henrietta and Charles both emigrated from Germany and met in East Saginaw, Michigan, where they married in 1884. William was their first son.

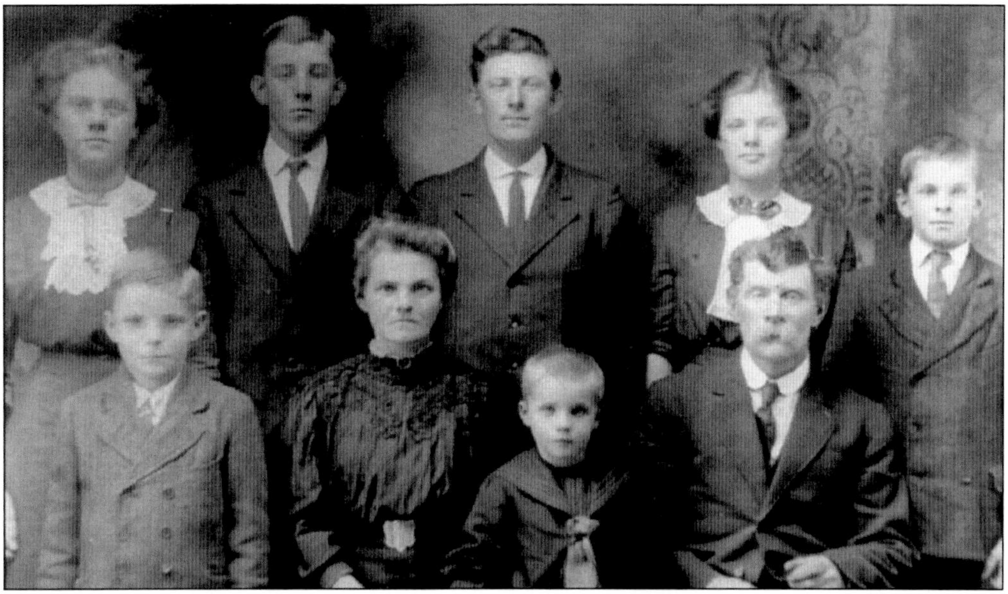

CHARLES G. CLARK FAMILY. The family pictured here, from left to right, are: (front row) Frank, Luella (mother), Bert, and Charles (father); (back row) Effie, Merl, Otto, Alice, and Sam. Luella was born April 9, 1869, to Samuel and Lorinda Hubbell, early Midland pioneers. Samuel brought the first shingle mill to Coleman. He was the first supervisor for Warren Township (1873–1876) and Justice of the Peace.

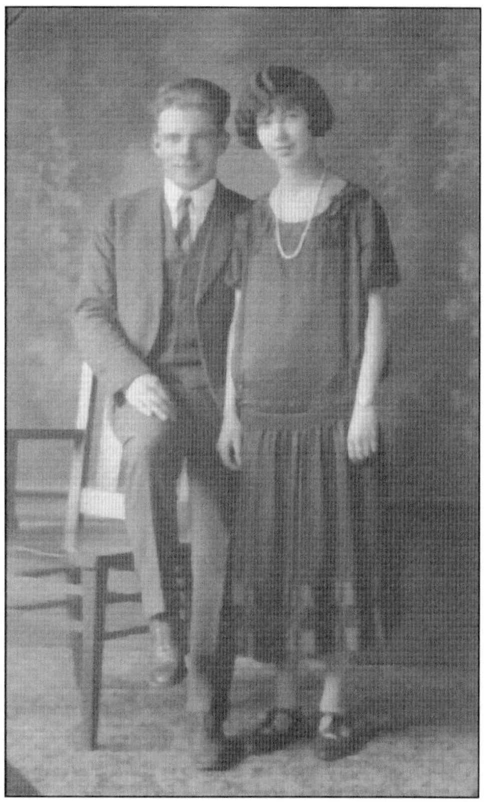

FRANK AND NELLIE CLARK. Frank Clark married Nellie DeJongh, January 2, 1925, in Coleman, Michigan. The DeJongh family moved to Coleman from Olive Center, Michigan, in 1907 when Nellie was six months old. Nellie was the second of nine children, five of whom are still living. Descendants of the Clark and DeJongh families continue living in Midland County.

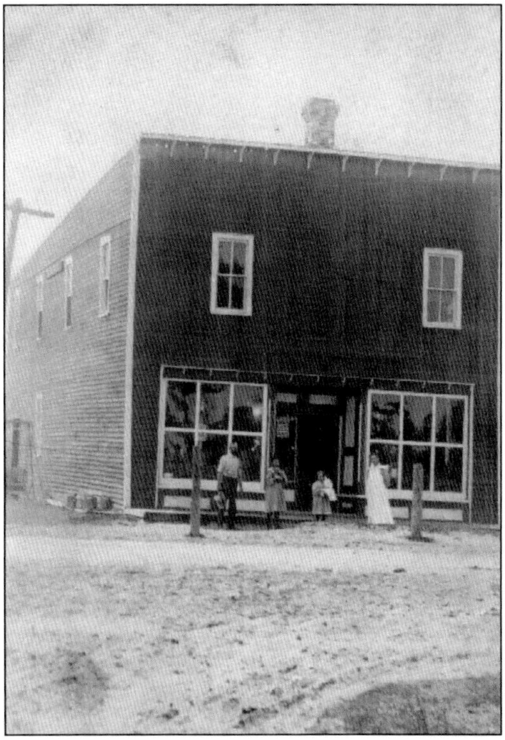

Haskell Hardware. Although their ancestors came over on the Mayflower, it wasn't until 1904 that John and his father Henry Haskell came to Sanford, Michigan. This is the hardware store in Sanford that they owned and operated from 1904 to 1917. In the picture left to right are John Haskell, Bessie, Bertha, and Alma Hill Haskell.

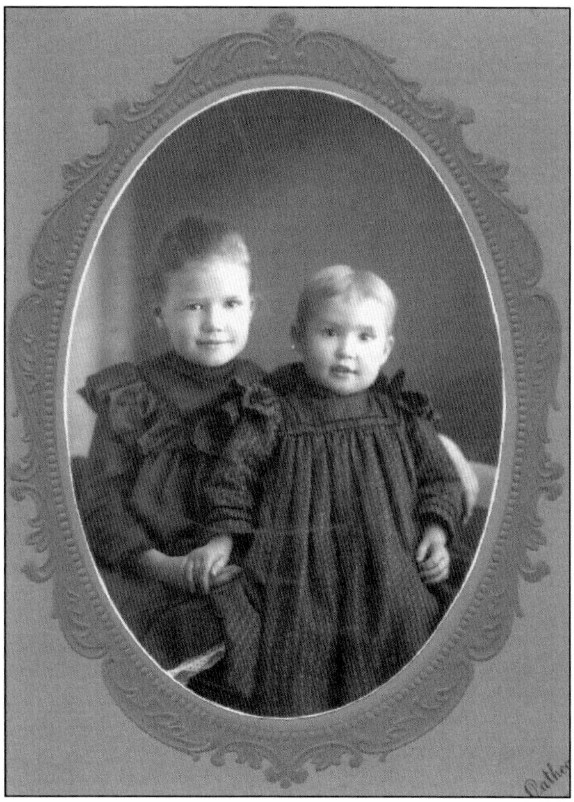

Bessie and Bertha Haskell. This is Bessie Haskell on the left and her sister Bertha born to Alma (Hill) and John Haskell. Attending high school meant a long day for Bessie. She left Sanford at 7 in the morning on the train and returned home around 6 in the evening. When Bessie was 19 she met her future husband Nels Peterson.

NELS AND IVA PETERSON. Nels and Iva Peterson were born to Alice Maxwell and Christian Peterson at the turn of the century in Sanford, Michigan. Nels learned as a small boy what it was like to assume a man's work after his father died suddenly when Nels was 10 years old.

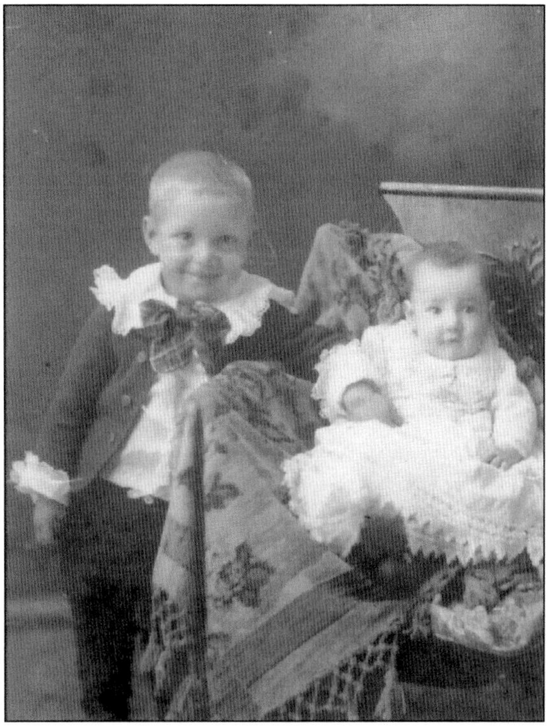

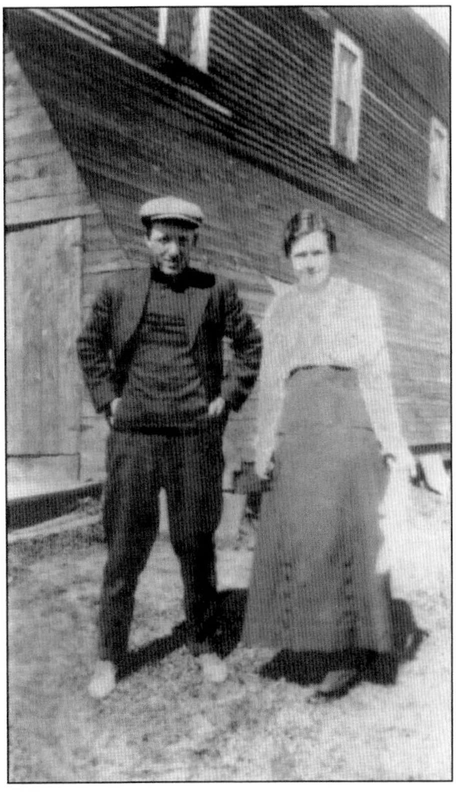

NELS PETERSON AND BESSIE HASKELL. Nels Peterson and Bessie Haskell were married on August 20, 1917. Their marriage was blessed with 8 children, 29 grandchildren, 59 great-grandchildren, and 16 great-great grandchildren. Nels passed away in 1971 and Bessie wrote: "It was the end of many happy years of marriage and my life from that day on was completely different."

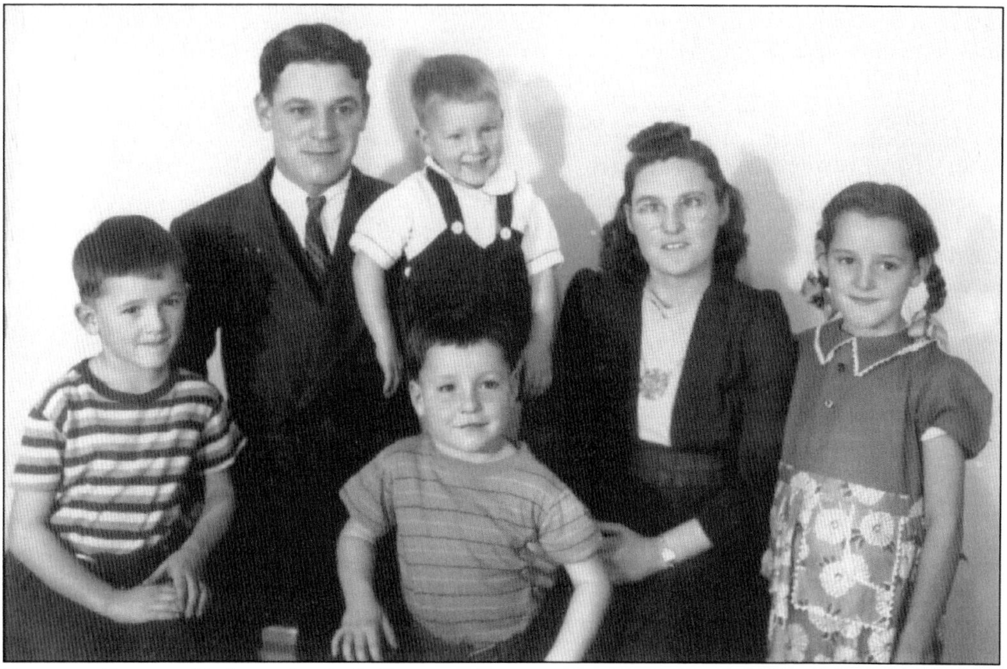

Everett Crosby. Early in the 20th Century, Everett Crosby, born in Midland County, married Nora Beardsley and raised five children here: LaNora, Howard Eugene, Wayne, Clair, and Keith. Today, Wayne enjoys success in business and community affairs. In the photo front left to right are Eugene (leaning against his father) and Wayne. In the back left to right are Everett (holding Clair), Nora, and daughter LaNora.

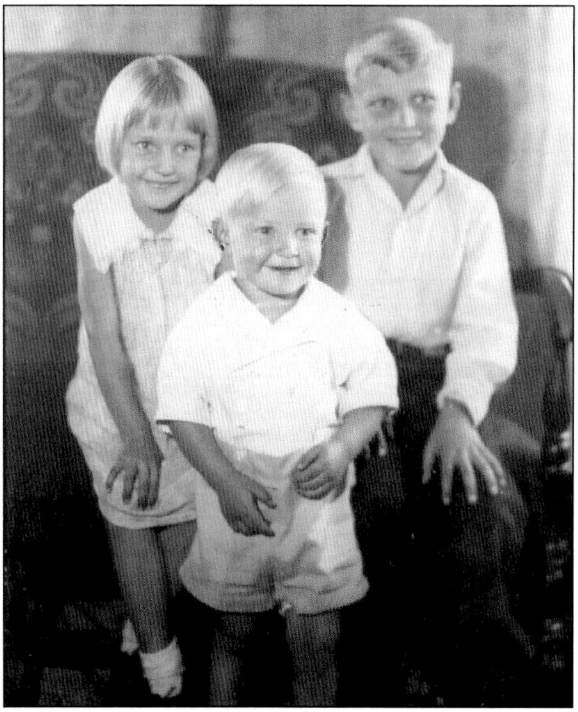

Townsend Children. This picture is of Marilyn, Bud, and Leo Townsend. Their heritage goes back to the earliest days of Midland. Their great-grandparents Joseph Townsend Sr. and Polly Cronkright Townsend came to Ingersoll Township in 1832. In 1841 they moved to The Forks. Their son, Joseph Townsend Jr., built the first frame house in Midland in 1856.

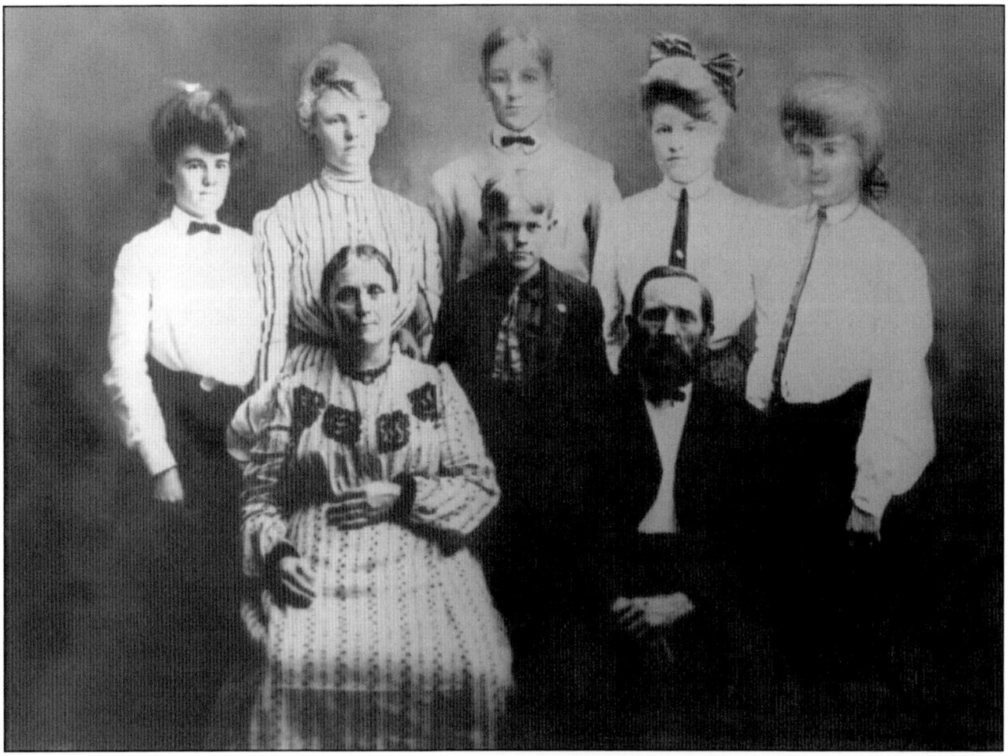

Fitzgibbon Family. In 1888 Ellen and Patrick Fitzgibbon came to the small town of Midland, Michigan, with five children. Three more children were born in Midland, two dying in infancy. This photo of the entire Fitzgibbon family was taken in Midland about 1900. From left to right, shown are: (front) Ellen, Jack, and Patrick Sr.; (back) Nellie (Dickson), Kate (Hunt), Patrick Jr., Marie, and Nora (Brines).

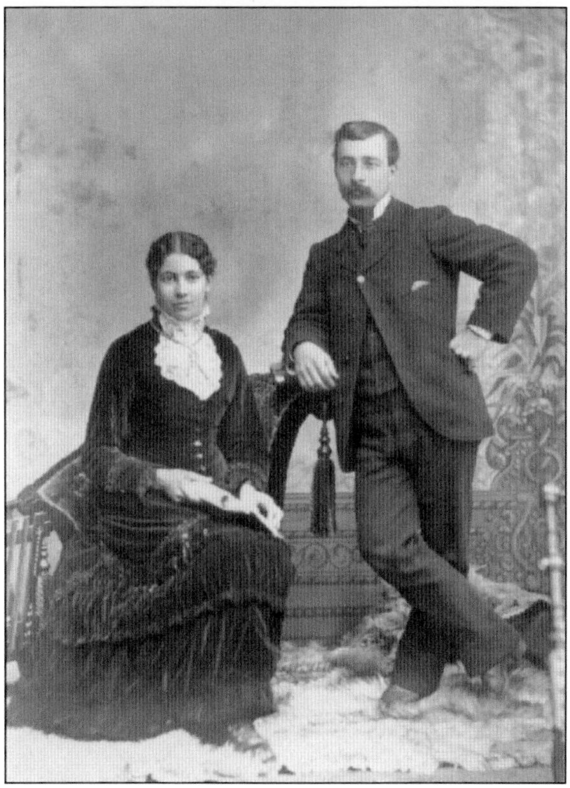

Thomas Hinds. This is a picture of Charlotte VanAlstine and Thomas Hinds. Thomas Hinds came to the Village of Midland City in 1872. He and Charlotte VanAlstine had four children: William, Vera, Daniel, and Dorothy. (Vera married Jack Fitzgibbon.) The stone house still standing on the corner of Ashman and Pine was built by Thomas Hinds.

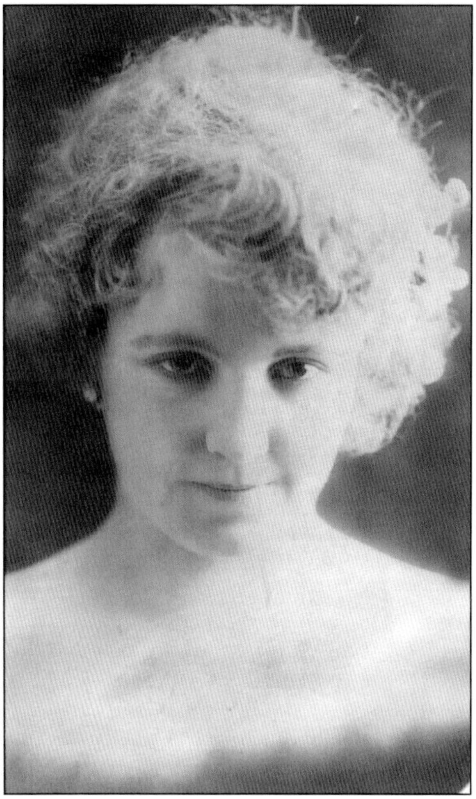

KATE FITZGIBBON. Kate Fitzgibbon, born in Limerick, Ireland, came to Midland in 1888. Her successful career on the stage was shortened by illness that forced her retirement from vaudeville and she returned to Midland in 1936 to spend her last eight years here. In her obituary E.L. Gardiner said, "I can hear her yet singing in the apple tree on a quiet summer night."

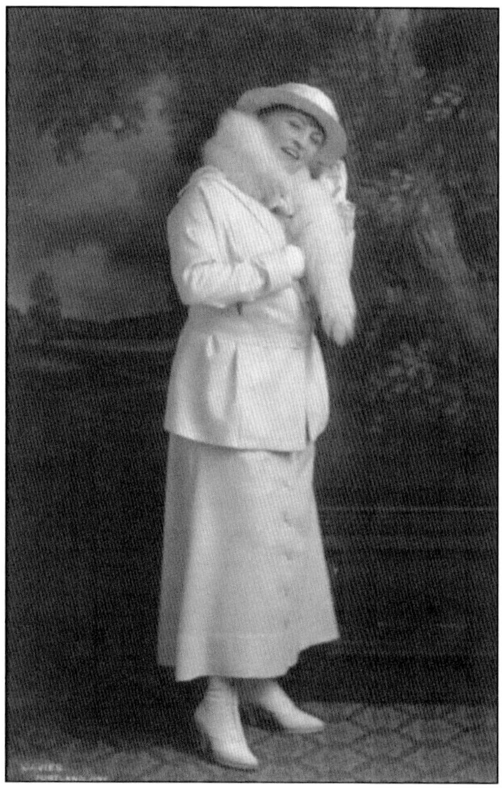

MARIE FITZGIBBON. Known for her Irish wit and humor, Marie Fitzgibbon, told stories of her hometown Midland to audiences from New York City to San Francisco as she played the Keith Orpheum Circuit in the heyday of vaudeville. When Marie died in 1927 Sophie Tucker, the famous actress known as the Red Hot Mama, came to Midland to attend her funeral.

WEAVER-BLAKE FAMILY. Weaver-Blake photo: left to right are Louis Weaver, his son-in-law Roy Blake, and his daughter Mary Weaver Blake with Mike, the family dog. In 1909 Louis brought his wife Katherine and daughters Mary and Henrietta to live on a 120 acre farm located off East Ashman. Louis Weaver hired a young man named Roy Blake and Roy would later become the Weaver's son-in-law when he married their daughter Mary.

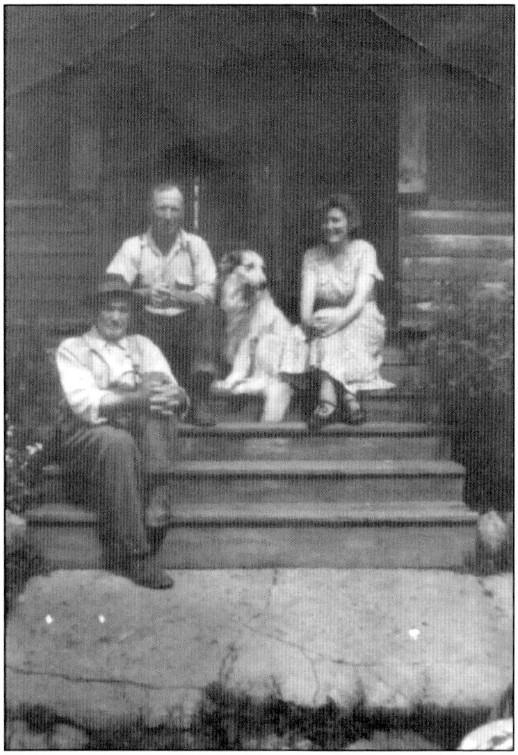

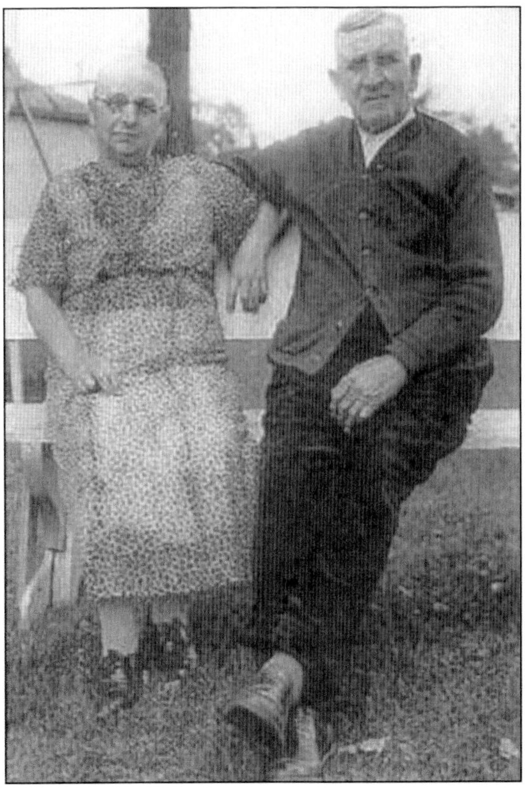

LUSHEN AND SARAH VARNER. Lushen and Sarah Bollinger Varner pose for their 50th wedding anniversary picture. In 1909 Lushen Varner and his sons came to Midland County in a covered wagon and homesteaded in Red Keg (Averill) with Sarah and her daughters coming on the train. Lushen and Sarah had eleven children: Effie, Ollie, Homer, Henry, Roy, Daniel, Charles, Victor, Mabel, Wilbur, and Clarence

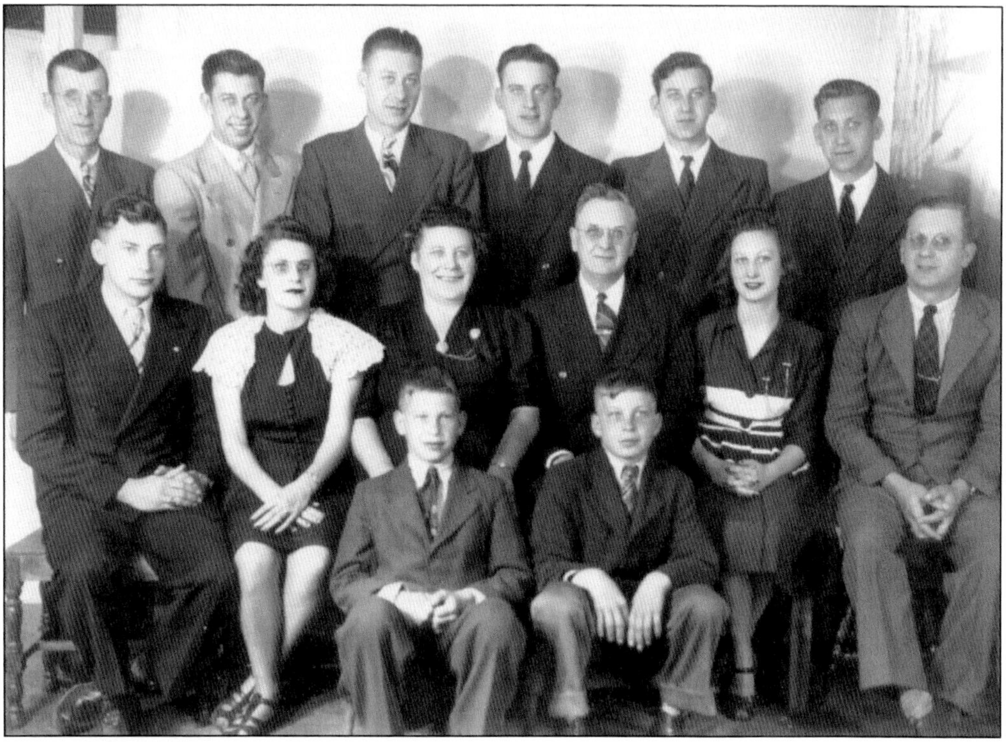

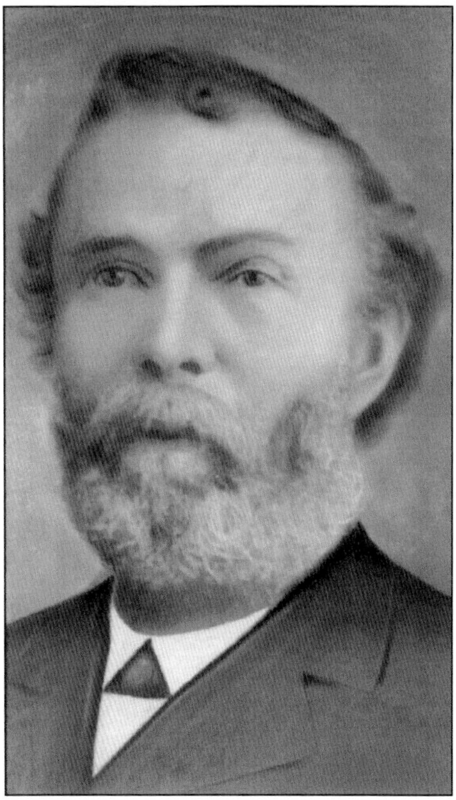

LEIGEB FAMILY. Immigrants have always played a big role in Midland's history. The story of the Leigeb family is no exception. Mary Winter came to Ellis Island on November 18, 1912, from Kapan, Slovonia (Yugoslavia). Michael Leigeb, born in 1890 in Hungary, arrived in Galveston, Texas, November 22, 1907. The 57 year marriage of Michael Leigeb and Mary Winter produced 12 children, 30 grandchildren, 53 great-grandchildren and 8 great-great grandchildren—a total of 103 descendants, all part of the huge melting pot that is called America. This is the Leigeb family taken in the early 1940s: (front) Joe and Harold; (middle) Ollie, Mary Adeline, parents Mary and Michael, Joanne, and Matt; (back) Mike, Paul, Tony, Elmer, Frank, and Ed.

WILLIAM H. GRANSDEN. Born in England, by 1859 William H. Gransden was scouting timber in Michigan. He married Mary Ann Elliott. In 1861 he and his family moved to Edenville. William H. and Mary Ann had 9 children, including William T. Having lived in various places, he returned to Edenville in 1890 and died there in 1905.

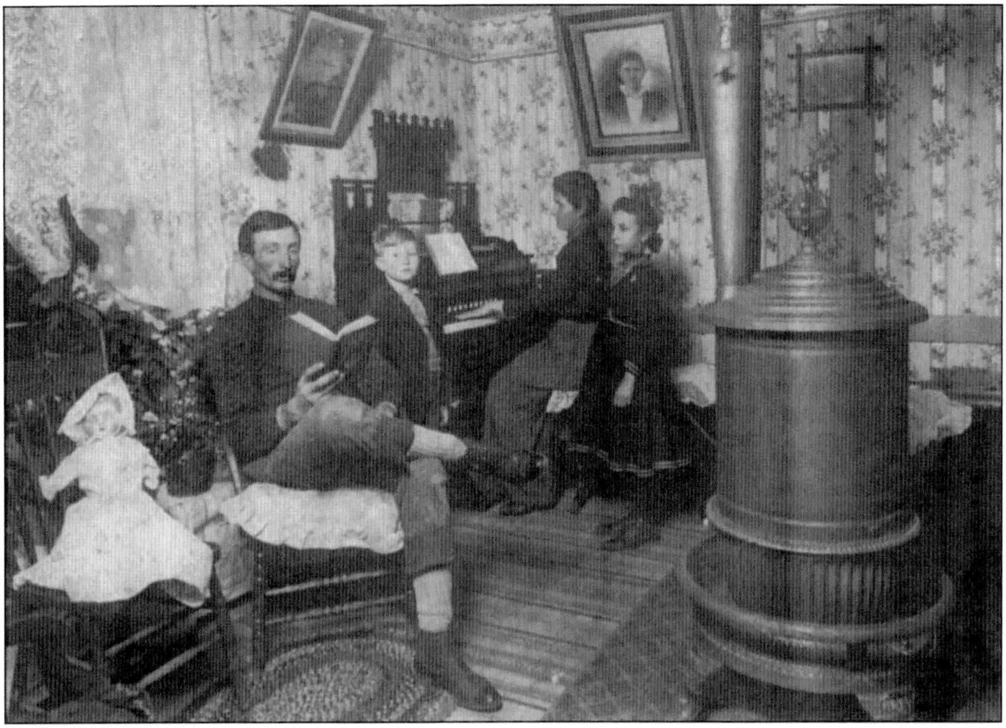

William T. Gransden. William T. Gransden married Margaret Wells in the little Methodist Church in Averill in 1892. Their children were Bessie, Lyle, Evabell, Arbutus, Lawrence, and Bertha. Lyle Gransden married Flora Swanton (a great-granddaughter to Elizabeth Ann Aiken Swanton) on June 18, 1919. This picture of the Gransden family in their parlor shows William T., Lyle, Margaret and Bessie.

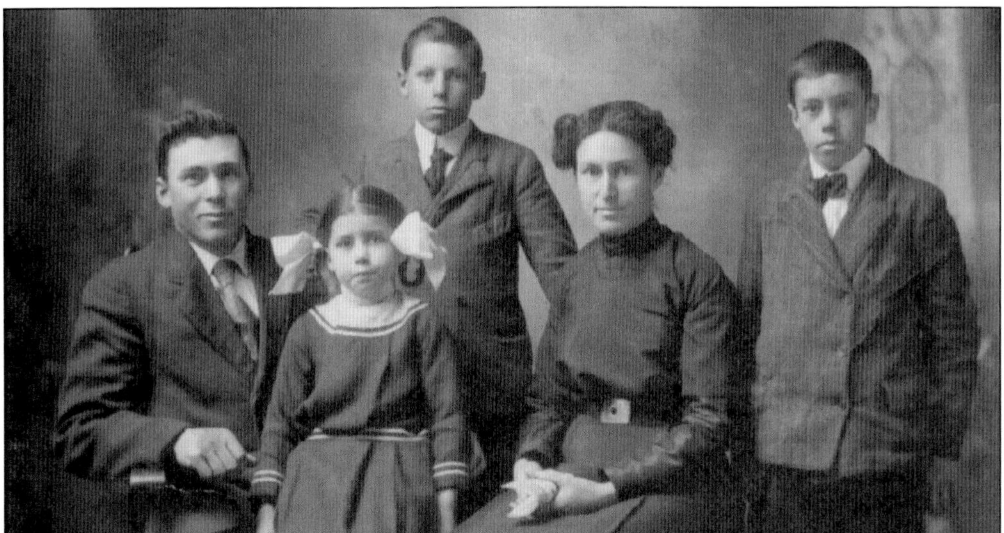

Sirrine Family. Thomas Abner and his wife Susie pose with their first three children. Left to right are Thomas Abner, Emily Grace, Susie, and Jimmie. In the back is Frannie, their oldest son. James Hubert Sirrine, Thomas Abner's father, came to Midland in 1875.

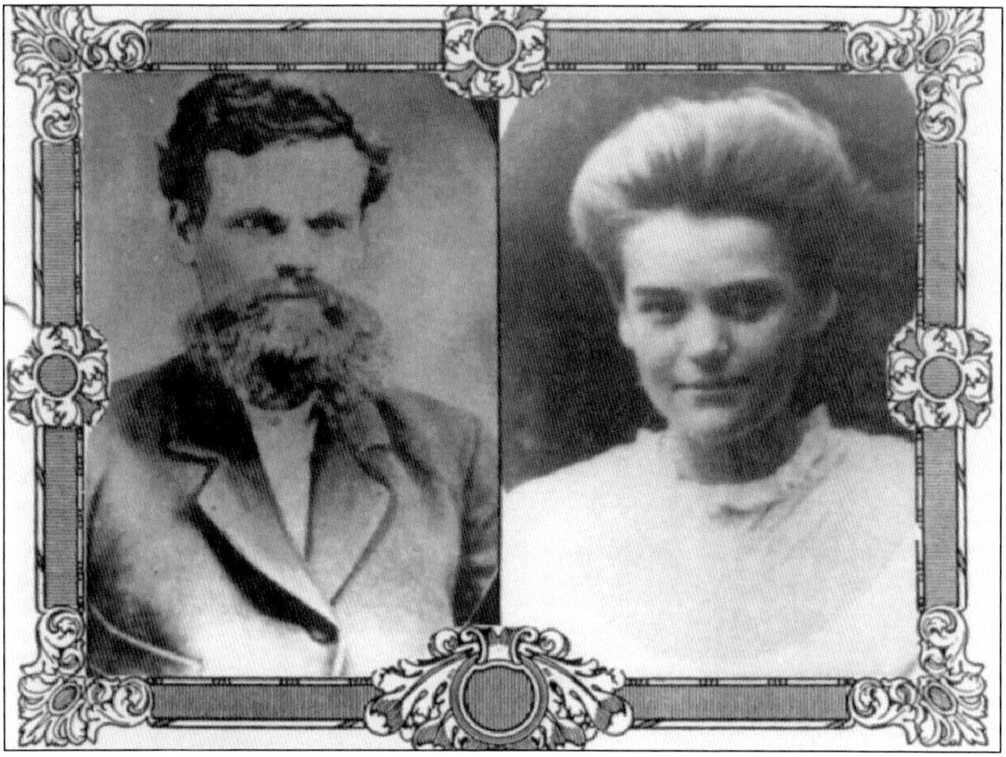

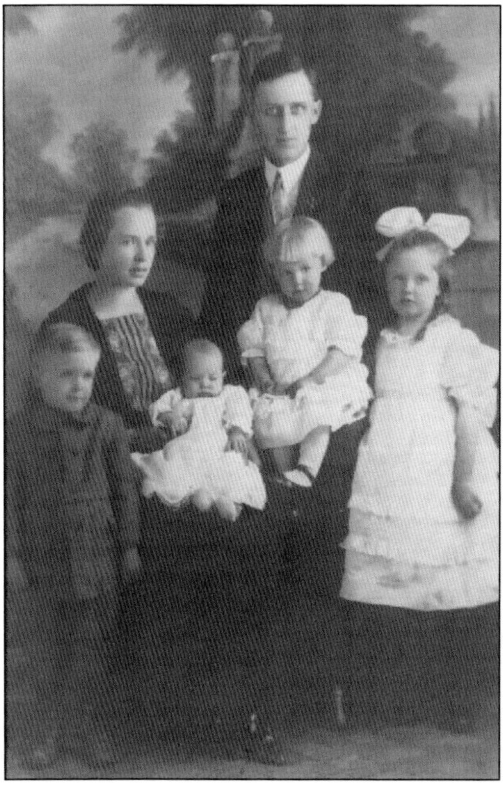

Finney Family. This is Jonathan and Mary Finney who had 10 children. After Jonathan's death in 1892, Mary Finney moved her family to Curtice, Michigan, a small town near Coleman. The Finney families have made Midland County their gathering place ever since. Their children were Alonso, Laura, Allen Harvey, Harry, Cora, Jeptha, Clarence, Bert, Hugh, and Inez.

Gay Family. Lexie Yeakle married Henry Gay in 1914. In the photo left to right are Harold, Wilma in her mother's lap, Thelma on her father's lap, and Lucille standing beside her father. Henry Gay died in 1939 leaving Lexie with ten children to raise.

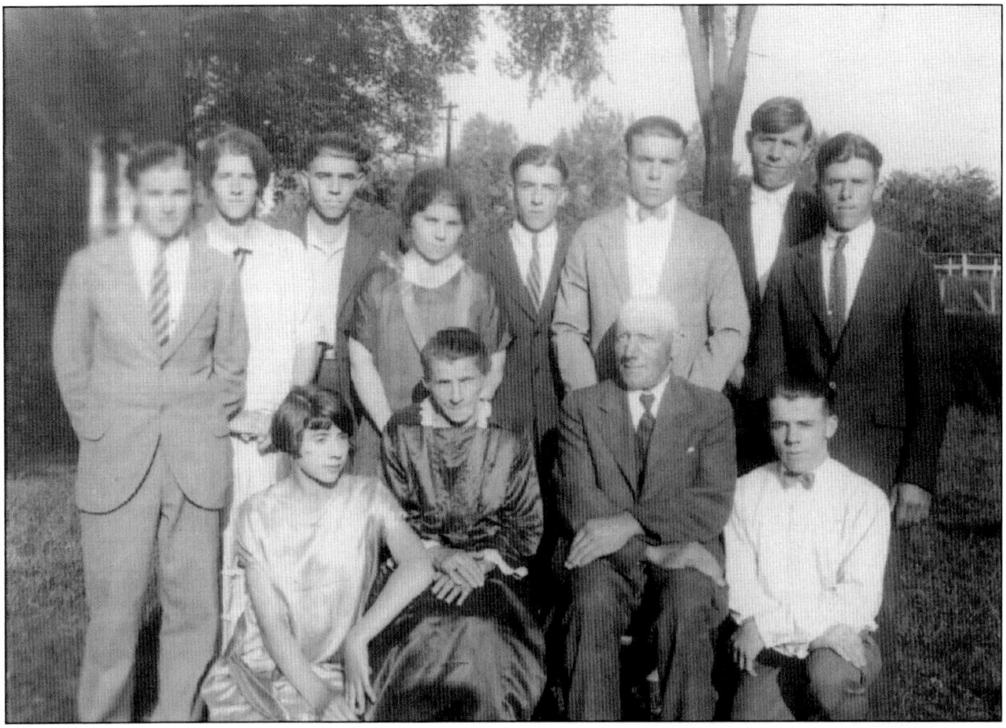

ASCH FAMILY. This is Katherine and Samuel Asch with their children in the early 1920s. Seated, left to right, are Mabel, Katherine (mother), Samuel (father), and Bill; standing are David, Liz, Ed, Edith, Sam, Albert, Chris, and Fred. Billy and Albert had grocery stores in early Midland. As a teen-ager, Edith was a waitress at the Stag Hotel, and was an accomplished musician.

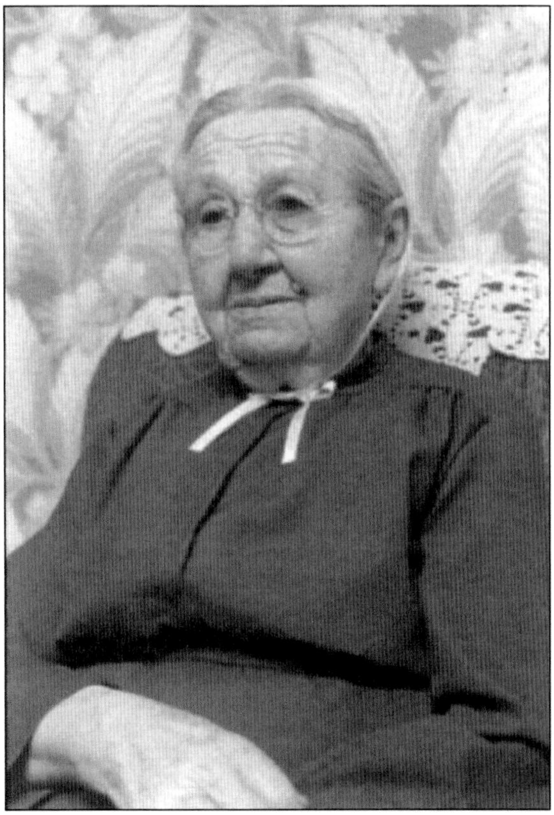

WYSE FAMILY. This is Abbiegail Baer. Born in 1878, she married Albert Wyse December 20, 1900. Their union was blessed with ten sons: Edwin, Daniel, Oscar, Monroe, Lester, Ray, Willard, Homer, Ora, and Lawrence. Albert and Abbie purchased 160 acres of land in the Gordonville area; 120 acres were ready to be farmed with 40 acres still needing to be cleared.

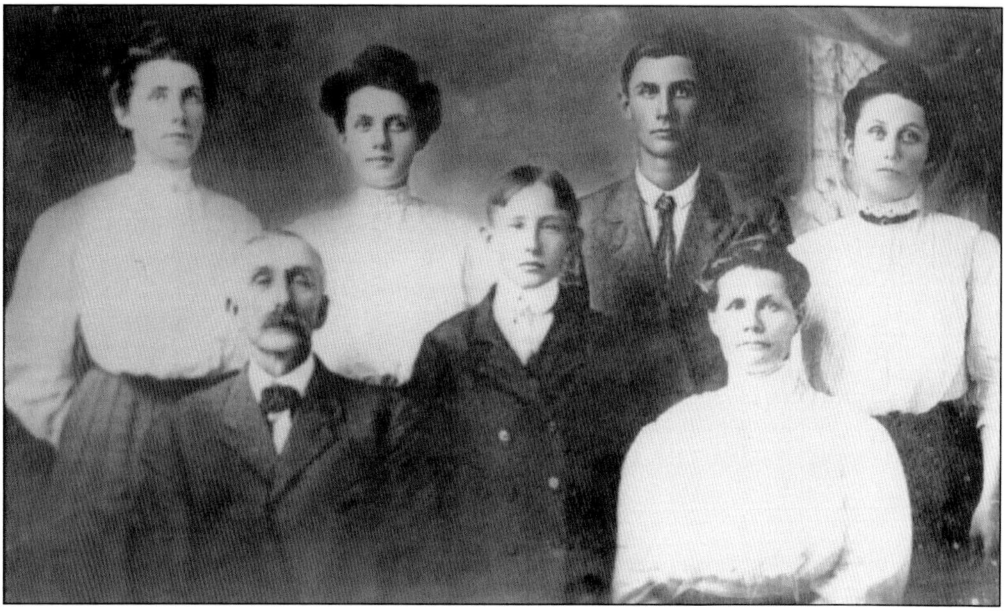

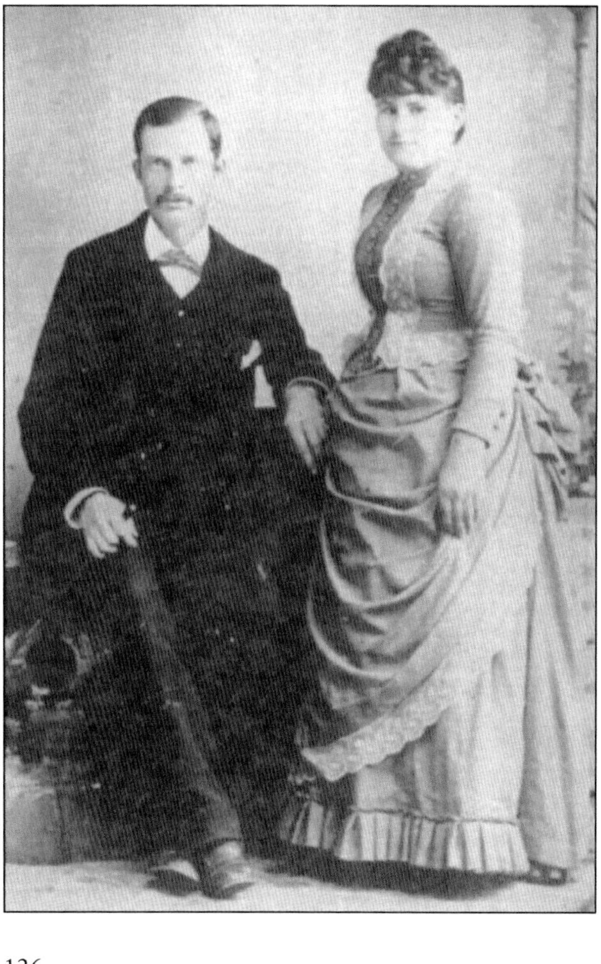

SINCLAIR FAMILY. David Sinclair came to Midland County in 1865. In 1881 he was united in marriage with Harriet McRae. Pictured, from left to right, are: (front) David (father), Harry, and Harriet (mother); (back) Alice, Blanche, John, and Anna. He was active in the Masons and Maccabees.

GEORGE AND RICKA NOLD. This is George Nold and Ricka Horn in a photograph taken at the time of their engagement. Ricka Horn married George Nold on August 19, 1887. They had six children: Nora, Anna, Charles, Arthur, Edna, and Martin. Their marriage ended tragically when Ricka died at 31. Martin was just four months old when his mother died and lived with his maternal grandparents, Frederick and Marie Horn. He eventually ended up in a Lutheran orphanage. In 1921 Martin Nold married Agnes Swallow. In 1923 Wilma was born, followed by Ernest and Frances.

INDEX

Picnics
093 SL Frank Wixom, Picnic Men
094 SL Lumberjack Contests

Making a City
095 SL Larkin & Patrick
096 LP Willard H. Dow
097 LP Alden B. Dow
098 SP Phil Rich
099 SP Man at desk
100 LP Towsley
101 SL Hospital groundbreaking
102 SL Hospital
103 SL Police
104 SP Sayles
105 SL Purol Gasoline
106 SL Purol Gas remodeled
107 SP Vogilsang
108 SP Tom Montgomery
109 SP Marville Kent
110 SL Nehil
111 SP Leland Doan
112 SP Ted Doan
113 SP Gilbert Cirrie
114 SL Vasburgh
115 SP Arbury
116 SP Bradley
117 SL 101 Bldg
118 SL Group at Service Awards dinner

Schools and Churches
119 SL Phetteplace School graduation
120 SP Post Street
121 SL Wright School
122 SL early Cody
123 SL Boarded up
124 SL Carpenter School
125 SL Carpenter Kids
126 SL School bus
127 SL McGill
128 SL Sr High
129 SL Girls' Basketball
130 SP Jack Cline
131 SL Track Team
132 SL Jr High
133 SL Jr High girls
134 SL Sr High
135 SL Boys Basketball
136 SL early Phetteplace
137 SL new Phetteplace
138 LL Methodist church
139 LP Presbyterian church
140 LP First Baptist church
141 LL Catholic church

They Served
142 LL Veterans
143 SP Pete Raymond
144 SP Israel Sayles
145 SP Charles Sinclair
146 SL Sinclair
147 SP Demske
148 SP Gerstackers
149 SP Roberts
150 SP Jack McCandless
151 SP Branson
152 SP Zondlak
153 SP Speakers
154 SP Earl Hoon
155 SP Bob Sinclair
156 SP Don Sinclair
157 SP Jack Sinclair
158 SP Eugene Smith
159 SP Dick Smith
160 SP Roy Blake
161 SP Rickard Blake, Harold Gay
162 SP Frank Liegh
163 SP Ollie Liegh
164 SP Tony Liegh
165 SP Ed Liegh
166 SP Elmer Liegh
167 SP Dale Crampton
168 SP Eldine Crampton
169 SP S.T. Crampton
170 SP Howard Smith, Henry Yeakle
171 SP George Gay

Settlers and Pioneers
172 SL Frank Sims house
173 LL Tippin family
174 LL The Hebners
175 SP John Andrick
176 SP Andrick
177 SL Bloom
178 SL Friedle
179 SL Craig
180 SP Craig
181 LL Bartos
182 LL Balcirak
183 LL Eastman family
184 SP Yeakle
185 SP Yeakles
186 SP Zondlak
187 SL Elna & Bernice Hoon and family
188 SL Speaker family
189 SL log farm
190 SL Clark
191 SP Clark
192 SP Haskell
193 SP Haskell
194 SP Two Peterson babies
195 SP Peterson
196 SL Crosby
197 SP Townsend

Settlers and Pioneers
198 SL Fitzgibbons
199 SP Hines
200 SP Kate
201 SP Marie
202 SP Weaver
203 SP Varner
204 LL Leigebs
205 SP Gransden
206 SL Gransden
207 SL Sirrine
208 SL Finney
209 SP Gay
210 SL Asch
211 SP Wyse
212 SL Sinclair
213 LP Nold